Suicide
and
Crisis Intervention

About The Author

Sheila A. Fisher, Ph.D., first developed her interest in Crisis and Suicide Intervention as chairwoman of the task committee to develop and create a telephone emergency service in her community. Recognizing an enormous gap in pertinent information relevant to these services, Dr. Fisher proceeded to institute a national study to enable others to benefit from research garnered. Dr. Fisher was the recipient of the Volunteer of the Year Award presented by the Mental Health Association of Stark County and is currently President of the Suicide Prevention and Crisis Help Service of Stark County, Ohio. Dr. Fisher received her Masters and Doctoral degrees from Case Western Reserve University and is presently in private practice as a psychologist. She has also been acting as a consultant to crisis services throughout the country, along with some extensive lecturing.

Because there has been a great proliferation and growth of Suicide and/or Crisis Prevention Services in recent years, this research was undertaken and developed to fulfill a vacuum for those desiring to create or make more efficient crisis services providing immediate response to people in crisis. The major purpose of this national survey is to define and synthesize material concerning both common and unique methods and techniques of operation of Suicide and/or Crisis Prevention Services. Some of the areas discussed concern purposes, goals, sponsorship, funding, recruiting, staffing, training, publicity, record keeping, community involvement, telephone method, type of contact and problem areas.

Data has been collected, tabulated and discussed concerning 192 services. Dr. Fisher's travels have taken her to 25 Crisis Services, and to workshops and institutes throughout the country to make this publication well representative and documented.

Suicide
and
Crisis Intervention

SURVEY AND GUIDE TO SERVICES

Sheila A. Fisher Ph.D.

Foreword by

Norman L. Farberow, Ph.D.

SPRINGER PUBLISHING COMPANY, INC.
NEW YORK

TO

Jack, Jeff, Barbara, and Pamela
and
all the volunteer workers who care
about people in crisis

Springer Publishing Company, Inc.
200 Park Avenue South, New York, N.Y. 10003

ISBN: 0-8261-1610-8
Library of Congress Catalog Number: 73-88106

362.22
F536s
1973

CONTENTS

TABLES

FOREWORD

There is something especially rewarding in participating in the culmination of an idea after having been privileged to take part as it was developed. This book is such an event, the end result of a number of discussions with Dr. Fisher over the past several years about the lack of a good source book on suicide prevention centers and hotlines to which a mental health or community worker could turn for information on organization, structure, and function.

The need for such a resource was great. Suicide and crisis had become recognized areas for focused concern in the 1950s and 1960s. The number of suicide prevention centers had been proliferating, and hotlines were springing up all over. Diverse professional, voluntary, and political forces were involved in setting up and administering the services, and new approaches and insights were developed. But it soon became apparent that a systematic overview of the field was very much needed. The experiences gained by one Suicide Prevention Center—successes and mistakes— which might have been invaluable in the development of another were available only with difficulty. Such a situation was a challenge to Dr. Fisher, for it went against the grain of her training and expertise in communication. And so this study is her answer: a handbook, manual, and guide that tells how, where, when, and what. Every center, new or old, will want it for its reference shelf, and researchers and other concerned individuals will find it an invaluable tool.

Throughout the country, 192 suicide prevention centers and youth services answered Dr. Fisher's requests for information. She visited more than 25 centers to collect extensive information about the way they were operating. From the data so diligently collected, summaries were prepared on initial aspects of center functioning, such as staffing, training, record keeping, etc.

Here the reader will learn the essential details for the effective operation of a center. For example, what should be recorded when a caller asks for help? What does a center want or need to know about its caller in order to help? Not only is there an exploration of the various kinds of data other centers have found useful, but there are also samples of record keeping forms used. Every good administrator knows how important adequate record keeping is; but ask any director to name his most persistent problem and he will inevitably answer: funding. This, too, is discussed at length, and the variety of funding resources and procedures may both surprise and enlighten.

Dr. Fisher has several advantages in writing this book. Not only is her expertise in the field of psychology and communication, but she has successfully administered a suicide prevention center for many years and has worked clinically with telephone callers and with patients in therapy and in counseling. Her book reflects an awareness of the needs and problems of all persons working in the area of suicide, crisis, and emergencies. Dr. Fisher more than identifies the problems; she also provides most of the answers.

Norman L. Farberow, Ph.D.
Los Angeles, California

PREFACE

When I first became involved in establishing a suicide and crisis prevention service, I soon realized that two major obstacles would have to be overcome. The first was immediately obvious: in order to obtain financial and moral support from people in the community, their initial anxiety concerning the discussion of suicidal and other self-destructive behaviors had to be dealt with. When confronted with this problem, I found that open and extensive discussions alleviated this anxiety and permitted emphasis to be placed on coping with the community's need for such a service.

Once we had achieved community recognition and support, the second major obstacle remained: how could we establish the most effective service possible? Because of extremely limited finances and the urgency of the task, it was necessary to learn what techniques had been tried in other communities and how effective they had been. In corresponding with other services, I found that our need for information was shared by hundreds of crisis centers throughout the country and that all recognized the need to learn from one another. Thus, I undertook a comprehensive nationwide survey of all existing services with the intention of providing thorough descriptions of methods and techniques of establishing and operating suicide and crisis prevention centers.

ACKNOWLEDGMENTS

I wish to acknowledge with special gratitude the participation of the many services that responded to this survey. Their cooperation, interest, and sense of purpose are making it possible for services to share up-to-date data. I am also indebted to the services that permitted examples of their materials to be published in the appendices, especially the Abilene Suicide Prevention Service for permitting me to use its excellent training manual. The mailing lists were a courtesy of Dr. Gene Brockopp of the Buffalo Services.

My thanks also to the directors of the 25 centers who, in spite of their demanding schedules, allowed me to visit and discuss the operations of their services.

My deepest gratitude to Dr. Norman L. Farberow whose sincere encouragement, from beginning to end, provided the impetus and motivation to conduct this survey.

Suicide
and
Crisis Intervention

CHAPTER I

INTRODUCTION

The major purpose of this work is to synthesize the relevant information concerning methods and techniques of operating suicide and/or crisis prevention services in the United States. It encompasses a variety of models and deals with a broad range of characteristics required to provide effective service.

The study examines every known service in the United States that could be identified through lists supplied by the National Institute of Mental Health, the Center for Studies of Suicide Prevention in Washington, the Suicide Prevention Center in Los Angeles, and the Suicide Prevention and Crisis Intervention Service in Buffalo.

The findings are based on two approaches: questionnaire surveys and on-the-spot interviews. The questionnaires requested basic information on method of operation, telephone set-up, telephone coverage, contact with callers, sponsors and funding, staffing, training, publicity, goals and purposes, follow-up of callers, length of time in operation, record keeping, and problem areas. The questionnaire also allowed room for "other" responses and solicited comments from directors. Tabulations based on 192 questionnaire responses constitute a major section of the study. In addition, visits and interviews at 25 centers provided further information and insight into the operation of various types of centers.

The study is based, in part, on research completed for a doctoral dissertation at Case Western Reserve University, and some sections were specifically designed to meet dissertation requirements. In order to make the findings available as quickly as possible, no extensive changes in format were undertaken.

A résumé of the chapter organization follows:

Chapter II describes how I became interested and involved in the delivery of suicide and/or crisis prevention services. It also discusses the rationale and need—national and international—for these services.

Chapter III provides a historical perspective on the need for suicide and/or crisis intervention services, and reviews the pertinent literature.

Chapter IV summarizes the methodology for the survey questionnaire and the responses to it.

Chapter V covers the methods and techniques of operations utilized throughout the country. The topical organization of the material makes it convenient for the reader to refer to specific points that may interest him.

Chapter VI summarizes the statistical survey data and sets forth some recommendations for determining the efficacy of an immediate response to the citizen in a crisis situation.

The Appendices present extensive examples of forms and publicity. Hopefully, this material will reduce the time and effort required when individuals or organizations are contemplating the establishment of such services.

3

Operational Definitions

1. **Suicide Prevention and/or Crisis Services (SPC):** Available 24 hours a day to persons of any age with suicidal or other crisis problems.

2. **Youth Services:** for a specific age population, usually 10 to 25 year-olds.

3. **Telephone Worker:** the person—professional or non-professional, paid or unpaid—who responds on the phone to the callers.

4. **Para-professional:** a non-professional telephone worker who has undergone training in crisis intervention by professionals and has gained knowledge from work experience.

5. **Gatekeeper:** any individual (other than a mental health professional) who is approached by troubled people for help.

6. **Significant Other:** someone who has an emotional tie or value to the person in crisis—for example, a spouse, a relative, a friend, or a minister.

7. **Lethality:** the degree of suicide intent—how imminent.

8. **Diverter or Divert-a-Phone:** a device that automatically conveys an incoming phone call from a central number to another number. After two rings the call is diverted to the new number, which has been set manually on the device.

9. **Patch:** a telephone switchover used by a central switchboard or answering service. This system permits the phone to ring; but by turning a manual switch, the operator intervenes and redials the crisis telephone worker's home phone. This permits a call to reach the workers at different numbers.

10. **Psychological Autopsies:** investigation of family and friends of a victim to determine the emotional climate surrounding a death that has been classified as accidental in order to determine if it was and should be classified as a suicide.

CHAPTER II

THE HUMAN REVOLUTION

Every day, every hour—in the United States, Canada, and Europe—thousands of concerned people pick up a ringing phone and say, "This is the Suicide/Crisis Service. May I help you?" They are aware citizens who are responding in a meaningful way to someone who feels desperately alone, helpless, and extremely hopeless about himself or some facet of his life.

Sometimes the caller is a man in a phone booth who has just slit his wrists because of an impending divorce. It may be a woman crying hysterically after physical abuse by her husband. And it could also be a teen-ager who suspects he has the symptoms of venereal disease. At times it is someone who simply, but tragically, feels all alone or wants to air his pent-up emotions and feelings. Often the caller wants to escape from a miserable situation—a drug problem, a boy/girl or marital disappointment; or it may even be a mother who feels so confined and unhappy that she sits by the phone holding a loaded gun and her child, trying to decide whether to kill the baby and herself so that they can both be spared a lifetime of utter misery.

These examples may seem extreme and dramatic, but they represent only a few of many, many thousands like them, some even more dramatic and tragic. Nevertheless, despite the wide age range and differing problems, all the callers share some common characteristics. They have decided to reach out, to call for help, in the desperate hope that someone will finally respond to their plea. Most callers feel that "no one cares if I live or die" and that "no one **ever** listens to me." What a tragic commentary on our society!

During a recent visit to Palm Beach, Florida, I read newspaper accounts of an act of brutality against a dog. The outpouring of citizen anger and demands for action was incredible. True, we should not stand by and see a helpless animal abused; but it is equally important that we not ignore people who are trying to reach out when they feel helpless and hopeless. We must be there to respond by providing **24-hour telephone** emergency suicide prevention and/or crisis services in every community. These around-the-clock services, manned by empathic and trained workers, should be backed up by a comprehensive network of professional mental health services.

The 1960s have been referred to as the era of anxiety, the era of depression, or the era of crime and violence. I would like to suggest that it also be called the decade of the human revolution, the era of caring, a time when people were genuinely concerned about other people who were hurting. It could also be spoken of as the era of volunteerism, when the volunteer worker began to gain respectability after years of being derisively called an "inept do-gooder." Today the volunteer has gained credibility by being trained, by competently filling vital services, and by freeing professionals for work requiring their special abilities.

Fortunately, the considerable growth of anxiety, depression, crime, and violence in our society has been matched by a growing recognition of the value of suicide prevention and/or crisis services which are staffed primarily by volunteers, both professional and para-professional.

Thousands of such volunteers, each contributing at least four hours weekly, are now available in dozens of communities in the U.S., Canada, and Europe. As telephone workers in 24-hour emergency suicide and crisis services, they are responding in a caring and meaningful way to persons who feel overwhelmed by the stresses in their lives.

I hope to act as a citizens' advocate in this book—to make you aware of the enormous day-to-day problems of living in our society, while at the same time not making you feel depressed by this knowledge and frank discussion. Rather, I hope to instill in the reader the sense of satisfaction that comes from confronting the challenge by working, each in his own way, for positive solutions. I urge you to join the human revolution, a revolution of people from different walks of life with a common ideal: concern for another human being who is experiencing a painful crisis. Our unselfish efforts can do a great deal to rid our communities of the stigma and shame that have hitherto been associated with emotional crisis.

My initial involvement began when I worked in the Community Mental Health Center in Stark County as part of a psychology practicum for Case Western Reserve University. The apparent loneliness, depression, and hopelessness of some of the clients seemed to be accompanied by the inability of their families to communicate with them in a supportive manner. About 30 - 40 per cent of the patients admitted to a previous suicidal gesture with varying degrees of lethality. Many others had in the past given very serious consideration to suicide. Their ambivalence about resorting to self-destructive means as a solution to crisis situations is suggested by the fact that these potentially suicidal persons left enough clues to insure being helped in time. Numerous phone calls to the Mental Health Association from potential suicides reinforced the need to help the citizens of Stark County find someone to respond to their "cry for help." I learned that other cities had established a 24-hour suicide prevention and/or crisis service, making it possible for people to communicate verbally their desperate situation to someone who is willing to listen.

Research has shown that over two-thirds of the people who complete suicide communicate their intent in advance (Robins, 1959). The modes of communication vary from subtle hints, such as giving away personal items and saying they would not be needed any more, to direct statements of intent (Murphy et al., 1968). Another study (Robins, 1968) found that of those who communicate their intention prior to the act, 65% utilize more than one means of communication and direct them to more than one person.

Farberow (1961) developed a thesis suggesting that suicidal behavior can be "viewed from the standpoint of communication." He feels that much of the suicidal activity has the specific purpose of communicating to others the desperate conflict and crisis situation the person is undergoing. He refers to the behavioral act as a "cry for help." The suicidal act is viewed by Litman and Farberow (1961) as an action of communication. Litman (1963) defines

> . . . .potential suicide as a situation in which one person, called the victim or the patient, communicates to another person, called the listener or the rescuer, that he is overly close to committing suicide, and it registers in an uncomfortable way with the listener. We can estimate that such a situation occurs at least 500,000 times a year in the United States. The person who receives a suicidal communication may or may not respond to it. (p. 68)

Every director of a suicide and/or crisis service that I contacted stated that the number of calls far exceeds the number of completed suicides—a range of from ten times the number of suicides and more. Dr. Litman reported (A.A.S., 1970) that the number of people who have phoned the Los Angeles Suicide Center and then completed the suicidal act is quite small in relation to the total number of calls received. It is estimated that in the past twelve years 250 callers have completed the suicidal act, whereas the Center received many thousands of calls during that period.

Dr. Litman (1966) noted that suicidal intentions are strongest during particular crisis situations which appear hopeless and insoluble to the person. The suicidal individual regards his present situation as intolerable, but he also wishes to be rescued or rehabilitated. An example of this ambivalence occurred when I answered a call from a woman at a suicide prevention center. She had the gas jets turned on and was going to kill herself. She told me she could no longer stand the "situation" and she wanted "out." When I asked why she was calling, she replied that she didn't know if this would really solve the problem and that she didn't want to hurt her family. Apparently, the woman did not really want to destroy herself; but suicide seemed to be a way out of her dilemma. I encountered this same type of ambivalence with at least two other callers during a training workshop. Mr. Heilig, co-chief social worker at the Los Angeles Suicide Prevention Center, has described such situations as very "common."

Bell (1967) observed that studies have shown that eight out of ten suicidal people ask for help, directly or indirectly. That 80% of suicidal persons try to communicate to their friends, relatives, and doctors about their self-destructive intent, manifests the ambivalence: the potential suicide gives clues to others about his self-destructive intentions, in the hope that someone will intervene to suggest a less destructive alternative.

The strong evidence that suicide or a suicidal gesture is a behavioral attempt to communicate justifies the establishment of a 24-hour suicide prevention and crisis service, an open channel—available at any hour, every day—where persons in trouble can expect a meaningful and timely response by a "helping" resource. The suicide prevention service also attempts to educate the public to be more aware of suicide clues and to the desirability of appropriate intervention by helpful persons.

Suicide prevention and/or crisis services are attempting to solve the problem described by Dr. George Albee (1970): "Actually there is no chance that psychiatry and psychology, as these disciplines are now defined, will ever provide the necessary amount of manpower for effective intervention" (p. 6). Dr. Albee's observation suggests the need to establish services designed to help the citizens of a community whenever they "call for help." If someone is available to respond with empathy, interest, and a sincere caring attitude, many serious crisis situations can be confronted and dealt with constructively.

As organizer and chairman of the Suicide Prevention and Crisis Help Service of Stark County, Ohio, I was confronted by the paucity of available information, both general and detailed, in such a sensitive and growing field of human concern. In a number of contemporary books on the subject of suicide, relatively few chapters deal with prevention services per se. I wrote for information to 45 similar services and made inquiries to The National Institute of Mental Health and the Center for the Study of Suicide Prevention. I visited six services for on-the-spot observations and talks. And my search for guidelines and know-how also took me to various workshops and professional meetings: the Suicide Prevention Center in Los Angeles, the University of California in San Francisco, and the American Association of Suicidology.

The 1971 Convention of the American Association of Suicidology took note of the proliferation, since World War II, of suicide and/or crisis services and youth-oriented hotlines. From 1959 to 1971, the former had increased from 10 to almost 200; and 600 hotlines were reported to be functioning. Unfortunately, but understandably, the growth was marked by an absence of exchange and its concomitant duplication of time and energy.

7

At a suicidology workshop in San Francisco, some participants who were in the process of setting up such a service expressed the same feeling of frustration at the needless waste. It became obvious that a synthesis and analysis of all existing services would be beneficial for all: by exchanging ideas, experiences and problems, center personnel could prevent some problems and deal more effectively with others. For example, even before the Stark County Service was established, I provided a small but significant bit of information concerning a telephone method that was unknown to many at the workshop who had been active in the field for some time. Many people in the workshops were not aware of the diverter or divert-a-phone as a valuable adjunct to the ordinary telephone system.

At about the same time, Dr. Norman Farberow, a pioneer in the field of suicidology and suicide prevention, expressed the urgent need for a synthesis of available information in order to reduce duplication and frustration. Dr. Calvin Fredrick, deputy chief of the Center for Studies of Suicide Prevention at the National Institute of Mental Health, also encouraged me to undertake this effort. Although the Institute received many requests for information, it could offer little appropriate and comprehensive literature on operational methods and techniques.

Furthermore, a communiqué from the International Association for Suicide Prevention (December, 1970), which reported on suicide prevention in Japan, Europe—Czechoslovakia, Yugoslavia, Finland, Belgium, Sweden, Denmark, the Netherlands, England—and Canada, emphasized the need for each country to provide an overall picture of its suicide prevention services. Models, ideas, and information could and should be shared throughout the world. The biannual meetings of the International Association for Suicide Prevention could provide an ongoing opportunity to exchange information on worldwide efforts to develop such centers. Research to determine their effect would be facilitated by reliable information that was international in scope. It was natural, therefore, that the challenge of my own step-by-step awareness, the consultations with others who had similar frustrating experiences, and the impact of the growing national and international services all led to this study.

CHAPTER III
WHY 24-HOUR SERVICES?

The unbelievable contrast between America's vast and complex technological advances and our tragic failure to advance in the area of mental health must be recognized. We have recently seen men walking on the moon—almost beyond human comprehension; yet in the course of that same hour young men were being killed and maimed in Southeast Asia, and thousands of people, young and old, were living in squalor and poverty. Finally, during that same hour, at least 3 - 6 people killed themselves—and approximately 60 - 80 people attempted suicide. Sad? Tragic? Unbelievable? Yes! And the most tragic aspect of it is that a great many of those people **do not want to die!**

Usually, the suicidal person is not rejecting life per se but, rather, an intolerable life style or a situation that seems to have no acceptable way out. His inability to escape from an intolerable situation makes him particularly vulnerable to feelings of inadequacy and despair, and a sense of complete hopelessness. He often feels impotent, and his ordinary coping mechanisms become inadequate because of a tremendous amount of ambivalence. In the midst of a crisis such a person is usually more amenable to empathic advice, and wise guidance at this time can often forestall self-destructive behavior. The crucial role of a "significant other" in the overall rescue process is one of primary importance.

The would-be suicide is generally subjected to great psychological stresses that are fostered by interpersonal relationships, excessive responsibilities, a rapidly changing society (religion, values), and general problems of living (financial, emotional). It is imperative that we be sensitive to every verbal and behavioral clue, whether overt or covert. The clues seem to indicate an "either/or" dichotomy of problem solving, neither of which is acceptable to the person immersed in the crisis.

Nevertheless, those surrounding the person who is giving the clues usually experience considerable discomfort and anxiety. The clues frighten and immobilize relatives, friends, and neighbors, preventing them from providing the emotional support needed by the person in crisis. Attempted suicide or suicidal threats often antagonize others (family, friends, professionals) and make them feel uncomfortable and inadequate; an angry response, or the failure to respond at all to the communication, exacerbates the sense of isolation. The suicide attempter needs total support and encouragement to find more socially accepted and appropriate problem solving techniques. He must be helped to expand his repertoire of constructive problem solving. The initial response should be done in a meaningful and caring manner; then emotional support from family, friends, and clergy should be mobilized, followed immediately by professional assistance or referral. It is vital that the continuity of care and response be maintained until the person has been helped to find a more satisfying way to live.

It is difficult to imagine that about three or four people kill themselves every hour in the United States. The recorded statistics suggest that 11 per 100,000 people in the United States—26,000 people—commit suicide each year. But experts in the field of suicidology maintain that conservative estimates of the true statistics put the total number of suicides at **50,000 each year!** Studies on Black suicides, car accidents, and psychological autopsies have begun to validate these new estimates.

Even more awesome is the fact that about one million people attempt suicide each year—20 times the number of completed suicides. The magnitude of the problem is so incredible, so repugnant, that we tend to scoff at the figures and to reject the reality of the situation. To some it is too distasteful to realize that suicide is the second cause of death for young people between the ages of 18 and 24 (the college years). Most disturbing is the fact that the statistics on young people in California have recently risen at an alarming rate. **Automobile accidents and homicide are less of a problem in our country than self-destructive behavior.** These figures, which have been substantiated by responsible researchers, are available from the National Institute of Mental Health in Washington, D.C. Mr. Heilig, of the Suicide Prevention Service of Los Angeles, estimates that at least three million people living in the United States have attempted some form of suicide during their lifetime. Hidden methods of suicide, such as autocide, drug abuse, and victim-precipitated homicide, contribute to the updating of previously inaccurate statistics (Yolles, 1968). Recent books by Lester, Grollman, and Dublin provide an in-depth analysis of the available statistics.

Before we examine the historical perspective, it is necessary to recognize that suicide data of the past are highly unreliable because of societal stigma, religious beliefs, and differences in methods of compilation.

Existing theories and concepts must now be re-evaluated because the statistics on which they have been constructed are often no longer valid. For example, the urban versus suburban dichotomy of suicidal behavior, which suggested that living in a rural country area is more beneficial to one's mental health, has recently been overturned by the research findings of Dr. Linden at the University of Georgia. He discovered that the statistics used to explain the theory are not valid, and that the rate of suicide in many rural areas is equally as high as that in the cities. Similar problems with statistics concerning the suicide rate of Blacks led to the theory of victim-precipitated homicide and indicated the gross inadequacy of true reporting in those particular areas of the city.

Historical Perspective and Literature Review

The National Save-a-Life League in New York, established in 1906, is acknowledged as the pioneer in the field. A young woman who had overdosed told Rev. Harry N. Warren that if someone had been able to talk to her, she would not have done it. Her dilemma so moved him that he organized the League with the help of a few determined citizens. Today, the National Save-a-Life League is funded by voluntary contributions of $55,000 per year and is staffed by seven daytime employees, plus 15 volunteers who work one night a week from 5 p.m. to 8 a.m. During the day, professionals provide face-to-face consultation (Blaher, 1970) and personal visits (1971).

It took five decades—a period encompassing two world wars, a depression, and unprecedented economic growth—for another significant breakthrough to occur in the field of suicide prevention. Federal funding provided the financial basis for Drs. Shneidman and Farberow to establish a pilot research project with Drs. Norman Farberow and Robert Litman as co-directors. Only a brief review of the agency will be presented since the Center has issued a considerable amount of materials and descriptions of its service. The staff, almost all of whom are paid professionals, offers face-to-face psychotherapy. As a research and training center, its efforts have in great measure been credited with giving birth to all existing centers. Nevertheless, their unique setup cannot and does not provide an overall approach to the variety and depth of problems encountered by services staffed solely by volunteers and functioning in small communities. Most of the existing services have learned from the experience of the Los Angeles Suicide Prevention Center and use either all or part of its training manual. In addition, to its research programs, the Los Angeles Suicide Prevention Center sells a Training Manual and lethality scale; it also rents films, sends speakers (at a fee) to conduct workshops, and sponsors training seminars in Los Angeles.

In 1959, Rescue Inc. was opened in Boston, Massachusetts, under the direction of the Rev. Kenneth Murphy. This service, fully staffed by volunteers, now has its offices in the fire station and is sponsored by the Catholic Church.

The past two decades have witnessed the setting up of over 180 suicide prevention and crisis services and 600 youth and/or drug hotlines. The present study concerns 192 services, of which 142 are classified as suicide prevention and/or crisis services and 50 as youth services.

Associations and Publications

A detailed list of associations and publications concerned with suicide prevention and crisis services is given in Appendix B.

Most of the published literature on the establishment and operation of suicide and/or crisis prevention services is strictly anecdotal describing what has happened in a particular service (Resnik, 1968; McGee and McGee, 1968). The Suicide Prevention Center in Los Angeles, an important pioneer in the field in the United States, is responsible for a great deal of valuable literature, however most of it is anecdotal in nature as well. A few studies offer extensive reviews of the methods of operation of several centers (McGee, 1968; Farberow, 1968; Moyer, 1971; and Haughton, 1968). Moyer's study is primarily concerned with youth services.

Since most of the research and operational information was made available by the Los Angeles Center, its widely duplicated literature will be reviewed first. At the International Society for Suicide Prevention in Copenhagen, Denmark, Farberow (1963) presented a paper describing the creation and organization of the Suicide Prevention Center in Los Angeles. He first discussed the fundamental question of why there should be a suicide prevention center. The answer, he indicated, lies in the fact that the suicidal crisis has special features and significance: it focuses on dramatically heightened intrapersonal and interpersonal emergencies in which life and death frequently hang in the balance. Focused resources are needed for this focused crisis. The suicide prevention service is conceived as an emergency psychiatric first aid center whose resources are geared to meet both individual and societal needs at the moment of crisis. Suicide is not only the individual's problem; it is also society's problem, and society has the responsibility of meeting the need of a suicidal person quickly and efficiently. The noted American jurist, Benjamin R. Cardozo, stated in 1923: "A cry for distress is a summons to rescue." This statement might well serve as the individual and societal **raison d'être** for suicide prevention services. Farberow describes his Center in terms of its five goals and three main activities: clinical treatment, training, and research. Some examples of its extremely valuable research follow.

Litman and Farberow (1961), in presenting a study of 60 suicide attempt cases, aim to help the suicide prevention center staff determine the seriousness of suicidal potential. They suggest that the findings of this study indicate a need for such services in the community. Klugman (1965) examines the characteristics of self-destructive persons, and the treatment techniques needed when crisis situations occur. Klugman describes the reaction to a crisis situation by the suicidal person, the person's ambivalence about dying, and some techniques for handling callers in the crisis state.

Heilig, Farberow, Litman, and Shneidman (1968) have published a valuable study for services that are staffed by non-professional volunteers. After a brief review of the literature, the authors describe in detail the procedures for selection, the criteria for selection, the volunteers selected, and the training program. They also examine the volunteer group a year later and offer views about their work, the pros and cons of the volunteers' effectiveness, and the problems encountered by volunteer personnel.

11

Another description of the Los Angeles Service (Litman, Shneidman, Heilig, and Kramer, 1965) presents the rationale, the operation, and the experiences of crisis-oriented short-term therapy. This short paper is very valuable as supplemental reading for volunteers in other centers who want to read some statistical data and to understand the communicative aspect of the telephone service.

The above-cited articles are based on experiences at the Los Angeles Center and are representative of some of the reviews published. Many of the articles are research studies that have some significance for operating a service, but are very specific in nature.

Farberow (1968), in discussing some of the basic concepts entailed in operating a suicide prevention service, states that most services are established as independent, autonomous services or are incorporated into an existing mental health facility, such as a mental health center. He points out that all services incorporate such common concepts as "crisis intervention, accessibility and availability, integration into the network of community helping agencies and maintenance of responsibility" (p. 4). Farberow expands each of the basic concepts and adds that "suicidal activity is essentially a communication process" that must be followed by an "action response" from the suicide prevention service. He emphasizes the absolute paramount need for community relationship and defines twelve liaisons that should be particularly sought in the community.

In the same study, Farberow notes the need for services to conduct ongoing research and self-evaluation and to train and educate gatekeeper groups. The three main characteristics of 74 services are briefly described: agency affiliation, funding, and type of staff. Farberow also examines four suicide prevention services—two in the United States, two in Europe—to demonstrate four different models of operation, distinguished principally on the basis of the professional or non-professional status of the staff. The Los Angeles Suicide Prevention Service is defined as a model incorporating "a large scale, multidisciplined, professionally organized and directed therapy and milieu centered agency operating in a major metropolitan community."

The Roanoke Rapids Suicide Prevention Service, which operates in a rural area in North Carolina, also has a non-professional staff aided by police telephone and professional advisory council consultation. The Lebensmuedenfuersorge, a service in Vienna, functions in a large city, uses professional staff only, and emphasizes, in addition to suicide prevention, such social services as home visits and an ongoing in-office psychotherapy program. The Samaritans in London are non-professionals whose principal therapeutic technique is a specially developed procedure of befriending potentially suicidal persons.

Haughton (1968) describes briefly some major aspects of 60 suicide prevention programs in terms of who directs the services, who sponsors them, what it costs to operate a 24-hour service, what they do, and who calls them. Haughton acknowledges that his survey is a brief overview (four and one half pages) and therefore somewhat superficial. He suggests that the programs "provide a service that is of unique and special use to their communities and which is of specific value to those who turn to it." (p. 29)

Three anecdotal studies have been done on the Crisis Clinic in Seattle, Washington. Cochrell (1967) completed a master's thesis on an evaluation of caller response and characteristics at the Crisis Clinic. A developmental study of the Seattle Crisis Clinic (funded by a National Institute of Mental Health grant) was written by Berg (1969). He describes the Clinic's unique development as it relates to Seattle. When requests for information are sent to the National Institute of Mental Health, the

Institute suggests Berg's study as the most comprehensive one they have to offer. There is certainly much value in this type of study, but since it is anecdotal, its scope is too narrow; it does not include the vast variety of existing models and ideas that should be disseminated so that others may make a suitable choice for their particular center.

Another master's thesis by Baatz, Haddad, Hartman, Richardson, Roller, and Stuart (1968) describes the Volunteer Training Program of the Seattle Crisis Clinic: how it was developed, what the program is, and, from the volunteer's point of view, how effective it is as a training mechanism. This survey is a valuable aid, but limits itself to a single approach to a volunteer training program.

Resnick (1968) discusses the operation of a service called Friends in Dade County: how the service was initiated; a review of the callers in a twelve-month period; and a description of the 25 workers, including the results of a series of psychological tests they completed. He recommends closer examination of the type of volunteer used. Unfortunately, this particular service is no longer in existence, having been replaced by another. An expanded and more detailed version of the above article can be found in **Suicidal Behaviors** (1968), edited by Resnick; the compilation includes about six additional articles dealing with suicide prevention per se and with suicide prevention in several other countries.

Anecdotal studies describing the establishment and/or operation of particular suicide prevention and youth-oriented services have also been completed by Fisher (1970) and by Jaffee, Beyer, Clark, Cytrynbaum, Quinlan and Reed (1971).

Dr. Richard McGee has been a prolific writer in the area of suicide prevention services. In an article published in 1965 he states that his major objective is "to develop an operational design for a suicide prevention center, and to show how each of the major components of a mental health program is demonstrated in its operation" (p. 163). He defends the community need for suicide prevention with a general review of the statistics and the hypothesis that suicide attempts represent a "cry for help" and not necessarily a rejection of life. To support his view that a cry for help must be answered, he cites Caplan's suggestion that in a crisis a person has a wish for help and is susceptible to another's influence. Farberow and Shneidman's research (1961) indicates that in 90 per cent of actual suicides some type of subtle or direct warning was given. McGee describes four functions of a center and discusses its personnel and the necessity for their having compassion and empathy. After presenting a brief overview of a proposed suicide prevention center, McGee discusses the proposed facility in terms of its relation to the community, and then describes the establishment of the "We Care" Suicide and Crisis Prevention Service in Orlando. In another article (1966) McGee emphasized four general principles that should be incorporated in all suicide prevention services: "utilization of non-professional manpower, participation in a broad base of community service, flexibility of mission and commitment to research." (p. 5)

In 1968, McGee presented "Some reflections on the character of suicide prevention centers," a study somewhat more comprehensive than any previous one. He studied 11 centers in the Southeast which he considered representative. The important characteristics he delineates include purpose, participation, procedures, and personnel. McGee stresses the need for very concerned deliberation when deciding on the purposes and goals of the service. Clearly stated goals help to define the service and enable evaluation of its effectiveness. Although McGee suggests that every center he visited can document case histories in which they have prevented a suicide, limiting the goal to suicide prevention would exclude 85% of all calls received in most centers throughout the country from people who have difficulty with the problems of living.

It is important, in his opinion, that the goals and purposes encompass a much broader scope of community service. Community participation and liaisons must be sought with all helping services in the development and operation of the center.

In connection with procedures, McGee discusses two telephone methods: contact with the caller—via phone or person-to-person—and a transfer procedure whereby the caller is turned over to and accepted by another service. He reports that callers respond with "gratitude" when they are followed up 30, 60, and 90 days after their initial call. The volunteer worker and back-up consultants are described in terms of their importance to the operation of the service. McGee concludes with the observation that "the preceding pages have represented an attempt to draw together, in brief introductory fashion, the conclusions and tentative findings which have emerged from a two year research project involving a close look at eleven existing prevention centers in the Southeast." (p. 25)

A master's thesis by Moyer (1971) on the Richmond Hotline analyzes the characteristics of the callers, the problems they present, the characteristics of the calls themselves, and the methods of handling the specific calls. The Richmond service is also compared with several similar hotlines. Moyer's study was done from the perspective of "the knowledge of preventive techniques used by occupational therapists in the community."

Recently, through their own **Crisis Intervention Journal** (Erie County), Brockopp and Lester have made available pertinent articles on the operation of services and on the problems encountered. This journal was distributed free of charge to all existing services. Brockopp's articles, published in 1970 and 1971, discuss such subjects as the caller who is a masturbator, the silent caller, the call itself, the training of the telephone therapist, and problems with repeat callers. He outlines seven predictions for the future of suicide prevention (1970):

1. Exploration of new methods for finding people in crisis and for bringing them into the network of assistance.

2. There will be changes in the pattern of patient care at suicide and crisis centers (from shorter to longer term intervention).

3. Marriage of the volunteer and professional into a team of mental health associates.

4. Exploration and innovation of new mental health services.

5. Suicide prevention centers in the 1970s will be funded by a combination of community and state money.

6. Post-vention will take on increased importance.

7. Integration of suicide prevention into the broader community mental health services. (pp. 2—7)

Dr. David Lester (1970—1971) has attempted to deal primarily with the characteristics and types of population who call the Erie County Suicide Prevention Service. His articles are informative and highly recommended.

One of the few very critical articles about suicide prevention services was written by Weiner (1969), who seriously questions the effectiveness of existing suicide prevention services. He compares the suicide rate in Los Angeles County before and after the establishment of the suicide prevention service and concludes that, "using only the factor of 'suicide rate,' there is little objective evidence to support the

14

assumption that present services and techniques used by the Los Angeles Suicide Prevention Center are effective in suicide prevention." (p. 360)

A thorough study by Bagely (1968) in England compared the suicide statistics in towns with the Samaritan Services (SPC) to those of similar towns that lacked the services. He concluded that the suicide statistics were lower in the majority of the cities with the Samaritan group or climbed only slightly. On the other hand, in towns without Samaritan groups, suicide statistics rose much more significantly.

The evaluation and effectiveness of the services will be discussed in more detail in Chapter V under the section on Evaluation and Research.

The foregoing review of the literature was narrowly designed to include material that is specifically pertinent to the operation of suicide prevention and/or crisis services. There are several reasons for this limitation. In the first place, the bulk of the literature written and more readily accessible concerns the theories of suicide, the historical views and taboos of suicide, and the psychology of suicide. Secondly, the specific category areas discussed in Chapter V will incorporate the present statistical data, personal experience, interviews, and relevant literature. Since this work will focus on the operation of 192 SPC/youth services, it must necessarily omit discussion of the theories, psychology, and historical views of suicide. To compensate for this limitation, the bibliography has been extended to incorporate a much wider range of literature.

CHAPTER IV

NATIONAL SURVEY AND RESULTS

A questionnaire containing twenty questions was sent to all the known suicide and crisis intervention services together with a request for as much information as possible concerning their methods of operation. Some services simply responded to the questions; others returned a complete description, including the materials used in their procedures.

Information was also gathered from personal visits and interviews at 25 services throughout the country (Appendix A). Knowledge acquired through attendance at previously mentioned workshops and meetings has also been incorporated.

Questionnaire Responses

The following information was abstracted from the responses of 192 suicide prevention and crisis services concerning their own operation. The replies, in their totality, provide an overview of the range of services throughout the United States. For those who may wish to examine the results in statistical tables, they are presented in Appendix A. A summary of the findings follows.

The primary goals of all the services is crisis intervention, with suicide prevention being stressed by the non-youth focused services. Lesser goals included information and referral, community education and, unfortunately, a lower priority in the area of research. Very few services indicated religious messages to be a significant goal; interestingly, however, those that do so seem to be youth-oriented services which are sponsored and funded by a church or religious organization.

Fully one-third of the services receive funds from three or more sources. The data suggest that the majority are funded by community organization donations, particularly for youth services. This contrasts with a few of the larger crisis services which are supported by large government grants. The nature of funding, which is a critical and ever-present problem for almost all services, has a direct impact on the quality of the services and on their administration, publicity, research, and staffing. This particular aspect will be discussed in more detail in the following chapter.

The setting or location often has a profound effect on the delivery of services and on organizational structure and telephone method. Most of the services have a separate or private facility; the next largest group utilizes their homes either exclusively or functions in conjunction with an office. About 12 per cent of the respondents use their homes exclusively for providing service.

The staffing pattern in the majority of services reveals that they have no paid staff (34%), or one to two paid staff (34%) at most. For the great majority, the total number of volunteer staff ranges from 11 to 120.

The very recent proliferation of suicide prevention and crisis services is demonstrated by the response to the question on length of operation. Fully 59% of the suicide prevention centers and 84% of the youth services were established less than four years ago. This rapid growth certainly underscores the salient need for research concerning the effectiveness of the methods and techniques used in these operations and their impact on communities.

The nature of the telephone method used in a service is critical, for it involves the effect on the immediate delivery of service and the response to the caller. Almost half the services (45%) use the direct telephone method, the most immediate type available. One third of the services report that they employ the direct method in combination with another telephone method. The use of two or more telephone methods is directly related to the number of locations used to provide service.

Almost all (93%) of the suicide crisis services provide 24-hour service and availability, while only 50% of the youth services do so. When they do not provide 24-hour service, they seem to focus on weekends and evenings only.

Approximately one-half (44%) of the total surveyed provide telephone-only services. In those services which offer direct contact, both professionals and non-professionals are used in almost equal numbers. The youth-oriented services tend to utilize more non-professional outreach teams in this capacity. There appears to be a recent trend toward establishing more outreach services.

Minimal record-keeping is conducted at all services, even if it is only keeping a record of the number of calls received. Suicide prevention centers tend to keep much more extensive records and case files than do youth services. The youth services invariably do not concern themselves with keeping a file of the name of the caller or any other identifying material. One small group suggested that they did so only when referral appointments or active intervention was needed. In response to the question concerning the tape-recording of calls, very few (8%) indicated that they do some recording, but only for purposes of training or evaluating the effectiveness of the telephone worker! There has been much controversy about this method, and the Task Force of the American Association of Suicidology has presented a position paper against the use of tape recording unless the caller is immediately informed. Complete confidentiality is strictly adhered to in connection with the tapes.

Less than half (43%) of the suicide prevention centers consistently follow up the calls during the first week. Most do very little followup, but, of course, this would be directly related to the fact that they do not keep files or attempt to identify the caller. Whatever followup is undertaken seems to be done for clinical reasons rather than for research purposes.

Tabulated data concerning telephone worker training suggest that 10 - 20 preservice telephone worker training hours is typical of many programs. The training, which varies extensively in content and method, will be discussed in the next chapter. Only a small minority of suicide prevention centers (5%) and youth services (2%) have no specific training program. Such services may be the ones that are an integral part of a mental health center or hospital that utilizes only four or five professional workers to answer the telephone. The majority of suicide prevention centers (58%) indicate they have inservice training once a month; almost half of the respondents of the youth group (44%) report that they have meetings every week.

The total sample responded to the question on publicity methods, and 75% indicated the use of four or more methods. The tabulation reveals the methods used, but in no way implies their effectiveness. Because the efficacy of the publicity methods is critical to the utilization of services, this area will be fully examined in the following chapter.

The responses to the question dealing with Problem Areas indicates that the chronic (repeater) caller (42%) and funding (42%) are the major problem areas for the suicide prevention centers. For youth services, while the same two areas are reported as major problems, funding (57%) is more critical. Volunteer dropout is the third largest problem area for both the prevention services and the youth services. It is

17

interesting to note that crank calls and obscene calls constitute the lowest percentage and are apparently insignificant problems.

The services which reported that they were involved in research on the impact on the community constituted only 23% of the total sample. Many were compiling a simple tabulation of calls received, but were not interpreting their statistics. The critical nature of this response will also be examined in subsequent chapters in view of the lack of research being done to show the efficacy of these services.

The response to the question concerning characteristics of callers presented difficult interpretation problems for a variety of reasons. Those interested in more detail can consult Tables 18, 19, 19b, and 20 in Appendix A. Tables 19 and 19b offer some general characteristics about the age of callers. Among the suicide prevention center services, 70% of those who submitted replies about total figures indicate that 1 - 30% of their calls come from the 10 - 20 age group. It appears that the 21 - 30 and 31 - 40 age groups are the most numerous callers to suicide prevention centers. At the youth services, the overwhelming majority of calls are received from the 10 - 20 age group, with some spillover to the 21 - 30 group.

Table 20 represents the percentage ratio between male and female callers to the services. The responses exhibit some very interesting trends: the younger the caller, the higher the percentage of male callers; but this consistently decreases with age for both the suicide prevention centers and the youth services. These figures should be examined together with the suicide statistics to determine whether the lethal population is, in fact, being reached or is responding. I shall discuss this point in the next chapter.

The majority of services receive up to 500 calls a month; 30% receive more than that number. In fact, several services receive up to 10,000 calls a month, but this occurs only in very large metropolitan areas such as New York City.

A very significant finding was the data collected on the time of day when most calls are received. We now know that the services receive the vast majority of their calls during the "leisure" hours of 4 p.m. to 1 a.m., when most other helping services or agencies in a community are closed and not available to the person experiencing a crisis.

As with the question on the characteristics of callers, the category of calls and the primary complaint were extremely difficult to tabulate or validate. However, the following is a brief summary of the findings (the tables are available in Appendix A). Based on the available data (and bearing in mind the possible limitations of their validity), some very tentative observations may be noted. In the suicide prevention center responses, 81% indicated that 1 - 20% of their calls concern suicide attempts in progress; the majority of these respondents were categorized in the 1 - 5% bracket. Sixty-nine per cent specified that 1 - 20% of their callers are involved in suicide attempts or have specific suicide plans. An overwhelming majority state that non-suicidal crisis situations constitute 21 - 100% of their calls. Information calls make up 1 - 40% of all calls received by the majority of suicide prevention centers. Third-party calls were mentioned by 42% of the suicide prevention centers as constituting 1 - 10% of their calls. The compiled data for the suicide prevention center group suggest that a complaint about marital stress of some form is the most frequent type of call received. Following closely are multiple problems, alcohol, drugs, and sex problems. Tabulation for the youth group data implies that drug problems are the primary reason for calling for help; sex and multifactor problems follow as reasons for primary contact. Analysis of the data reveals that a great many of the categories overlap and that many have been subsumed under multifactor problems.

18

CHAPTER V

SELECTED CATEGORIES CONCERNING OPERATION TECHNIQUES

In terms of selected categories concerning the operation of Services, this chapter will consider the results from the questionnaire survey, pertinent literature, and information and knowledge from workshops, meetings, interviews and personal experience.

The whole area of statistics about suicidal populations and suicide theories will for the most part be excluded from consideration. These areas have been adequately documented by many writers, and the following are recommended as very interesting and informative books: Lester and Lester (1971), Dublin (1963), and Grollman (1971). Additional articles can be found in the bibliography by Farberow (1969) or in bibliographies included in the **Crisis Intervention Journal** and at the end of this thesis.

Goals and Purposes

What do the Suicide Prevention and/or Crisis Services really **do?** What are their purposes and goals? These questions are frequently asked about these relatively new services that deviate from the norm in the provision of mental health services to the community. The primary goal is to provide an "immediate response" to people, twenty four hours a day.

The following acrostic was written by a caller to a suicide prevention and crisis service after its immediate response to her suicidal crisis. It defines what these services really do and mean to callers.

WHAT "SUICIDE PREVENTION" MEANS TO ME

S   is for Service they give without pay,
U   is for Understanding they have every day,
I   is for their Interest which will never end,
C   means that they Care and want to be your friend.
I   is for Important; that's the way they make you feel,
D   is for their Devotion, and you can be sure that it's real.
E   means they are Eager to do what they can.

P   means they are Patient and will understand.
R   is for the Reassurance they will try hard to give.
E   is for the Effort you must give to live.
V   is for Victory you see they are sure you will win,
E   means they will Ease the pain you have within.
N   means they will NEVER ever say no,
T   means you can Trust them, and I ought to know.
I   is for Instantly that's how soon they are there,
O   means simply that they Obviously do care.
N   means their help will NEVER end,

And believe me in them I have found many a friend.
Put all of these letters together in a line
And I'm sure the words
Faith, Love and Friends you will find.

Regardless of the stated goals of the Suicide Prevention and Crisis Service, the above acrostic defines what the service meant to a specific caller.

The **raison d'etre** of these services is based on some common assumptions, many of which have been researched and documented. Dublin (1963) proposed that "frequently the counsel of a kindly and understanding confident acts as an antidote to suicide." In such periods of stress and strain, human kindness and sympathy are preventive measures. Wise guidance "at the moment of crisis may often forestall the impulse to destroy oneself." (p. 179)

There is very general consensus that the acts of suicide or suicide attempts can be a serious attempt to 'communicate' that one is in a serious crisis state with a lack of alternative coping techniques. The act, essentially can be viewed as a "behavioral communication" (Farberow 1961) acknowledging one's rejection of an intolerable situation rather than a sincere rejection of life itself. This behavioral act is often felt to be accompanied by feelings of helplessness, hoplessness and by severe ambivalence, "a simultaneous wish to live and to die." (Walzer 1971) A further reason for intervening is the assumption that crisis (a special stress) often is a temporary state or a situational one. The anxiety and stress that accompanies a crisis situation seriously interferes with and impedes ordinary coping mechanisms and limits the extent of the previous repetoire of techniques. Caplan (1964) suggested that people in crisis are usually feeling helpless, hopeless, alone, confused, fearful and suspicious, thus are quite willing to accept advice and counsel which can help them redirect their lives. Noyes (1970) stated that:

> The view that most suicides occur during crisis has formed the basis for a belief that this can be a rational and successful approach to prevention. Litman notes that self-destructive persons are highly ambivalent and that they provide for the alert respondent verbal and behavioral clues to their suicidal consideration. (Litman 1966) When such respondents are readily available and take appropriate action a suicidal crisis may be successfully surmounted. (p. 361)

Recognition by Harry M. Warren (1906), the Samaritans (1956) who do "befriending," Rescue, Inc. (1959) and the Los Angeles Suicide Prevention Center (1958) that people in crisis can be responded to in a meaningful way particularly when they reveal 'clues' to the crisis state they are experiencing is tantamount to providing this response. Ventilation of emotion to a concerned and empathic listener can often reduce suicidal tendencies or feelings. Farberow and Shneidman (1956) discovered that completed suicides do in fact communicate their self-destructive intentions to at least one other person. Bell (1967) states that studies have shown that eight out of ten suicidal people ask for help in some direct way. They are looking desperately for someone with whom they can talk about their problems. The fact that 80 per cent of suicidal persons try in some way to communicate to their friends, relatives and doctors about their self-destructive intent seems to be a manifestation of the ambivalence that surrounds a fatal solution. The ambivalence about death as a solution to problems causes the potential suicide to give clues to others about his self-destructive intentions. This seems to indicate the individual hopes that someone will intervene with a less destructive alternative.

The myths (Appendix D) and stigma that have surrounded suicide for many years interfered with the response to this crisis state. The motives behind suicidal behavior are very complex and unique to each person but there is general agreement that interpersonal relationships have a profound effect as does a complex and stressful society. Albee (1969) stresses that it is necessary to replace the medical model definition of emotionally disturbed behavior with a "social-development" one before it will be possible to provide "large scale intervention and prevention of human misery . . . . through nurturance of strength and social engineering to strengthen the family." (p. 46) The worker at the Suicide Prevention Center and Youth services often acts as a concerned "surrogate" for an exhausted family who do not understand or who become part of the exhausted family syndrome. Societal changes, especially rapid ones, appear to be among the contributing factors. These societal changes include the change from the extended family to a nuclear one without much support; technological stress; excessive mobility with a resultant lessening of community neighborhood or religious ties; questioning of previously accepted morals and values; and, a lack of friendly and supportive resources.

Responses to the questionnaire concerning goals and purposes denoted some difference between the youth and SPC in terms of emphasis (Table 1) but essentially the major goals indicated by both included suicide prevention, crisis intervention, community education and referral. A minor discrepancy occurred in the category of research as a goal or purpose with more of the SPC's responding affirmatively to the area of research. This will be discussed as a separate category.

There are some generalizations that may be drawn from the 192 respondents. Essentially the purpose and goals of the services described by the 192 respondents are to provide a free, easily accessible open line of communication 24 hours a day (although Youth services often provide less) permitting any person regardless of age to call for help with or information about such problems as interpersonal conflict, hopelessness, crisis, drugs, and/or loneliness. The services generally offer an instantaneous, concerned and empathic response from a worker whose sole purpose is to actively listen, evaluate and formulate with the caller a therapeutic plan of referral or intervention, whichever is deemed necessary and appropriate. All of this is done as the worker attempts to establish a trusting relationship to alleviate the enormous feelings of worthlessness, helplessness and inadequacy felt by a great many of the callers. The telephone worker endeavors to help the caller find alternative solutions to his problem and to mobilize resources to provide emotional support for him. Crisis intervention is the most important of the three major goals of the majority of SPC and Youth services.

Referral, a second major component of the services requires an intimate knowledge of all the available community services that can be utilized. The majority of Suicide Prevention and/or Crisis Services provide the telephone worker with a book that lists all the available helping resources and attempts to define which resources would be the most helpful and appropriate. Knowledge is usually gathered by sending the resource services a questionnaire requesting a definition of services (Appendix E) they provide or by personally visiting and evaluating the services. Some SPC/Youth services, then send referral forms to determine whether a caller who was referred did in fact, go to the referral source and, if so, whether it was an appropriate referral. These referral forms are considered a beneficial way of determining whether the scope of the resource agency is truly understood.

The SPC's and Youth services can provide two services to the community when referring: they can maximize the use of the existing services and define the "gaps" in community services. With the proper recognition and credibility, the SPC and Youth services can act as important catalysts and play a viable role in helping to provide the kind of services needed by the citizens, as the citizens themselves define their needs.

Community education, the third major role of the SPC/Youth service focuses attention upon educating the community to recognize the "clues to suicide and crisis." Such education should help to destroy the age old myths and taboos long associated with suicide and emotional crisis. The services attempt to educate the citizens to be sensitive and responsive to those verbal and behavioral communications about feelings of helplessness and hopelessness. The following activities of the services are most important in community education.

21

1.   Speeches and talks to schools, organizations and other groups and agencies.

2.   Publicity materials such as brochures.

3.   Sponsoring workshops for professionals and gatekeepers in the community.

The purposes and goals of these services are affected, sometimes unfortunately by sponsorship, location and funding.

Hall (1969) in Cleveland, Ohio has suggested that the effective creation and operation of these programs depends on the acknowledgement of three basic facts. These include the shortage of professional personnel, the lack of adequate funding and the increasing awareness of the need for providing twenty-four hour help to people in crisis.

Specific goals and purposes as well as budgetary limitations will necessarily determine the number and the proportion of professional and non-professional, paid or volunteer staff members in any particular service. The Corpus Christie, Texas service has observed that the cost of its staff, if paid, would be $98,122. In this service, which actually received $8,500 through grants and donations, the volunteer staff performs a vital and critical role in the provision and maintenance of community mental health services. Although matters of staffing and operation will be discussed in more detail later in this thesis, it is important to note here some general structural characteristics and needs. A total of 85% of the services specify that they use volunteers, professional and non-professional on their staff. Some 50% utilize them through the medium of the telephone and the other 50% provide some type of personal face to face contact. In those 50% which do provide face to face contact, both professionals and non-professionals are utilized equally at a central location and/or with outreach teams.

Many services indicated that they have outreach teams for emergencies, many others implied that lack of outreach teams presented frustrating problems, especially when no other community services provided this type of help. Richard and McGee (1971) outline the **rationale** for and functions of the Care Team (outreach) at Gainesville, Florida. The team responds to serious crisis situations particularly when police intervention is illegal or inappropriate and yet personal contact would be helpful.

The structure of the service usually includes an executive policy making board and an advisory board. The advisory board is generally composed of representatives from significant helping sources and agencies in the community and ordinarily meets once or twice a year. Serving primarily in an advisory capacity they do not make policy but do provide two way communication and feedback both to the SPC and their own agencies. Furthermore the advisory board is to facilitate cooperative liaisons with the total community, an important function that cannot be overemphasized.

The executive board functions as the policy making board and is responsible for the operation of the service. Some services have representatives of the staff attend meetings; others incorporate staff, telephone workers, and board members. It is vital to include on the board mental health professionals able to function as trainers and back-up consultants. Occasionally, a separate professional consultant board consisting of psychiatrists, psychologists, social workers and clergy is established. They assume active roles as trainers, consultants to telephone workers, and advisors, but do not function as policy makers. The executive board ordinarily meets once a month although several respondents suggested that their boards meet every second month, four times a year, or whenever needed. Other services indicated that they meet every week when they are intimately involved in the operation and function of the service itself. Examples of several authority structures are located in Appendix F.

Various services investigated are not in complete agreement about some important matters of philosophy and procedure. There still remains much controversy over whether the service should initiate contact with someone who has not called the service. If a "third person" calls and is worried about another person some services indicate that they will call the "person in crisis" and others tell the third person what he can do to help or insist that the "person in crisis" himself must call if the wishes help. The controversy also includes calling attempters reported to the SPC's by police or emergency room and contacting remaining family members of a suicidal victim. While there still exists some serious controversy, there appears to be a trend towards more involvement and broadening of the scope of intervention.

Controversy also exists concerning the name of the service. Shneidman and Farberow when establishing the center in Los Angeles felt that the name should include **Suicide** because it was time for the taboo problem and its attendant stigma to be brought out into the open where it could be acknowledged and dealt with openly and constructively. There are some who state that the term "suicide prevention" limits the scope of service by indicating that a person must **qualify** to receive its help. Others say that since most of the callers (between 80-85%) are not specifically suicidal, the term "suicide prevention" is a misnomer. On the other hand still others feel that since suicide is the ultimate crisis, the term allows the caller to speak about the otherwise forbidden feelings. Wetzel (1971) concluded from results of a recent study that the name of a service is not a significant factor in reaching suicidal people. He reported that there was much similarity between callers to both the SPC and Crisis Service although the callers to the SPC were more concerned with lasting and significant relationships. He further suggested that the SPC may attract more callers who have had several depressive episodes and who exhibit family pathology. There was a significant difference in the number of callers who were in the midst of a suicide attempt: 25% at the SPC and 6% at the Crisis Service.

The greatest majority of the services guarantee the caller confidentiality. In most cases this guarantee is seriously adhered to, although possibly it is misinterpreted. Most services use this appeal, especially to the Youth who apparently feel very uncomfortable with the "establishment" and those others who appear to fear exposure, at least in the beginning. There is some legal question about the fact that the service could not be truly confidential if records were subpoenaed by the law, but records are rarely likely to be subpoenaed, if ever. There is a supreme effort to guard the confidential aspect of the call. There is a possibility that some services are not even trying to get more information or names because of overreaction to the confidentiality guarantee. Concern about confidentiality does interfere with research and follow ups concerning the service's effective impact on caller and community.

Some services visited stated that they had very specific goals and yet others indicated they were broadening the scope of their purposes and goals in response to need. The variety of purposes and scope is apparent in the sample descriptions of services presented below.

1. Is designated as a Selective Service Program for conscientious objectors (SPC of Alameda County, California)

2. Provides a "life line" chain of callers for shut-ins or elderly (Rescue Inc., Boston) (Portsmouth, Virginia)

3. Conduct crisis training for police recruits (Stark County, Ohio) (Dallas, Texas)

4. Encourages suicidal pen pals (San Francisco, California)

5. Conducts "Psychological Autopsies" (Gainesville, Florida)

6. Provides consultation to "gatekeepers." (Erie County (Buffalo) New York)

7. Provides short term counselling and therapy. (Erie County, New York) (Philadelphia, Pennsylvania)

8. Sends youngsters, from a family where a suicide occurred to a summer camp for a week. (National Save-a-Life League, New York)

9. Dispatches someone to the home of the caller to provide help and support. (Cincinnati, Ohio) (Van Nuys, California) (Gainesville, Florida)

10. Goes with police to home of attempter. (Gainesville, Florida)

11. Conducts extensive and systematic follow up of callers (Gainesville, Florida) (Orlando, Florida)

12. Acts as a temporary catalytic agent inducing the community to provide services and then the SPC will self-destruct. (Erie County, (Buffalo) New York)

13. Fosters and sponsor Youth Hotlines (Gainesville, Florida)

14. Offers parent counselling (Mt. Clemens, Michigan)

15. Trains workers to go back into the community--keep them on staff for only one year (Columbus, Ohio)

16. Provides impetus to start a drug drop-in facility (Amarillo, Texas)

17. Offers group therapy program (Dallas, Texas)

18. Conducts rap groups (Sunland, California)

19. Conducts research on volunteer effectiveness (Gainesville, Florida)

20. Helps the family of suicidal person understand and cope with the problem.

21. Offers opportunity for field work with credit for graduate students.

22. "Baby sit" and outreach for drug problems (Santa Ynez, California) (Palm Springs, California)

23. Christian Oriented Message (La Puenta, California)

24. Conducts research concerning rumors (Moscow, Idaho)

The diversity of approaches listed above characterizes some of the unique interpretations each service defines for itself relative to community needs. Essentially, the growth of the services has been fostered by the model and purposes presented by the Los Angeles Suicide Prevention Center; nevertheless each service has recognized the need to be autonomous and to fulfill the needs of its own particular community.

The foregoing discussion implies that the **purposes and goals are manifold,** each one crucial in and of itself but it is Shneidman, quoted in an article by Asbell (1970) who defines the primary task of all services by stating:

When a man is floundering a lifeline must be
thrown to him. It is neither the time nor
the task of the rescuer to teach the drowning
man to swim or to improve his stroke . . . .
the first telephone interview often spells the
difference between life and death.

Sponsors and Funding

The two items, sponsors and funding were grouped together in the questionnaire and will be discussed as one category because of their often overlapping functions.

Sponsors

The absolute necessity to secure sponsorship by some credible sources, agencies, association or persons was cited by an overwhelming majority of services that were interviewed. They emphasized the need to incorporate, on a planning or advisory board, representatives from a great many community agencies when initially planning and establishing the service. Emphasis on this factor is related to community acceptance, funding, and, of course, use of the agencies for referral purposes. Sponsorship can occur in several ways. An SPC or Youth service can be sponsored by any specific group, agency, or organization such as the Mental Health Association, Mental Health Center or Clinic, Hospital, Ministerial or Council of Churches association.

Sponsorship by a group may be either "integral" or "autonomous." Integral refers to a type of sponsorship whereby the SPC or Youth service becomes a part of the sponsoring organization and is governed by its structure and board. Integral sponsorship affect flexibility of operation, but may make it easier to obtain funds. If a service is "autonomous," sponsoring organizations publicly endorse the service, its purposes and goals, but do not have any real power over policy making.

An example of an "Integral" sponsorship is the Mental Health Association or Mental Health Clinic, whose board makes all policy and provides funding. McGee (1971) discusses some of the particular aspects of sponsorship through the Mental Health Association. He acknowledges the very helpful role of the M.H.A. in acting as a catalyst to fill in the gap in community service. Although the Mental Health Association was the active organizer and legitimizer of services in the community (Stark County, Ohio; Abilene, Texas; etc.), McGee suggests that sponsorship of a certain type can be detrimental to growth and delivery of services. Having identified three patterns of Mental Health Association sponsorship, he concludes that the

Mental Health Associations should be encouraged to take an active and
vigorous role in the stimulation and initiation of suicide and crisis services,
but that they can only do irreconcilable harm to the program, and perhaps

to their own internal organization, unless they set about very early to make the program completely independent of the association itself. (p. 66)

In an "autonomous" type of sponsorship the sponsoring groups would not intervene essentially in policy making, but would indicate their approval of the service and work towards providing funding and credibility. Whether "integral" or "autonomous," crisis intervention services should include on the advisory or planning board the following people: representatives from the medical association, police departments, all community service agencies, and fire departments as well as coroner, psychiatrists, psychologists, directors of the hospitals, directors of emergency rooms, and representatives from the welfare department, courts and legal associations, legal aid, Ministerial Associations and Universities. It is critical to ask these agents in the planning stages for suggestions, ideas, and involvement. Good liaison with these representatives will certainly seriously affect delivery of services by the SPC and Youth services. There must exist a sense of mutual cooperation in providing service to the citizen rather than one of competition for clients and community funds. This cannot be over emphasized if there is a sincere commitment to delivery of immediate and effective service.

Funding

The survey data indicate that a major source of funding for both the SPC and Youth services comes from private donations. Forty-three per cent (43%) of the SPC's and 71% of the Youth derive their funds from private sources. The problem of funding is indicated as a major problem area by 42% of the SPC's and 57% of the Youth services; a total of 32% receive funding from three or more sources. Private donations and donations from organizations are the primary source for the Youth services. From comments on the questionnaire, the following have also provided funds to some degree to services: P.T.A., Y.M.C.A., Y.W.C.A., service organizations, O.E.O. grants or contracts from city, county, state and federal governments, Mental Health Associations, private foundations, industry, United Funds, Universities, Churches, Health Departments, Mental Health and Mental Retardation Boards, general or psychiatric Hospitals and Mental Health Centers.

Some other fund raising ideas include Rock concerts (Philadelphia, Pennsylvania), (Orlando, Florida), board member donations, society dance benefits, plays, speakers bureau charges, letters sent to churches, charitable dinners, and student associations. The Jaycees organization sponsors a "Gold Rush" walk where people walk up to 20 miles and secure pledges of money from friends, per mile; one half of the collected money goes to the Wilderness Center and the other to a personally chosen and designated non-profit service. The service in Stark County has received several hundreds of dollars this way. The service in Santa Ynez, California has memberships with a contributing membership costing ten dollars and a supporting membership, fifty dollars. The service in Dallas, granted also the use of an old house, is funded by donations from two persons. The house has been donated to the Mental Health Center for expansion purposes with the proviso that the Center will provide rooms for the SPC in the new building. In Muncie, Indiana, a plea for furniture brought very good response.

The CSSP of N.I.M.H. is also another source of funding for research, training and demonstration projects only; they do **not** fund for direct service.

In spite of the above lists of possible sources, funding remains a critical problem. For example the service in Pueblo, Colorado mentioned that they had requested $19,800 from the United Fund and received only $100. The service in San Raphael, California approached 15 foundations and, so far, had received eight negative responses.

In summary, then, it must be noted that funding and sponsoring can affect effective delivery of services, location, staffing, and research. It is evident from the survey and interviews that the greatest majority of services are working with budgets ranging from $100 to $20,000. Most are fortunate if they have enough money to pay a full time director and part time clerical help. Haughton (1968) in a study examining the cost of operating sixty 24-hour services also found that a number of services existed with budgets under $500 per year while many of the services had annual operational budgets of between $8,000 to $15,000. Apparently this finding is still appropriate, with more of the Youth services in the under $500 category. Only a few services in the country, like Gainesville, Los Angeles and Buffalo are receiving more substantial funding which is primarily for research purposes. When applying for funds, services must seriously consider the following:

(1) The need for accountability.

(2) A complete description of the program including the rationale for its existence.

(3) A thorough study with the needs of the community fully documented.

(4) Evidence of support from credible sources including liaisons with existing services.

(5) Thorough knowledge of experiences of other services in the country with national and local statistics available.

(6) A detailed and documented realistic budget.

(7) The need to support your beliefs in policy where necessary **but** be open to suggestions and be somewhat flexible when flexibility will not be detrimental to the program.

Location

A discussion of the location or the physical setting of a SPC or Youth service must of course be examined in light of the purpose and goals, funding or sponsorship, and telephone system. All the above play a significant role in determining the location of a service.

Goals and Purposes help define the method of delivery of services, whether it be through a "telephone contact only" method or a combination of "telephone and personal contact." Obviously, if a telephone-contact-only system is adopted, there will be a greater flexibility of possible locations. When a "telephone only" service is decided upon, then there is in most cases an attempt to keep the location of the service unknown to the general public to prevent casual drop-ins by callers. Drop-ins are discouraged because the staff is not trained to handle face to face contact adequately and also for security reasons. A "personal contact" method will narrow the scope of choices of location because it will be necessary for it to be easily accessible and available to the callers. Limitations of location, of course, do **not** imply that "personal contact" is less desirable. As a matter of fact the general trend is moving towards providing face to face contact.

The telephone system that one must use also restricts the location of a service. If the service will utilize only a "direct" method, then **one** central location is possible. A decision to provide service originating from several places, (e.g. office and homes) demands the consideration of the availability of different telephone systems such as the patch systems, answering services, or diverters. An example of the interactional effects is demonstrated by some services who state that although its original goal was to provide 24-hour-telephone-only direct service, staffing problems at a central location from 2 a.m. - 9 a.m. elicited a need for the "patch" system during those hours. Since in Ohio the patch can be done only by a non-profit switchboard, the choice of location was limited. It became obvious that the general hospital would be the ideal spot because its non-profit switchboard could "patch" into a home if necessary. The hospital offered additional advantages: accessibility, all night parking, and 24 hour operation providing security.

Funding or sponsorship is also a factor affecting location, for a service often needs to keep rent costs to a minimum. Many services surveyed indicated that their location had been donated by organizations or individuals. The data collected demonstrates that 38% of the SPC's and 50% of the Youth services use a separate central office facility, some of which are in, but not affiliated with, other services, clinics, churches, and universities. Using both the home and another location in combination was indicated by 19% with a group of 12% who utilize their homes **only** for delivery of service.

Types of locations used by services in the United States include, churches, general hospitals, mental health departments, police department, fire station, Y.M.C.A.'s, universities, family service organization, psychiatric clinics, community mental health centers, mental health associations, individual homes, emergency rooms, public mental hospitals, out patient departments, storefront clinics, and old donated storerooms or houses.

Some considerations when choosing location(s) includes

(a)   Telephone contact-only method

(b)   Telephone and personal contact

(c)   Telephone system availability and effectiveness

(d)   Central or multiple locations

(e)   Space for records, phones, desks, files

(f)   Accessibility

(g)   Parking ease

(h)   Staff security

Problems and Advantages

One Central Location--Staffing in one central location can present problems particularly when requiring a staff member to be there or come there in the middle of the night. Some services provide a comfortable cot, coffee, soft drinks, small refrigerator, radio, and TV to make the center as comfortable and inviting as possible. A few centers (Buffalo) have experimented with paying their night staff but have since dropped this procedure. Others have developed husband and wife teams to staff at night providing "good" company and a sense of security. In case of severe weather problems, there can be difficulty having someone reach a central location. This is usually handled by requiring the person on duty to **remain** until relieved. Having a "diverter" device on hand in case of such emergencies would make it possible to receive the calls at home. Usually the night shifts are expanded to eight, ten or twelve hours in length to avoid constantly changing staff during this period. The **rationale** is that it is simpler to take a longer shift during the night and thus serve that shift less often.

Advantages of a central location appear to far outweigh the disadvantages. The ease of reporting and filing plus the availability of files and referrals is cited as a major advantage. The central location also aids in more complete effective record keeping. The atmosphere of the office "for work" without a variety of distractions or interruptions seems to increase the staff's effective response and meaningfulness. The office provides the opportunity for the staff member to perform other clerical duties or follow-ups between calls or to read new materials. The immediate accessibility of a file on a repeat caller is at times crucial to the outcome of the response. Being at a central location also allows the worker to read up on cases and types of incoming problems and the way in which they were handled. In an office some worker interaction is possible; staff members leaving or coming may discuss cases and/or methods and thus acquire a sense of belonging. Probably the most critical advantage is the multiplicity of phones available. Most services have at least two incoming telephones receiving calls and one outgoing for use when help must be summoned, be it emergency police or consultation. Included in this critical advantage is the ability to provide immediate and direct response to the callers. One central location also permits the setup of taping or monitoring devices to evaluate staff response and effectiveness.

Multiple Locations

According to the data, multiple locations usually involve use of a part time central office which is open and manned during the daytime hours, 9 a.m. to 5 p.m., and use of homes by individual staff members during the 5 p.m. to 9 a.m. hours. The lack of two or more phones in most homes is a major disadvantage. It does not allow more than one call to come in at a time and, in a critical circumstance, does not permit emergency help to be summoned without breaking contact with the caller. Some services evaluate the crisis nature of the call and, if a non-crisis, ask the caller to call back when the central location is open. Some deal only with crisis calls and do not stay on the phone for any length of time. There are no files to refer to about previous callers, but some services indicate that each worker is provided with a referral manual and repeater's bulletin to offset some of these problems. Evaluation of the staff member's effectiveness and response by taping the call or monitoring it would be impossible. Record keeping can be seriously hampered by using homes because call report forms often are not turned in to the office immediately, if at all. The next staff member on duty often is not aware of calls or recurrent problems handled by previous staff that day. This particular problem has been recognized and dealt with in several ways: one service insists that the staff worker must bring in the call report forms within 24 hours after his shift and rewrite it there. Other services require a "call in" report as soon as possible (when center opens) followed by a mail-in report. Some services require that a staff member have at least 6 months experience before handling the home calls; another service insists that the worker must serve in the central office once for each shift he serves at home. Home shifts also interfere with the families' social use of the phone, and prevents anonymity of workers since they must explain why they cannot converse with a friend. It is felt by others (Brockopp, 1971; McGee et. al., 1970) that the use of homes is far from desirable.

The fact that 12% are providing total telephone coverage through use of homes with 19% utilizing this location in combination with an office suggests that there certainly is a possibility that some services may be coping with the disadvantages very well and may still be providing important, effective service that might not be in existence if the homes were not in use. In a discussion Grigliak (1970, Pueblo) and others indicated that much effective service was being provided through home phones. An advantage of home use for location was cited by the Abilene (1971) service in terms of maximizing the use of excellent staff who would not otherwise be available to go to a central location. It was also suggested that the method provides families, especially the children, with an excellent education in caring for one's fellow man.

In summary, it appears that location is affected by other factors of operation and organization and that one central location with a direct telephone system would be, by far, the most desirable. This conclusion **does not** suggest that use of multiple locations, including homes, should be equated with ineffective delivery of services. It merely implies that the one central location would have fewer disadvantages. If a decision is made to use a home location alone or in combination with an office, then it is crucial to be aware of all the possible disadvantages and to actively seek answers and coping techniques. In discussing the disadvantages of using home phones, the vast majority cited problems involving the telephone system.

Several of the centers using multiple methods indicated their desire to eliminate the partial use of home locations and were working toward that goal. Several others felt very uncomfortable with their multiple location system and were not anticipating a change in the near future. The use of the diverter or the "patch" system then would be more efficient than the answering service, which requires both a caller name and number and a call back from the volunteer. The answering service which takes longer than the other two methods, does not allow the caller to be anonymous. A few services mentioned that they utilize the "patch" at home but, because of the disadvantages after they have established a trusting relationship with the caller, they get a number and recall the person directly.

Telephone Service

The establishment of the twenty-four hour telephone service was based on the recognition that effective crisis intervention focuses on meeting the client's needs at the time when problems occur. Until very recently mental health community services have always forced the client into seeking help during a nine to five schedule rather than when it is most needed. Established delivery of services in the past could be aptly described as "come and get services when we're here if you qualify." Providing 24 hour telephone emergency service greatly changed the existing bureaucratic model. Using the telephone as a medium for services maximizes the availability of service to the citizen when the citizen perceives his greatest need of it and provides an immediate, accessible channel. With these facts in mind, the variety of telephone methods used in 192 services will be described and discussed in terms of definitions, effectiveness and problems including statistical data.

As a result of the survey the following statistical data was gathered about the existing services. Table 22 designates that the greatest majority of calls are received by the SPC, 71% and Youth, 84% services during the time period of 4 p.m. through 1 a.m. This demonstrates that the majority of calls are coming in during "leisure" hours when traditional helping services are closed. Table 8 reveals the specific use of telephone methods by the services. Seventy-four per cent (74%) of the SPC's and 90% of the Youth services indicate use of the "direct" telephone system. The "patch" system and "answering services" are used by the SPC's much more often than the Youth services.

Definition of Telephone Systems Used and Problems Encountered

The Direct Telephone System

A system whereby the call is received directly, usually in an office, by the crisis worker without any intervening variable or interference.

Survey data indicate that "Direct" service **only** is used by 38% or (54) of (142) SPC's, 66% or (33) of (54) Youth services. A total of 45%, (87) out of a combination Total of (192) SPC's and Youth services, use "Direct" service exclusively. Thus we see that under 50% of the SPC's and Total group use this method **only,** but over 50% of the Youth services do, in fact, use only a direct service system.

In terms of providing an immediate response to those people who call for help, direct service is felt to be the most effective response method. At the American Association of Suicidology meeting (1971) McGee stated that the effectiveness of response was defined by the amount of time it took to reach a crisis worker in 19 southeastern services. He concluded that reaching a crisis worker through the "direct" method of telephone service requires the least amount of time (6 seconds), and is the most efficient method. The only problem associated with the "direct" system is the problem of staffing and location. It is necessary to find staff who will be willing to come to a central location.

The Divert-a-Phone or Diverter

This method, not used very widely is a mechanical device that automatically conveys the phone call from a central place to another phone. Such a device can be rented or purchased. The device is connected to the original phone, the worker's number is dialed or programmed onto the device; when the original number is called, it rings once or twice, but the call then automatically switches over to the new (pre-dialed or coded) number. This system is similar to the "direct" method, for it too is without the intervening variable. The main advantage of this system is that it permits calls to be taken outside the office without the problems encountered by the other systems. Problems encountered with the Divert-a-phone method include availability of device, cost of renting or buying, and need to recode the number manually if there is a change of crisis worker or shift during the night. The latter difficulty can be obviated if the original phone is placed where some responsible person is available to recode the number manually, if necessary. For example, a nurse could do it if the office is in a clinic or hospital setting. The Diverter can be used on only one incoming telephone line; any other lines must be disconnected. It requires phone jacks to be installed for the incoming and outgoing lines in order for the device to be workable. The diverter is presently being used some of the time in the San Francisco, Sacramento, Berkeley, California and Greensboro, North Carolina services. There are two other diverter types of systems available in North Carolina. The Special Emergency Transfer arrangement is currently being offered by The Southern Bell Telephone Company and permits after-hours calls to be diverted to any of nine alternate lines. This allows full time coverage on emergency lines during periods when qualified staff members are not in

31

attendance or when the emergency is unattended. The Teletron Corporation of Tallahassee, Florida has developed a "Call Transfer Unit" a forty (40) capacity unit that can be installed. They indicate that the rates will be in the area of $40.00 per month.

The "Patch" Telephone System

This particular method, a common one, utilizes a central switchboard or answering service. The system allows the phone to ring directly into a switchboard where, by turning a manual switch, a switchboard operator may dial the crisis worker's phone number. The system is particularly useful when it is impossible to staff a one location number; nevertheless, many inherent difficulties impede immediate quality response.

The "Patch" type of system, according to FCC rules, may be utilized only by a non-profit specified switchboard, for example, a hospital or police station. McGee (1971) notes that some commercial answering services are doing this for convenience of the crisis service but may jeopardize their position.

There are some other very serious difficulties when using this method:

(a) The system "opens the line," thus interfering with the clarity of tone and ability to hear.

(b) It requires constant monitoring by the operator, who may be busy or may forget to disconnect the line. The line must be disconnected before another call may come in or before the worker can make an outgoing emergency call. The delay can be crucial and frustrating. When the operator monitors the call there is often a soft clicking sound that may be perceived by the caller as a sign that the conversation is being taped, traced or listened to, all of which may destroy any sense of relationship or confidence about confidentiality.

(c) It, in fact, does allow some breach of confidentiality because a third party is, in effect, listening.

(d) Several services indicated they were having difficulty with being "cut off" inadvertently.

The advantages of using the patch system are similar to those of the divert-a-phone. Some centers say that it allows them to use, in their home, good qualified crisis workers who would not be available if it were necessary for them to go to one central location. Another advantage cited by some is that a trained operator can detect when there is a call that should be traced or emergency service sought and she can initiate the action while the worker is conversing with the caller. (Peoria, Illinois) In response to a question posed about the availability of only one line (usually) the answer was that it was possible to have two or three back up numbers that the operator could "patch" into, if needed, and thereby provide more service. Another rationale given is that if backups are not available the operator can respond to the caller, explain that the worker is on another call, assess whether it is an emergency nature and determine whether to intervene on the on-going call or suggest that the caller, recall later. The feeling expressed is that some response is better than a cold "busy" signal. Orlando and others prefer to get a telephone number from the caller, if possible, to eliminate the patch problems. Some workers feel uncomfortable about tying up the line in case some one else is waiting.

The data collected from the survey indicate that those services using an Answering Service or Patch System are as follows: 28% (40) of the SPC's; 24% (12) of the Youth services; 27% (52) of the Total sample. It is interesting to note that response indicates a combination of telephone systems (two or more) are often in use: 41% (58) SPC's, 28% (14) Youth, and 38% (72) of the Total services use two or more methods. It appears that the Patch or Answering Service method is used most often in the evening or night hours when staffing is more difficult. McGee (1971) stated that services using this system took one minute and thirty-five seconds to reach a crisis worker. When using the "patch" method it is important to decide if the switchboard is going to respond and, if so, how she is to do it. Recognizing the role of the operator in terms of effecting quick response to the caller, some operators are asked to participate in the training program. The Amarillo, Texas service has found this to be very beneficial. They also suggest that they have a **silent** monitor switch and that a single button push by the worker will summon the operator.

The Answering Service

McGee (1971) suggests that this method is perhaps the most inefficient and ineffective one. The system involves an operator answering a call and requesting the caller to leave a name and number or, at least, a number and informs the caller that a crisis worker will return the call. McGee noted in his study that immediate response was not always forthcoming and sometimes took several hours. He implied that it required a minimum of twelve minutes to reach a telephone worker. Since his sample was small and thus anecdotal, some services using this method were asked to comment. In defense they stated that their workers were always available and on duty and delays could be due to a busy call. Of course the caller has no way of recognizing this and may just feel that no one wishes to respond. The operator might be instructed to call the caller back and inform them that the worker is busy but will call back shortly. A major disadvantage of this system is the need to provide a number and name: such a request is often immediately threatening, particularly to the young population. Only 6% (3) of the Youth services indicated the sole use of an answering, while 16% (23) of the SPC's use it as their only system. One advantage cited by a service was that this was a good and easy opportunity to acquire some pertinent information, a name and number. One other service informed us that if the caller refused to give a number, rather than lose the caller they would give the number of the crisis worker to the caller and ask him to redial. They did not elaborate about the possible problems the worker encountered once the caller knew his home number.

The above mentioned telephone systems direct, diverter, patch and answering service are by far the most popular but there are some other types that should also be briefly mentioned.

The Message Machine

A recorded message that can be heard automatically when the number is dialed is most often used by those services which do not provide 24-hour service. The message usually informs the caller when the service will be open and in some cases tells him what other appropriate services are available and open. One Youth service has included the name and number of a 24-hour SPC service and also information regarding social functions available during the week. The recorded message device is used by some to provide the caller with the phone number of a worker on duty.

Receptionist Response

Having the call answered by a receptionist and then switched over to a crisis worker is a method employed in a Mental Health Clinic type of operation more often than in other services. This type of operation may lack the warmth and immediate acceptance of the caller, even though there is only a few moments delay.

Comment on Relevant Factors

Visiting the centers enabled one to perceive that most were utilizing more than one telephone system. When more than one system was used it was generally for the convenience of night phone shifts. The patch, answering service, and diverter methods were most commonly used during the "after business" hours of offices, from 5 p.m. to 9 a.m. The majority of services had two incoming lines and one business or outgoing line used especially for emergencies. Some services make use of the new automatic card dialing phone for reaching emergency numbers or consultants easily and quickly while still on the phone with the caller. Others use push button outgoing phones because they are easier and less noisy. There are services that have spokesman units and monitor systems attached to their phones to permit periodic supervision of the volunteer and his effectiveness. The monitor also provides the opportunity for a consultant to hear what is transpiring, thus permitting him to plan his intervention when and if needed. Zanesville, Ohio, has an interesting set-up that allows certain professionals to receive calls at home (in the early a.m. hours) via special extension phones placed in their homes. These extensions also permit a 3-way professional, worker and caller involvement when a crisis worker feels the need of it. The extensions do not ring when a crisis worker is manning the phone but an available signal circuit can summon the back up professional, at any time.

There are some methods in use that permit each call to be automatically taped when the receiver is lifted. It is extremely important to emphasize that this is done only for training purposes and a review of crisis worker effectiveness. Those who use this method (only a few) stress their dedication to complete confidentiality.

Many of the services interviewed stated that they will accept long distance calls; others do not because of the cost factor. The feeling is that this has not been a major problem. The Stark County Service includes an Enterprise number which permits toll free calls from anywhere in the county. Zanesville accepts collect calls from the six county area for which it is responsible.

Recognition of the crucial aspect the telephone system plays in the effective delivery of service through an immediate response to a call for help suggests that the best method would be through the direct system. It is necessary to acknowledge that many services are, nevertheless, providing quality service using other systems. In some cases, service would be nonexistent if other telephone methods were not available. Although direct quality service is the ideal, vital services less than ideal certainly should **not** be abolished. As a matter of fact, during interview sessions, "direct," poor quality response could be observed and "indirect," excellent quality response also could be noted. It is recognized that other variables are at work; an indirect response might be better than no response.

The relevancy of many other facets of the services to the telephone system chosen will be discussed later in this chapter. The following factors, to mention just a few, affect and are affected by the phone system chosen: location, funding, staff, hours of operation, and record keeping.

Since it is sometimes impossible for a back up consultant always to be immediately accessible, especially if the telephone worker does not have an extra line, a pocket paging system or Citizen's Band radio could be most helpful.

Hours of Telephone Availability

An overwhelming majority, 93% of the SPC's specified that they provide 24-hour telephone coverage. On the other hand, only 50% of the Youth services provide coverage less than 24-hours a day. Of those Youth services that provide less than 24 hour service, 32% are available every evening and 10% are open on the weekends. Six per cent responding to the "other" category cited unique hours. The data demonstrate that the Youth specifically define the focus of their service and apparently provide service when they feel the particular population to which they are appealing will be available and needing help.

The hours of availability and type of service appear to have a direct effect on telephone systems that are employed. As stated previously, 66% of the Youth services use a "direct" telephone method. Reasons for this choice possibly are a result of the limited time coverage, recognition of the absolute need for anonymity if desired, the use of a central office and problems of using home phones, and the youth workers' willingness to go to a central place until 2 or 3 a.m. The fact that there are usually more than 2 or 3 on duty at one time may also provide the impetus to go to a central location.

On the other hand, the SPC's usually offer 24-hour service. Since the hours between 2 a.m. and 8 a.m. are not usually busy, one crisis worker is ordinarily sufficient. The majority of SPC services using more than one telephone method do so to allow the telephone calls to be taken during the evening and/or early a.m. hours at home.

Most of the SPC services interviewed expected the telephone worker to work one four hour shift a week. Of course, there are some variations, such as a six hour shift. Some who take all calls at home work one full day or weekend once a month. Night shifts often last for eight to twelve hours twice a month. In the Youth services not providing 24-hour service, shifts are usually designated by evenings rather than hours. Workers are often responsible for one evening, once or twice a month. Some services require a worker to commit himself to the same specific shift each week, while some others are constantly flexible and changing. The statistics on telephone availability and coverage suggest that the population one is attempting to serve determines in a large part the hours of availability.

Community Involvement and Referrals

"No man is an island unto himself," John Donne's reflection is pertinent to individuals and agencies engaged in SPC and Youth services. The service must have a good working relationship with community agencies, services, gatekeepers and professional associations. The importance of interrelations has been emphasized consistently throughout this thesis; and it has been emphasized by almost all the responsible people in the field, including Rescue Inc., Boston, Mass., Dublin (1963). Shneidman (1970), Garrad (1968), Shneidman, Farberow and Litman (1961), McGee (1968), Litman (1971), Sudak, Hall and Sawyer (1970), Resnik (1968). The services must be able to refer callers and know that they will be effective referrals. Community interest and support are important also for funding the services and for helping callers through coordinated action.

As stated in a previous section total community involvement must begin when the service is in the initial planning stages. It is crucial to alleviate hostile feelings that might arise if the already existing services feel that they are being ignored and that they are in competition with the new service for funds and clientele. The best approach is to contact each agency and group at an initial meeting, presenting tentative proposals for the service but allowing and asking for suggestions so that the established agency will consider itself engaged in the planning. Whether the service planned is considering telephone only contact, or telephone and face to face contact, there is no possible way for one service to provide all the help the callers will need. Community liaison and involvement are paramount. Before one approaches the community, though, it is necessary to define the needs and gaps in service to determine if creating the SPC/Youth service will, in fact, provide a viable service to the citizens. By **initiating** a relationship the SPC service can demonstrate its good faith and a desire to have a continuing relationship with two-way communication encouraged. As a matter of fact, it it wise to initiate a review meeting at least once a year, more frequently if a problem arises. Farberow (1968) in his article about "Concepts and Conceptions of Suicide Prevention Services" lists eight essential liaisons and four desirable ones, some of which will be discussed on the following pages.

Liaison with the Community Psychiatric Hospitals, or Psychiatric Wards of General Medical Hospitals, State Mental Hospitals and Emergency Room Services

Farberow suggests that since there will be some clients or callers who must be hospitalized immediately, arrangements should be made to effect easy entry. This has been a particular problem with many services that were interviewed. The difficulty stems from the unavailability of a psychiatrist who will respond, especially in the middle of the night, to admit a patient. This problem is particularly evident when there is a shortage of psychiatrists on the staff. Some services report that often the psychiatrist on call will prescribe tranquilizers and send the person home (all done in a phone conversation with the resident on duty) if there has not been a very serious attempt or if there is a "welfare case" problem. When people are undergoing serious crisis, not taking their communication seriously can provide more impetus for a successful suicide next time. Some cities also have problems with the general hospitals accepting only "economically stable" patients; the rest are shunted off to a state mental hospital, even if the crisis is a temporary situational one. There has also been some problem with the lack of an empathic response from emergency room personnel to clients when they come in. These types of problems seem to occur more frequently in smaller communities where other 24-hour resources like psychiatric clinics or community mental health centers do not exist. A serious attempt must be made to anticipate and deal with these problems **before** they occur.

The author suggests that there be a separate discussion meeting with the hospital director (for hospital policy), the Emergency room director and head nurse, and director of the psychiatric wards in general hospitals. Presenting the problem and asking for help may elicit some excellent response. Only after discussion can very clearly defined procedures be outlined to prevent the problems from arising. The Stark County Service discovered that certain procedures were being conducted by the hospital because of "police policy;" when the police were questioned, they indicated the procedures were "hospital policy." Clearly, it is important to determine who is responsible for policy, if actions are being taken that are detrimental to the caller.

Relationship with the Police

This is a most important relationship because there are functions that no other agency in the community can perform without the aid of the police. When there is a call to the SPC service from someone who has attempted suicide and must be rescued, the police are the only ones who can break down the door if necessary. Furthermore, when there is a hazardous situation with a person waving a gun threatening to kill himself, the police, preferably in plain clothes and accompanied by a trained crisis worker, are the ones sent to the rescue. The implications of the above testify to two very important facets of the police-SPC/Youth service relationship. Since most of the calls police receive involve families in crisis, then relationship with the service can be truly cooperative. The police should be completely aware and knowledgeable about the organization and goals of the service; they should be made to understand, accept and realize its seriousness of purpose; and the police and the service should establish a defined relationship: **When** to call the police (what they can and cannot do), **who** to call, **how** to call and what clear and concise information they need should be clearly outlined. Arrangements can be made to define a certain procedure to gain follow up information.

As a case in point, the liaison between the police and the Stark County, Ohio service will be used for illustrative purposes. At every training session for new telephone workers, a policeman outlines procedures, policies, and relationship; in turn, the service provides a speaker (the director) for the Police Academy training program to suggest how to approach people in crisis and to inform them about the inner nature of the service. Letters of thank you are sent to the individual policeman and the captain when the police are called upon by the SPC service. Wallet size cards and some brochures are given to police to hand out when appropriate. The police have at times expressed gratitude to the service for being there and helpful to them when they have called upon the service. Discussion has also taken place concerning the problem with young callers because of their inordinate fear of the police.

Because some persons in crisis fear police, many services have formed outreach teams that can respond to a person (youth or adult) in need. Although such groups as the "freak squad" (a Mobile Drug Crisis Unit in Spokane, Washington) and Night Walk (clergy who go into the city during late night hours, Spokane, Washington) certainly can provide efficacious service, there are times when police must be called; therefore emphasis is placed upon the necessity for all services (SPC and Youth) to form a viable relationship with them. The Gainesville, Florida service often sends a crisis worker out with the police, to aid them and to alleviate inappropriate threat and fear on the part of the caller.

Another important reason for creating and sustaining an excellent relationship with police is the possibility of providing or initiating some crisis training in the police academy course. Mann (1971) discloses that the police receive very few hours (if any) of training about the handling of people in crisis or about existing community services. Mann further observes that since the policeman's "primary commitment is to the protection of society," the policeman "responds first to whatever threat the behavior of the individual may pose to the social order, and only after that threat is under control may he give attention to the needs of the individual." (p. 121). His effective response to the needs of the individual depends on his training. Mann further suggests that "the behavior of individual policeman is strongly influenced by the attitudes and examples set for him by command-level officers." Mann's study strongly supports the need for providing training and involvement of the command-level officers in a mutual relationship with the SPC services. Litman (1966) recommends to police that when confronted with a suicide attempt or threat they should move slowly, cautiously, and thoughtfully, recognizing that sometimes conversation and interest can be more effective than aggressive action. Because of the unique position of the police and their

37

involvement with people in crisis, it is critical for them to become sensitive and alert to suicidal communication. Peck (1969) reports on a training program instigated by the Los Angeles Suicide Prevention Center, which provides only three hours of training. The training includes information about reasons for suicide and suggests that the policeman respond with a "firm, helpful concerned attitude," which may help the person in crisis to seek appropriate help. Peck concludes that while there has been no detailed studies demonstrating the effectiveness of this type of training there are many anecdotal situations that strongly suggest its positive value. The police sometimes have called the SPC/Youth lines about people who have attempted suicide, and some of the SPC/Youth services such as Gainesville and Amarillo in turn call or write the attempters to tell them about the service afforded them by the SPC and Youth services. There are some services also which send letters or call the family of a completed suicide victim to encourage them either to call or seek help if they feel the need. A list of names is often supplied by the police or coroner. A study conducted by Murphy, Walbron, Clendenin and Robins (1969) on an analysis of 380 consecutive suicides and suicide attempt calls answered by police substantiate the notion that "the police are in a crucial position with respect to suicidal individuals, and that a close working relationship between the police and SPC/Youth services is of fundamental importance." (p. 269)

The data received from SPC/Youth questionnaire (Table 16) indicates that only 14% of the SPC/Youth services felt liaison with the community agencies and/or police to be a major problem area. Services indicated more problems with agencies than with police. Several services interviewed, mentioned they had an excellent relationship with the police; indeed, the SPC in Dallas is applying for a grant to provide training for police and public health nurses.

Relationship with Community Helping Agencies

Developing a mutually beneficial relationship with community helping agencies requires a supreme and continuing effort essential to providing meaningful and helpful response to the citizens. As stated before, no one SPC/Youth service can stand alone and provide all help to all people; referrals in some manner to some other agencies will be needed. Some agencies that are most often involved are Mental Health Centers, Family Service, Legal Aid, Welfare Agency, Salvation Army, Fish, Planned Parenthood, Public Health Department, State employment office, alcohol abuse agencies, Goodwill Industries, drug drop-in centers, drug programs and poison control centers.

Without any doubt the community agencies should be involved in the planning stages since they will have the most to fear from competition for funds and the possibility of the SPC/Youth services acting as evaluation sources. These fears should be dissipated immediately. Ideally the director of the SPC/Youth services should, after an initial large meeting, request an appointment with each director to discuss coordination of effort between them, to benefit the caller.

The SPC/Youth services must be aware of the specific services and purposes of each agency so they can refer to the most appropriate service to aid the caller. It is a good idea to visit each referral agency to determine the exact process the client must undergo so that the telephone worker may allay the caller's fears. It would also be very wise to attempt to evaluate referral resources in terms of their credibility in the community. A referral book must be thoroughly compiled, constantly updated, and immediately accessible to the telephone worker. To compile pertinent information, the Stark County, Ohio service has sent a specific questionnaire to each agency; the questionnaire provided space also for other useful and available information. (Appendix G) With the questionnaire providing a guideline, the information is available in the same place for all services.

In an effort to develop a mutually beneficial relationship representatives of the various community referral agencies were included in the pre-service training programs to describe in detail the function of their agency. This was not as beneficial as anticipated because there was too much overlap; moreover each director took too long while attempting to "sell" himself and his agency. Assigning one person to collect the appropriate information concerning all the various agencies was thought to be more effective, although a representative from a community resource might be asked to speak at an in-service worker meeting, especially if the resource is new or if there are gaps in information and procedure policy.

There is a tendency for telephone workers to refer to one specific service, although several facilities may offer the same service, if that agency responds well and immediately. In Stark County, Ohio, the Mental Health center and the Catholic Community League, have made special staff arrangements so that one staff member if always available to accept an immediate crisis referral from the SPC, thereby helping to provide immediate response when necessary. The service attempts **not** to abuse this arrangement unnecessarily because it is so important to eliminate a 'waiting list' in an emergency. This kind of collaboration is to be commended. In an effort to assess the efficacy of the referrals, a form is sent out to the referral agency when an appointment is made for some caller, to inquire if the caller kept the appointment and if it was an appropriate referral. Concern is appreciated and the agencies sometimes don't even wait for the follow-up form, but call in a report to the SPC service. (Appendix H) In order to check up on all referrals, a code number might be used to find out if the caller did make an appointment at a referral agency. The code can be given to the caller who in turn will give it to the agency. This will help to insure confidentiality of callers who do **not** appear.

It becomes very evident that the establishment of a good working relationship with community resources agencies is necessary if providing meaningful response to a caller is a primary goal. The mutually beneficial aspect of this relationship can be demonstrated by the fact that some agencies and professionals suggest that some of their clients call the SPC/Youth service on weekends and after hours if a crisis or problem develops, since the agency or professional is not available at those times.

Relationship and Involvement of the Health and Mental Health Associations and the Coroner

Excellent relationships with the psychiatric, psychological and medical associations is critical to existence and provision of service. By involving these people immediately, with sincerity, a service may gain their endorsement and, with that endorsement, credibility in the community. Even more important is the response they provide in crisis situations. It has been established that if people or associations publicly commit themselves to something, they usually take an active part. There is no doubt that their help is absolutely essential.

It is important to establish the relationship, clearly define the role and involvement permitted, make provisions for open two-way communication, and suggest that the relationship can be mutually beneficial. The medical association will possibly be somewhat apprehensive about the use of volunteer and non-professional workers, but this skepticism can be obviated by defining the screening and training procedures. Psychiatrists and psychologists may feel threatened because of competition for clients, expectation of being called all night, and anticipation of possible complaints about them from disgruntled clients. Representatives of the organizations should wherever possible be included on the executive policy making board and the advisory board. The SPC/Youth services have to rely heavily on these professionals to provide training and back up consultation for telephone workers as well as professional services in serious crises. Total and intimate involvement in the program by these resources will be required if a service is to exist and to deliver services.

Comments from those interviewed indicated that the "lack" of mental health professionals (Psychiatrists and Psychologists) presented a vast problem particularly in a community where there was no 24-hour psychological service except the emergency room of a general hospital. Also cited as a significant problem by a few was the lack of mental health professionals who were willing to respond, even to telephone calls, after office hours. There are, of course, a great many who will, in fact, respond at any hour of the night to the crisis telephone worker or caller but this is usually a result of a firmly established relationship. An excellent example of involvement in the community is provided by the Metuchen, New York service, whose staff members "regularly participate in nurses training at the city hospital, social work student training, psychology intern training, police officer and probation officer training. Plans for training of medical students at Rutgers University is contemplated for the future."

The coroner's office can provide the SPC/Youth service with the statistics needed to understand the suicide problem in the community. A relationship with this office will enable a service to procure names and numbers of completed suicides, information which will make it possible for a service to begin to evaluate its **immediate** impact on the suicidal population. These statistics will also allow the service to determine whether they are **reaching** the more lethal populations and just **who** those populations are. There will be further discussion of these questions in the category of record keeping and evaluation.

Educating and Involving the Gatekeepers

As mentioned previously, gatekeepers are people who, either because of their profession or their proximity to people in crisis, can respond meaningfully. Such people include clergy, probate and juvenile courts, lawyers, nurses, personnel in universities and schools, counselors and, in fact, the total community. The emphasis with this group should be an educational one. Primarily they should be informed about the overt and covert "clues to suicide" and should become aware of the myths about suicidal behavior (Shneidman and Farberow 1961). The education process should include a thorough knowledge about the SPC/Youth services and the actions the gatekeepers can initiate on their own. Responses to suicidal people should be discussed and demonstrated so that they may respond in a concerned, empathetic, and responsible way. The educational approach to suicide and crisis prevention should also include presenting statistics and defining specific lethal populations.

Even though the clergy are included in this category, they deserve to be acknowledged specifically because they are primary gatekeepers. They most often come in contact with people who have just undergone a "significant loss" or are facing an intolerable situation. They are often the **first** ones the people in crisis turn to; the type of response by the clergyman can and does affect the outcome. The clergyman must become extremely sensitive to the "cries for help" that come in many forms. They must receive more training to prepare them to respond to subtleties. Ideally, the seminaries should include psychological and pastoral counselling in its curriculum (McGee, L.L. and Hilger, 1968). The SPC/Youth services can in the meantime provide special educational workshops, such as those offered in Stark County, Ohio and Abilene, Texas, by the Mental Health Association.

The relationship between the clergy and SPC/Youth services goes beyond an educational one. There is a need to have available to the SPC/Youth services a group of clergy who have had adequate counselling training including the above mentioned education. There is a significant group of SPC/Youth services callers who wish to speak to a clergyman, **but** not their own! The 24 hour availability of qualified counselling clergymen will be a consequence of the involvement and relationship between the service and the ministerial association. An interesting example of the vital role of the clergy was related by Harry Warren, Jr., director of the National Sav-a-Life League, New York (Interview, 1971). He described how his father established the above service in 1906 as a result of a young woman's suicide attempt and of her comment that she would not have taken the overdose if a clergyman had been available to talk to her.

The clergy can be utilized by SPC/Youth services for recruiting of their parishioners, for educational purposes through sermons and for dissemination of information in church bulletins.

The need for a firmly established relationship with the **total** community is considered to be a paramount factor in the continued existence of the SPC/Youth programs and their effective service and response to people in suicidal and other crisis situations. Because of the number of third-party calls from people other than the person in crisis (see Table 25) the involvement of the total community is necessary so that they understand the nature and availability of the service and become sensitive to those people around them who call for help. An ongoing, mutually advantageous relationship should be maintained with all the above groups (Fisher 1970). The demise of the Antisuicide group called "Friends" in Miami may possibly be linked to their independent and autonomous philosophy which rejected community involvement (Resnik 1968).

There is almost total agreement that a firm and sincere liaison must be established in the community with all those groups, agencies, professionals, and individuals who are concerned with the mental health of a community. The SPC/Youth services can play a dual role by seeking this kind of meaningful relationship and by acting as a catalyst to coordinate and maximize the use of the existing services. The comments from services interviewed cite the **lack** of available services, rather than relationships, as the more important problem. Without effective liaisons, including knowledge of the service provided by the SPC/Youth services, a problem of duplication of service arises. In one metropolitan area where 16 hotlines were identified, few knew what the others did. Very recently the newspaper announced a fund raising drive, supported by a prominent judge and other community people, to establish a 24-hour hot line! With total community involvement and education such duplication probably would not occur.

The total community and especially the mental health community should be involved and included on the advisory and executive board. Appendix F shows the structure of some boards and some letters sent initially to involve the community in the program.

Publicity

According to the tabulated statistics in Table 15, the great majority of services (over 74%) have publicized their existence through the newspaper and radio media, posters, pamphlets (brochures) and speeches. T.V. has been used as a method of publicity by 58% of the combined SPC and Youth services. Use of billboards and wallet cards has been indicated specifically by a rather small percentage.

Purpose of Publicity

It seems obvious that if a service is attempting to make its services available, people must know of its existence. The service cannot be utilized by lethal, crisis, or any other populations unless its purposes and goals are also known. By simple questioning of taxi drivers, housewives, professors, doctors, etc. in several cities with SPC services, it was discovered that a great many people do not know these services exist! For this reason the area of publicity must be investigated thoroughly and maximum use be made of the information gathered here. It would be wise to progress slowly with publicity campaigns or promotions in order not to "overload" the wires and thus interfere with effective service. Promotion and staffing should be coordinated. It is extremely important to define the specific populations one is attempting to reach and to be positive that the publicity is appropriate and well placed. For example, many urban poverty people do not receive the newspaper; hence, appealing to them through that medium would produce few results.

Much of the media publicity has been donated to fulfill public service requirements stipulated by the Federal Communication Commission. Some advertising agencies have willingly donated their services to design brochures, posters and symbols; this was the case with the Stark County, Ohio service. Some companies will donate the services of their advertising departments, and some printers will donate wallet size cards or provide ample discounts. It would be worth while to investigate these avenues. After the discussion about methods, a more detailed description will follow concerning the brochures and cards. Several research studies about publicity will also be briefly noted. There are samples of some of the publicity in Appendix J.

Methods of Publicity

Newspaper publicity is the most popular method being used by 93% of the services. This publicity manifests itself in a variety of forms. Daily or almost daily 'sig' cut symbols are run free of charge as 'fillers' in Stark County, Ohio and Zanesville, Ohio. The telephone number of the service is run each day with a listing of other emergency numbers in Peoria, Illinois; Buffalo, New York reports good response from ads run in the personal columns, as does Abilene, Texas which runs daily ads in the classified section. Feature stories have been an integral part of the publicity campaign by most services. [Caution: provide a news release to all newspapers at one specific time.] Rivalry in the newspaper business is extreme. It is important to provide newspapers with feature or news releases that are brief, timely, and pertinent. The concerns of the service make good "human interest" copy so their facilities should be used whenever possible. Some newspapers are so receptive that they will provide daily or weekly ads free of charge (Portland, Maine, Stark County, Ohio); some other services unfortunately have obtained no such interest and response from local newspapers. To approach the newspaper through a large advertiser or popular political candidate is one suggestion; another is to make them fully aware of the need in the community.

Both **Radio** and **T.V.** are excellent media sources because of the FCC ruling about free public service. Many are willing to flash a slide or read a brief message if you provide them with the copy for it. Make it as easy as possible for them and try to change the copy often so it will be pertinent and timely because they will discontinue using the same message after a short time. Interviews and talk shows are another excellent source of publicity and education but do not wait for them to call you, rather, you suggest the idea to the program director.

Telephone directories are another primary source used to make the service visible and easily accessible to a great number of people. A study done by Brockopp and Lester (1971) of 129 telephone directories reveals that 25 [19%] services had their telephone number listed on the front cover of the telephone book with other emergency numbers. The use of this method varies with the policy of the telephone system in each state. In Ohio almost all services are so listed, but the requirement is that they be referred to as "Suicide Prevention" services, as, for example in Stark County, Ohio. Use of the telephone directory as a method of publicity in a variety of ways is felt to be essential. Many centers have multiple listings in bold face type in the white pages section, under C for Crisis, S for Suicide and H for Hotline. In the yellow pages some are listed in as many as five places as is the case in Manhasset, Long Island. The purpose is to make it as easy as possible for the person in crisis to find the number and appropriate service very quickly.

Brochures, Wallet Cards, Stickers and Posters

Brochures come in a great variety of shapes, sizes, colors and designs. The major purpose of these is to introduce the public to the name, number, and scope of the service, describing clearly what services they offer and to whom they are appealing. A great many of the brochures double as an educational tool by providing a brief resume of national and local statistics, a description of the erroneous myths surrounding suicide or severe crisis, and concrete suggestions for action. Some of the brochures incorporate on the cover a symbol that is representative of their service and then use that symbol constantly in the advertising media. The range of symbols includes some form of telephone, out-reaching hands, a picture of an obviously dejected or troubled figure, and geometric designs, most of which include a prominent display of the telephone number. It is vital to make the front fold of the brochure self-explanatory, just in case the person does not read any further. Some services include in the interior of the brochure an appeal for volunteers and/or an appeal for monetary contributions to support the program. Most of the brochures are about 9" x 4" after a 3 fold. Some brochures are smaller, 6" x 3½", so they may be easily inserted into a suitjacket pocket or a purse. The most important facets of a brochure are eye catching design and color, easily understood and self-explanatory cover, and a clearly defined description of the services. The language used in the brochure should be familiar and easily understood by everyone. When the brochure was being designed for Stark County, Ohio, the top heading over the symbol was "Emotional Crisis?" After a sample of citizens had pointed out that they never use those words or expressions and that when a crisis arises they describe it as a "personal problem," the heading was changed. Some of the brochures designed especially for youth incorporate colorful psychedelic patterns that are particularly appealing to that age group, examples are Teen Age Hotline in Pittsburgh, Pa., and Youth Line in Des Moines, Iowa. Samples of some brochures will be in Appendix J.

Wallet cards (approx. 2 x 3½") are used by many services and usually include only the symbol, name, phone number, and time open, although some also include information concerning other emergency helping agencies. This seems to be especially beneficial when a Youth line like Manhasset, Long Island is open less than 24-hours.

Small stickers with peel off paper are used to place on telephone books, booths, and other distribution points. These usually include only name, symbol, and phone number. They are usually smaller than the wallet cards, although several (Galeta, Calif., Pittsburgh, Pa.) have combined the two by making them wallet size with a sticky peel off back. The wallet size sticker/card may of course be too large to place it conveniently on the phone handle or the phone itself.

Posters are often enlarged copies of the front of the brochure or wallet cards, although may incorporate more information. The posters should be large enough for people to read and see from a distance.

Distribution and Placement of Publicity Methods

As previously stated, publicity **must** be directed to that population one wishes to serve. If it is the desire of the service to be available to everyone, then a great variety of methods must be employed. Distribution of brochures, cards, stickers and posters can be accomplished in many ways. It is impossible to list each service using each method, but if it is different from others, then the service will be mentioned when appropriate. The listing that follows is a testimony to creative thinking about distribution methods:

Small, compact and sturdy clear plastic holders were acquired for about 50¢ each by the Stark County, Ohio service for distribution to public facilities. The holder contains 50 brochures; a card with a name and number to call for refills was pasted to the back. The holders, which may sit on a counter, also have a stick-um back for use on bulletin boards. These can be placed in libraries, banks, doctors' offices, bus stations, laundromats, airports, hotels, motels, rooming houses, YMCA's, YWCA's, barber shops, beauty parlors (Gainesville, Fla.), bars, schools, universities, factories, pharmacies, gas stations (Palm Springs, Ga.), emergency rooms (Amarillo, Texas), law enforcement agencies, welfare departments, and trailer parks (Richmond, Va.).

Wallet size cards are given to police and firemen who often respond to marital strife calls. When the violence or suicide gesture is controlled, they leave a card suggesting that the person or family call the service. Cards and/or brochures are also given to taxi drivers (Peoria, Ill.), high school classes, welcome wagons (Stark County, Ohio) and boards of Realtors (Amarillo, Texas).

Brochures have been included in Bar Association mailings (Akron, Ohio). Use of advertising on books of matches (Contact, Harrisburg, Pa.) is clever because the population using the matches are already indulging in self-destructive behavior.

Posters are used in busses and subways (Buffalo, N.Y.) and on bulletin boards in schools, factories, and churches. Billboards are sometimes donated by industry. Publicity has been obtained by the Listening Ear, Mass., through distribution of bookmarks in the library; in Gastonia, N.C., through enclosure of brochures with bank statements; in Stark County, Ohio, through enclosures with industry paychecks, since industry is interested in the relationship between mental health and production; in Jacksonville, Fla., through enclosures with light bills; and in Orlando, Fla., through enclosures of brochures and stickers with phone bills. Orlando, Fla. publicizes also by means of car bumper stickers, news items in the Power Company newsletter, and ads in the T.V. guide and other T.V. programming lists.

Stickers have often been placed in public phone booths, although it is wise to get permission first. The Stark County, Ohio service put on displays in conjunction with Mental Health Association booths at the county fair and home and garden auditorium shows. Another service has an ad on the cable T.V. time and weather station; the W. Palm Beach, Fla. service has a weekly booth (or table) in a shopping center mall. Those services located near military camps make certain that they place publicity in this area. Sponsoring mental health workshops and developing an active speakers bureau are excellent ways to publicize a service and its purposes. In Amarillo, Texas, the Board of Realtors hands out a multifold pamphlet which includes emergency numbers and a description of the Suicide Prevention Service.

Another effective publicity technique used by Buffalo, N.Y., and Stark County, Ohio is door to door canvassing. Some of the Youth groups are very willing to participate in this as a group project, as have the Y Teens in Stark County, Ohio. In Amarillo, Texas, the Boy Scouts put stickers in the telephone booths; in Gainesville, Fla., the Mental Health Association provides the publicity.

An extremely unusual newspaper ad by the Suicide Prevention Center in San Francisco, Calif. requested that phone-shy potential suicides write for help; as a result, the center has some suicidal pen pals. (**Behavior Today,** 1971).

In summary, it should be recognized that publicity must be considered as an integral facet of the suicide prevention service; if people are not aware of the existence of the service, they certainly cannot utilize it.

It has been found that continuous low-key advertising in the mass media will sustain the number of calls or increase them gradually and will make the service known (American Association of Suicidology, 1970). The low-key continuous advertising eliminates the excessive spurt of calls that result from very large dramatic publicity. The enormous number of calls resulting from the "big splash" type of advertising usually cannot be handled effectively by the suicide prevention service (American Association of Suicidology, 1970).

Advertising on the front page of the telephone book and under several different headings throughout the book is felt to be beneficial. Other advertising should be placed in areas that have been designated through research as ones possibly containing people that might be higher suicidal risks. These might include university areas, the military camps, the cheap hotels containing single, white males (Heilig, 1970), and doctors offices. Over 60% of all completed suicides had seen a doctor within the previous three months. A study by Tuckman and Lavell (1958) demonstrated that 43% of the suicides were reported to have been in poor health; thus the "physician is in a key position to recognize potential suicides and refer." It would be wise, then, to have brochures in the waiting rooms and to provide information to doctors. It is particularly important to select the appropriate publicity methods and media that will appeal to a specific lethal population or to a population that the service is attempting to reach. For example, a rock music station or underground newspaper is an effective medium for an appeal to Youth.

In a study of suicides in Detroit during a 268 day newspaper blackout, Motto (1968) recognized the potential harm that sensational news media treatment of suicides can have on the female population under 35 years old. During the media blackout, "female suicides in the 15-24 and 25-35 age ranges were dramatically reduced." (p. 88) Motto also states that "Prominent students of the suicide problem such as Friedman, Dublin, Ringel and Durkheim agree that it is not the reporting of suicide per se but the exploitative manner of reporting that stirs the imitative impulse in vulnerable persons." (p. 87) Results of this survey could possibly be generalized to discourage presentation of **excessively dramatic** feature stories about Suicide Prevention Services or exciting rescues with accompanying sound effects.

A few general principles of restraint in publicizing should be observed. It is critical not to overdramatize publicity or feature stories since they might be misunderstood and obscure the serious message one is really attempting to convey. When establishing a new service, proper timing for initial publicity is extremely important; extensive publicity should be postponed until the service is functioning smoothly and efficiently. Proper and effective publicity is essential, of course. Several studies have indicated that many people are not aware of the existence of an SPC/Youth service in their community or, if they are, they do not completely understand the purposes or goals. It seems possible to conclude that if a service is to be used, it must be known!

Recruiting and Staffing

The results of the survey demonstrate that the overwhelming majority of respondents (86%) utilize and rely on volunteers in some capacity. These volunteers may be professional or non-professional. A sizeable number, 33%, revealed that they have no paid staff; of those that do, the majority have indicated only one to two are paid. (Table 4) Louis Dublin (1969) recognized

> The lay volunteer was probably the most important single discovery in 50 years of Suicide Prevention. He had the time and qualities of character to prove he cared. With proper training, he can make an approach to the caller and with knowledge of available community services the volunteer can tide the caller over his crisis period. p. 45

The existence and proliferation of the SPC/Youth services in recent years has depended largely on the use of "volunteer" staff. Research completed by Rioch (1963), Reiff and Riessman (1965) and Heilig et al (1968) attest to the efficacy of the lay volunteers (non-professional) provided they receive the appropriate training corresponding to the task.

There is an unfortunate tendency to equate the term "volunteer" with the adjective non-professional, although the services surveyed designated that the volunteer includes both professionals and non-professionals. Facing the reality prospect that there will never be enough professionals in the mental health field (Dublin, 1963, Albee, 1968), the SPC/Youth services discovered a constructive alternative. A small minority of the established services use only paid professionals to staff the center but the trend even with this group is to move toward more involvement with volunteer staff. (McGee 1970) Those services which use only professionals are often incorporated into a professional structure, like a mental health center or hospital.

It is possible to delineate several different types of staffing patterns for SPC and Youth services throughout the country. These include paid professionals, paid non-professionals, volunteer professionals, volunteer non-professionals, and various combinations of them all.

The most popular model specified by response to the survey was the combined use of volunteer professionals and non-professionals as well as one or two paid staff. The role of the volunteer professional is most often one of providing back-up consultation and training for the volunteer non-professional. Providing the telephone response to the community is most often the role occupied by the non-professional volunteer.

In an attempt to remove the implied "incompetency" or "inadequacy" connotation of the term "non-professional volunteer," services have variously called their volunteers clinical associates, staff aides, para-professionals, telephone workers, and mental health associates.

The following discussion will focus upon the volunteer worker utilized in the majority of SPC/Youth services.

As of this date there is no documented research that demonstrates the specific characteristics of the effective volunteer in these services. McGee and Richard (Gainesville, Fla.) are in the process of making a critical evaluation of the non-professional volunteer and assessing his performance in order to develop a scale for effectiveness. This scale will be published in the forthcoming Bulletin of Suicidology (Fall 1971). Steve Girard, a Suicidology fellow, is currently attempting to delineate specific personality characteristics of those workers termed "most effective" by the directors of the services. Carkhuff and Truax suggest that empathy and warmth are primary qualities needed to establish a relationship. Their scale can be used to determine the level of empathy and warmth exhibited. There is some suggestion that professionals do not score as well on this scale.

The personality characteristics and qualities sought in the telephone workers include maturity, responsibility, sensitivity, motivation, empathy, genuineness, warmth, capacity for growth, stability, flexibility, willingness to learn, reliability, intelligence, perceptiveness, acceptance of training, and ability to get along well with others. A non-judgmental attitude and a great deal of flexibility are crucial because of the exposure to a great variety of cultural value systems. The maturity of the volunteer provides him with a tolerance for frustration and the ability to recognize his own limitations when attempting to help a caller. The nature of the work shifts demands the trait of dependability and the desire to do more than what is required in case someone does not appear for a shift. Handling calls of a suicidal type requires a volunteer who has a low anxiety threshold and who can be calm but interested. The traits found to be characteristics of the more successful volunteer included a need for further self-development and learning and an interest in working in a direct way with people in crisis situations (Heilig, et al, 1968).

The San Francisco service includes ability to listen, voice quality, awareness of self, control over impulses, and acceptance of others as prerequisites for telephone volunteers. Amarillo, Texas intimates that their workers are "busy" people who are not looking for a social vehicle through their volunteer work. McGee (1967) suggests that the best volunteers "feel comfortable with themselves, love life and live it to the fullest, have a capacity for influential leadership and actively experience a social existence."

Research completed by Rioch (1963), Reiff and Riessman (1965) and Heilig et al (1968) attest to the efficacy of the lay volunteers (non-professional) provided they receive the training appropriate to the task. Response comments on the survey constantly refer to effectiveness of the non-professional volunteer, while a few suggested they were even more effective than some professionals who tended to have less patience and lose interest in the project more quickly. A recently completed study by Ansel and McGee (1971) suggests that the non-professional telephone worker in the suicide prevention and crisis services has a more positive attitude toward the suicide attempter than do psychiatric residents, psychiatric nurses, emergency room personnel, police and the lay public. Professional groups displayed more negative attitudes toward the suicide attempter when responding to the survey instrument. This study has many implications for further research, training and staffing. There is, as yet, little empirical data to support the suggestion of the non-professional worker as being more effective, and until research is completed it is anecdotal evidence. A very recent study by Knickerbocker (1971) implies that "non-professional volunteers offered significantly higher levels of warmth $(p. < .01)$ empathy $(p. < .10)$ and total conditions $(p. < .05)$ than professionals over the phone." (p. 8 Knickerbocker and Fowler)

47

The development of a Technical Effectiveness Scale by Fowler and McGee (1971) is to provide a method of measuring the telephone worker's communication skills, his assessment of the crisis condition and his ability to formulate an appropriate plan of action. These studies along with the results of Girard's study (1972) concerning effective telephone workers should begin to define and evaluate the worker's performance.

The role of the professional volunteer in the SPC/Youth services is ordinarily that of back-up consultant or trainer rather than telephone worker. Because of the importance of providing the trained non-professional volunteer with available professional knowledge, professional volunteers are usually assigned shifts to serve as a resource person for the worker on telephone duty. The professionals also function in the capacity of interviewee, trainer, counselor and evaluator of non-professional performance.

McGee (1971) proposes that the professional, whether in the role of consultant, telephone worker or trainer, should also receive crisis intervention training. He implies that it is incorrect to assume the professional has knowledge and expertise concerning suicide and crisis intervention. He further submits that there are three different types of consultants but suggests the most desired one "maintains an ancillary but supportive role which encourages independence." (p. 15)

McGee postulates three excellent approaches to recruiting and training of professional concultants:

1. Consultants must be evaluated and selected just as carefully and with just as much deliberation vis-a vis the goals of the organization as are the non-professional volunteers (p. 15).
2. Consultants must be given some training opportunities and exposed to the same training material that is provided for the non-professional volunteers (p. 15).
3. Consultants must be given a realistic role appropriate to their skills and consistent with the responsibilities which they can reasonably expect to fulfill. (p. 16).

He concludes that there is a trend towards more use of non-professional volunteers even by services who used only professionals previously.

Services which rely primarily upon paid or volunteer professional staff to provide a response to the community include SPC's in Atlanta, Georgia; Cleveland, Ohio; Louisville, Kentucky; Quincy, Illinois, and Grand Forks, North Dakota. Some of these services use professionals exclusively and others use them mostly during the day. The professionals include psychiatric nurses, psychologists, social workers, clergy, pharmacy students, and medical residents.

In general, very few services pay their telephone workers. One service formerly paid for night shifts (Erie County, N.Y.), but has since discontinued the practice. The director has indicated that the quality of worker and his performance has improved since discontinuing compensation. This fact does not, of course, imply that paid workers are less effective. Some services do pay students nominal sums to work nights or weekend shifts, but this occurs in a small minority of cases.

Recruitment Methods

Several methods of recruiting staff are employed by the SPC/Youth services. Growing in popularity, possibly because of certain advantages, is the "mass media" method. The appeal for volunteer telephone workers is spread through the news media, brochures, bulletin boards in churches, and industry--in short, through any agency that seems effective (Dallas, Tex.; Akron, Ohio; Orlando, Fla.; Atlanta, Ga.; Cincinnati, Ohio; San Francisco, Calif.; Miami, Fla.). Some of the advantages of mass media include immediate mobilization of prospective workers and community education about the existence and purpose of service. Responses from services imply that the average duration of service of a volunteer is approximately a year; hence, services are acquiring and training staff constantly. The major disadvantage of mass media mentioned by proponents of other methods is the enormous screening responsibility that becomes necessary to eliminate the unsuitable applicants. Those services using the mass media method point out, nevertheless, that their screening process takes care of the situation easily. Several disclosed that 25% of the applicants from this method become volunteers.

The second most popular method is that of "personal selection" by a director who approaches individuals from specific groups or organizations. This is often accomplished through speeches to organizations or appeal to psychiatrists, psychologists, physicians, clergy, and gatekeepers who might suggest potential workers. The major advantage of this method is the quality of performance one might expect. Disadvantages include the length of time it takes to select specific workers and the possibility that their involvement will be a result of mild pressure or coercion. (Manhasset, N.Y.; Abilene, Tex.; Amarillo, Tex.) Another method used although much less frequently is "organization sponsorship" whereby an organization agrees to staff the service with the members from the organization itself. This appears to be the least advantageous approach because it relinquishes complete supervisory power, raises questions concerning divided loyalty and the motivation and commitment of the worker to the service.

Interesting but perplexing is the problematic relationship between retention of staff and the method of recruiting volunteers. Three services in Texas (Abilene, Amarillo, and Dallas) testified that they experienced very little staff turnover or discharges. Reviewing their recruiting methods in an attempt to discover one reason for this phenomenon of a stable and enduring staff, one discovers that two services used the "personal selection" method while one service utilized "mass media." It might be inferred, therefore, that the recruiting method may not be the crucial factor in maintaining effective staff over a long period of time.

Screening

The screening process is seen as a critical factor in providing effective telephone workers. The process acts as a device to help people recognize they are not suited for this type of work. Completion of the whole process requires motivation, perseverance, and sincere interest. It provides an opportunity for others to observe the applicant function in a variety of settings. Recognition of certain procedures commonly employed in the screening of volunteers is useful to anyone with either a theoretical or a practical interest in crisis intervention services.

The application form is used by almost all services as part of their screening process. The form includes inquiries concerning current and past emotional and physical health, reasons for wishing to volunteer, attitudes toward suicidal behavior,

49

personality traits, psychotherapy, and reactions of their family to becoming a worker. Most applications are brief one page forms; others are quite lengthy. (Appendix J) Several services require references from a family physician, therapist (if there is one), and two other persons. Other services use this form as a method of securing an agreement concerning the worker's role responsibility; still others include a confidentiality agreement. If the application is accepted, a personal interview usually follows; then, sometimes, testing takes place.

Psychological tests used by some services include the Minnesota Multiphasic Personality Inventory and/or the Sixteen Factor Personality Cattell Test. Cincinnati uses a battery of tests by Peabody. Screening processes may include a written quiz eliciting immediate responses (Bangor, Me.); a stress role play at the first interview with three professionals (Dallas, Tex.); participation in a training course lasting for about 20-30 hours; and evaluation of actual performance on the phones. Several services indicated they do not require psychological testing because they regard the tests as not particularly helpful; others disagree, asserting that the tests are useful. Some use the testing results during interviews and training to stimulate discussion of strengths and vulnerabilities. (Dallas, Tex.; Stark County, Ohio).

The majority of services mentioned the use of the personal interview conducted by the director and/or psychologists or psychiatrists. Several services require more than one interview, at different stages, and insist that the interviewers agree on the suitability of the volunteer. The service in Atlanta also conducts a group interview to determine why the individual wants to help and what he feels he will get out of the experience. These interviews are very important in interviewer decision and self-selection.

Many services advise that it is essential to have **personal** contact when informing a person that he or she is not suitable for the telephone work. In order not to damage egos and to soften the rejection, some services attempt to find other more suitable volunteer work for the applicants.

The variety of approaches to screening procedures is extensive and is defined by each unique operation in relationship to its stated purposes and goals. Some services will require a written request for an application form; others insist upon a telephone request. Each method is used to define certain characteristics. For example, writing for an application requires more motivation and displays the person's ability to express himself. On the other hand, a telephone request allows the director of the service to hear the tonal quality of the voice, assess the flexibility of response, and determine some degree of ability.

Finally, there are a diversity of approaches surrounding the provisions for training. There are services which do extensive screening and eliminating before the training sessions and others which allow everyone to take the training because of its educational value. Two factors influencing these opposing decisions are the educational value of reaching more people by allowing everyone to participate and the need to preserve the anonymity of the volunteers. Services in smaller towns (Amarillo, Texas; Stark County, Ohio; Manhasset, N.Y.) often require that workers keep confidential their association with the SPC/Youth services because knowledge of their participation could prevent a neighbor, friend, or relative from benefiting from the service because of fear of exposure. Volunteers in these services use only first names or code names if they are well known in the community or have distinctive names.

The survey indicated that problems of staffing and/or volunteer drop-out were significant for a total of 42% of the services. Recognition of this as a major problem area suggests the importance of discussing this area in more detail. Mary Swanson (1970) designates the following reasons why people do volunteer:

1. To become responsibly involved in their community.
2. To help selves or members of their families.
3. Leisure time.
4. Satisfy needs for personal contact.
5. Alleviate boredom of automated jobs.
6. "Belong" to a group.
7. Newcomer to community.
8. Self-respect
9. To be wanted.

Some factors that were mentioned and also observed in services that did not have a serious staffing problem included enthusiasm generated by the director, maximum involvement of the workers in policy-making decisions and/or representation on the policy-making boards and committees (Dallas, Texas), and involvement in several ways such as having all clerical work done by the volunteers (West Palm Beach, Fla.). Maximum utilization of volunteer time through added responsibility and involvement is important (Jacksonville, Fla., Dallas, Texas). Involvement tends to instill a sense of responsibility, pride, and importance in the job. In Jacksonville, Fla. groups of volunteers painted the telephone worker rooms, and another group made curtains! This type of involvement encourages a sense of belonging and of being 'needed.' The importance of an "open door policy" allowing the workers to complain or suggest and to receive respectful attention cannot be over-emphasized, for such a policy provides an important outlet for mixed feelings and prevents festering problems.

Various methods are used to continually motivate and fulfill the needs of the volunteer. These include the following techniques:

(a) Promotion, after six months, of qualified workers to "clinical associates" acknowledges their competence and provides them with additional responsibility. (Erie County, Buffalo, N.Y.)
(b) Day to day verbal or written praise for competence by the director, either privately or publicly. (Jacksonville, Fla.)
(c) Making them aware of the importance of their participation in maintaining the service. (Abilene, Tex.)
(d) Fulfilling personal growth needs by providing interesting workshops on a community, state, or national level based on competence and/or length of service.
(e) Social affairs or parties held at Christmas or other times. (Dallas presented volunteers with small Christmas gifts.)
(f) Recognition of hours of service; awarding certificates at a special ceremony (Appendix K) (Zanesville, Ohio); presenting pens inscribed with "people who care" and placing names and hours of service on a large permanent honor role board that is constantly updated and displayed at all volunteer meetings. (Stark County, Ohio); presenting plaques and trays to recognize and acknowledge specific volunteers. (Dallas, Texas)
(g) Permitting experienced volunteers to take an active part in training and supervising new group of applicants.
(h) Recognizing when volunteers become stale or tired and encouraging short vacations or even turnover. (Ken Beitler, Y.E.S., Columbus, Ohio)

There seems to be little doubt that the volunteer has become an important and critical facet of providing mental health services and will continue to take increasingly more important and valued roles. Recognition of the invaluable contribution of volunteer efforts in our society has been spearheaded by Ellen Sulzberger Straus **(McCalls,** 1972) who will dedicate a monthly column "toward a new understanding of the worth, the rights and the problems of the volunteer." She suggests that there should be a tax deduction for the volunteer and will discuss the "proper relationship between the volunteer and the paid professional."

A general picture of the staffing pattern may be drawn from comments and interviews describing the volunteer in the SPC/Youth services. The professional volunteer ordinarily functions as a back-up consultant and resource for the non-professional who is on front line duty as a telephone worker. The professional also helps to provide proper and adequate training, but it has been suggested that he also needs the original training. Many services require all volunteers and workers to go through the screening and training procedure regardless of their designated function, or professional or non-professional status.

It has been mentioned by some services that a volunteer generally functions in the service for approximately a year. Seventy per cent are women, and the average age range is thirty to forty years of age for the SPC's and teens or early twenties for the Youth services. The majority of volunteers consist of middle or upper middle class persons, regardless of age, with, unfortunately, relatively little participation from blacks and the poor.

Once the volunteer is accepted, he then must attend all the required training sessions and is not usually fully accepted into the program until he has completed the training requirements. The training program is seen as another screening device where the volunteer is being observed carefully during the program.

Training Program
Response from the survey reveals that the majority of services provide some type of pre-service training for their workers. Only 5% of the SPC's and 2% of the Youth stated that they offer no training program at all. The SPC's of this group were staffed by professionals regarded as already knowledgeable. Results of the survey further demonstrated that an equal number of SPC's have training lasting 1-10 hours (22%), 10-20 hours (24%) and 20-30 hours (22%). The Youth services concentrate their efforts within training programs lasting 1-10 hours (30%) or 10-20 hours (32%); only 20% of the Youth services demand 20-30 hours of training.

There is general agreement that the pre-service training program is a prerequisite to effective service, especially for the non-professional worker. There is some controversy concerning the need also to train the mental health professionals because of the specificity of focus on suicide and crisis intervention. McGee and many others suggest that it is unfair to expect the professional to know everything concerning this unique and new approach.

The format of the existing programs are limited only by the lack of imagination. The range of training program hours and format includes the following definitions:

(a)　Twelve 3 hour sessions held weekly. (Bangor, Me.)
(b)　Three all day sessions (Great Falls, Montana)
(c)　Three evenings (2½ hours each) once a week followed by a sensitivity session on Friday evening and all day Saturday (Albuquerque, N. Mex.)
(d)　Four half-day sessions, two days a week

(e) Three Saturdays, 9 a.m. - 2 p.m., two consecutive and a final one three weeks later. (Peoria, Ill.)
(f) Three nights in one week for three hours each night.
(g) All day workshop with a coordinator responsible for five trainees.
(h) Sixteen weeks, once-a-week (W. Palm Beach, Fla.)
(i) Two day Weekend-Workshop, 10 a.m. - 4 p.m., followed by a private fifteen minute interview. (Cincinnati, Ohio)

The respondents indicated a variety of approaches with the majority having about six weekly sessions, two and a half or three hours in duration. They also specified that they usually require from 2-4 observation and participation shifts. Many suggest that the training is ongoing and constant through counselor meetings with the worker, observation of new workers by experienced workers, and in-service meetings held, usually, once a month.

The **in-service training meeting** provides an opportunity to present new information concerning new services and also permits more training in more depth. The most valuable function of the inservice training is to air specific problems concerning chronic callers and difficult calls. Through discussion of these problems specific plans for approach can be defined and the repertoire of response techniques can be expanded after exposure to unique problems. It is also an excellent method to foster a sense of community concerning a common goal. It should permit two-way communication concerning the problems the workers encounter or breaches of rules and should provide an opportunity to ventilate anxiety. As noted from the data (Table 14) the majority of the SPC's (58%) have inservice meetings once a month; 44% of the Youth services reveal that they hold inservice meetings every week. There is an interesting discrepancy in this area. Although the Youth services tend to provide less preservice training, they are obviously more involved with inservice training.

In personal interviews respondents indicated that while inservice training is **required** and desired, there is some difficulty in finding appropriate meeting days, especially in the SPC's. Very often the telephone workers are busy people with many other commitments that interfere with their attendance. This problem is coped with in various manners. One service holds the same meeting three different days in one week to accommodate those who are busy. Another service polled the group and divides them into smaller groups who meet on specific nights for three months; the fourth month they all meet together. Rotation is encouraged within the groups whenever feasible. To encourage attendance, another service serves coffee and cookies and counts attendance at meetings as hours served for recognition awards.

The problem of finding a time convenient for all will constantly exist; nevertheless, experience reveals that these in-service meetings serve a very valuable function in maintaining effective service to the community. These meetings permit the telephone workers to vent some of the anxieties concerning certain calls or callers and their own sense of adequacy. Several services include, in the in-service training, individual meetings with the director or assigned counselors to permit guidance and discussion about problems.

Training Format and Materials

The training manual from the Los Angeles Suicide Prevention Center has been the basic tool used by services providing training. In recent years the individual services have modified or altered the basic text, and some have developed their own complete program. In general, most require attendance at all sessions.

213-381-5111

The following outline of content of the training program will be a compendium of the responses and materials gathered from over 192 services:

Orientation includes a general overview of the philosophy of the service and a definition of its goals, purposes, and organizational structure. The orientation usually includes a brief definition of the role and responsibilities of the telephone worker. Defining expectations has been emphasized by several directors. Policy and rules for staff and working are outlined. General statistics, local and national, are discussed. Professional ethics and confidentiality should be outlined.

Crisis Theory and intervention is emphasized. Definitions, identification and evaluation of crises situations are explained and thoroughly discussed. Included in the category are the characteristics of the suicidal crisis, depression, anxiety, neurotic symptomology, evaluation of lethality, psychosis. This section should also include thorough discussions concerning crises of drugs, as well as alcohol, marital problems, sex deviations, legal and job problems. The feelings of helplessness, hopelessness, ambivalence, and hostility accompanying the crisis situation should be examined and explained.

Role of the Telephone Worker

Many hours of the training should involve the worker's role and responsibilities.

The art of listening with empathy and concern has been stressed constantly. There have been many references by respondents to Rogers' technique of non-directive reflection, although some others have indicated a definite need at certain times for a more authoritarian stance. Listening allows the caller to ventilate some of the pent up emotions and to help clarify the situation in relationship to the precipitating stress.

Training should focus on the development of interview skills and techniques, with special emphasis on the interactional process of communicating without the benefit of face to face encounter. Discussion of the purpose of the interview and the establishing of a relationship through various approaches is important. There is stress by respondents on training techniques used to gather necessary information concerning the caller and the focal problems without interfering with the warmth and trust of the relationship. The worker is taught how to respond with concern and empathy, establish a relationship, identify the major stress or crisis, and begin to formulate a helping plan. The worker is also taught how to cope with the range of emotional responses of the caller and the worker himself. These include, for the worker, recognition of his own biases and judgments concerning values and moral issues as well as his anxiety about the responsible nature of his role as helper.

The characteristics of certain types of calls including prank calls, third party calls, obscene calls, and information requests as well as the usual calls of people in crisis should be reviewed in the training session. A discussion of these should include response techniques available for the telephone worker.

Resources. Information should be immediately available to all workers concerning the complete range of possible resources available to help the caller in need. After the crisis problems are defined and focussed upon, the worker must be able to suggest or contact the most appropriate helpful resource if needed. He must learn the complete gamut of available resources including family, friends, gatekeepers, clergy, mental health specialists, police and community helping agencies. Specific emergency procedures should be outlined. The worker might be helped also by some explanation of the procedures in the referral sources. Knowing details about referral sources will enable the worker to describe what will occur when the caller goes to the referral source and thus perhaps alleviate some apprehension and fears.

Office Procedures: Office procedures, particularly the record keeping are explained in detail in training sessions. The record keeping system should be explained to the worker so he will not only know what to do but also understand the rationale of the recording and office procedures. The worker should become familiar with the forms he is to use, the telephone system, and all the tools available to him.

The training programs are most often conducted by a variety of professionals in the community along with the director and those involved in the operation or on the board of the service. Since these professionals are usually in a volunteer capacity, problems sometimes arise. Sometimes the professional is not adequately trained or prepared to handle the specific training program unless provided with the appropriate information and definition of role expectations. In many services, experienced telephone workers take an active role in the training classes. The engagement of the experienced workers in training sessions appears to have multiple benefits: the new worker benefits from the worker's experience; moreover both workers experience a sense of interaction and involvement; and the experienced worker's ability is recognized.

Training Materials and Procedures. The basic format of the training in the responding services includes lectures, small group discussions, demonstrations, and role play. Although a few services indicated the use of sensitivity type experiences, Neleigh, Newman, Madore and Sears (1971) allude to their agreement with Riessman (1967) that sensitivity groups are less useful as a training technique with non-professionals.

Role play demonstrations were cited by trainers and especially by the telephone workers as the most beneficial method. In responses to training evaluation forms (Appendix L) the workers suggest that they would have liked much more of this method used both in pre-service and in-service training. They feel that it helped to relieve many feelings of anxiety concerning the initial phone call and their ability to respond adequately. Through the use of "teletrainer" phones, available from the local telephone company, the trainees may play the part of the caller or telephone worker in a simulated call. The value of this technique is stressed because of the benefits derived.

Tapes and records of actual calls are played and trainees are allowed to respond at various intervals to foster a discussion of "individual" response. If tapes of actual calls are used, it is wise to delete any identifying information for the sake of confidentiality. Tapes of the trainee's first calls are often listened to by the trainee, the counselor and/or the groups to determine effectiveness.

One of the most valuable aids is the use of an individual training manual given to each worker for rereading at his convenience. The Los Angeles training manual has been utilized extensively; its use has given birth to a great many other manuals with a slightly different style and emphasis. Some of these other manuals include creative approaches, brief suggestions and itemized "dos" and "don't," reminders and tips on call responses. (Abilene, Texas, Appendix M).

Taping of lecture sessions by many services permits **repeated** listening by volunteers and makes the "tape library" available to all experienced volunteers. Specific books and articles are distributed with emphasis on response techniques and more detailed information. A list of some books and articles used can be found in Appendix N. One service provides a three ring binder for each new telephone worker to encourage the compiling of an individual reference book containing hand outs. Another service provides articles and then tests briefly for content.

Movies such as "Cry for Help," "The Physicians Role," "Counselling Techniques," "Suicide" and video tapes of previous speakers (especially if from out of town) are also used as adjuncts to the training program. The play "Quiet Cries" (N.I.M.H.) has also been used effectively in a variety of settings for educational purposes.

Several services allow gatekeepers, police, switchboard operators and mental health professionals to participate in all or part of the training program even if there is no intention on their part of becoming a telephone worker. There is some diversity of opinion concerning this technique as some services stress the need for small group involvement in the program to derive the most benefit. They prefer to have the training for the workers only and educate the others through specific seminars and workshops.

Recognizing the worth and goal of training programs, Nancy Bourne (1969) from the Erie County Service (Buffalo) in New York suggests that the

> Goal of training has been that of facilitating each individual counselor in the most creative use of his or her own style of helpfulness while developing knowledge and skill about the problem solving process, including as flexible a variety of counseling techniques as is possible.

Examples of several training program formats can be found in Appendix O.

The training program is conducted because the telephone worker must be provided with appropriate knowledge and techniques so he may feel adequate to cope with the problems; otherwise the worker begins to feel incompetent, hostile and angry.

Several services provide the new workers with a questionnaire concerning their evaluation of the training program (Appendix K). (Seattle, Wash., Jacksonville, Fla.). Results of the evaluative questionnaires and anecdotal experience signify that the telephone workers wished to have many more role play situations, more specific response techniques, more detailed information concerning resources, and, especially, more supervised shifts including evaluation feedback on their handling of calls. These responses seem to reaffirm the need for an adequate and ongoing training program.

Record Keeping

Responses to Question 9 (Table 12) and Question 10 (Table 13) on the questionnaire present a rather clear picture of the type of record keeping practices in existence. An overwhelming 93% mentioned that they do record incoming calls, but less than half (47%) of the total combined services, (SPC 51%; Youth, 34%) attempt to keep files for all. A significant difference in percentage response by the SPC and Youth services involves response to (c) attempt to get all names and other identifying information, and (d) Don't bother with names; 67% of the SPC's, but only 18% of the Youth services attempt to get all names and other identifying information; only 10% of the SPC's, but 46% of the Youth services, do not bother with names. Responses to these questions certainly exhibit a substantial difference in policy that ultimately affects record-keeping. A great many comments accompanied these questions; they will be included in this discussion.

The Log Sheet or Book

As indicated above, a great majority of SPC/Youth services use some type of method to record all calls on a log sheet. Logging a call usually involves recording the date, worker's name, sex of caller, time call begins and ends, type of problem, type of response and information about whether it is an initial or a request call. Some services (but not many) include other more pertinent information like age, marital status, and employment status. Other services keep a separate log sheet for prank calls, hangups, information, wrong numbers, business calls. There is some general feeling that the above types of calls are unimportant, but personal experience reveals that this does not always seem to be true. Through these methods of hangups, pranks, and wrong numbers, callers can be testing the response of the service. Several callers have apologized for that kind of behavior, explaining that it took some time for them to become trusting of the service. Examples of some different log sheets can be found in Appendix P.

Case Filing System and Report Forms

Those services which do attempt to get names and identifying information ordinarily use some type of case report form. These forms vary greatly in kind. Some are very structured, covering two or three pages; others rely mostly, except for vital information, on a narrative type of report. There is a sample of different forms in Appendix Q; the variety of types is self-evident. Whittemore (1970) in a study of 1,000 callers discusses the benefits of the call report form, its construction, and purpose. He suggests that it is important to decide which information would be vital; each question on the form should be there for a specific purpose. He recognizes the possibility that a complicated and detailed form may interfere with the worker's meaningful response to the caller and also that much of the information is not valid for research because not enough of it is consistently gathered. Whittemore further suggests that the gathering of the data has three purposes:

1. For facilitating assessment of the situation presented
2. For administrative purposes
3. For research purposes (p. 51)

After a review of the Atlanta, Ga. form, that service deleted 14 questions which seemed to serve no useful purpose.

A study completed by Kohler and Katz (1971) defines a specific area of information that should be sought: age information. The suggestion is made that "when age is not obtained, the call tends to be handled loosely." (p. 37)

At a workshop on Data Collection in San Francisco, Litman (1970) specified the following reasons for collecting data:

A. To remind the worker of various areas that need to be dealt with in talking with a caller, thus to help in the emergency therapy;
B. To keep track of the patient. If someone is calling repeatedly, probably his problem is not being satisfactorily met;
C. To monitor the operations of the Center;
   1. To evaluate the workers' performances;
   2. To keep track of the frequency of calls and the time necessary to respond to them in order to know how many workers to assign for duty;
   3. To note changes in the sources of referrals and in the types of patients.

57

D. For evaluation of effectiveness of the service:
  1. To keep track of dispositions of the callers;
  2. As a starting point for follow-up studies
E. For "research." These data are used to test hypotheses and formulate new hypotheses (p. 27)

Numerous services revealed that they use call report forms and case files only for those specific few callers they see in person or when they take immediate emergency action. Others stated that they began with several complicated forms, but have since changed to simpler and/or narrative types of forms. (Amarillo, Texas; Atlanta, Ga.) The service in Gainesville places high stress on the attempt to get all names and identifying information, short of alienating the caller, of course. They do not attempt this at all with their teenage line.

A description of the process of filing the case report forms at the Stark County, Ohio service might apply generally to many of those services which do keep case files. The telephone worker fully completes the case report form during and after the call, then writes up a brief resume on a form that is provided. If a follow-up is felt to be beneficial, a form designating when and how the call should be made is included also. Both these forms are then placed in a 24-hour file if no immediate action must be taken, so that the staff workers coming in on the next shift may see immediately what calls have been coming in. The worker also fills out the Log Book at this time. The director of the service reviews each case report form in the 24-hour file (an excellent way for him to be knowledgeable about all cases and briefly assess volunteer response) and assigns a number to the file. A Roladex file card is then filed alphabetically, according to last name, code name, or nickname, if the precise name is not available, and the file number is included. The case report form is then placed in a folder, the resume form is stapled to the inner cover for quick reference, and the folder then is filed numerically. If a follow-up form was included, then this is placed in a daily follow-up book and the worker who will be on duty at the follow-up time, proceeds to make the follow-up call. When it is completed, it is filed in the numerical case file; if another follow-up is indicated, that worker makes out another follow-up form and places it again in the book. If a referral appointment is made for the caller, then a follow-up form is sent to the agency to determine whether the caller kept the appointment and whether the referral was appropriate. Examples of the various forms are to be found in Appendix G.

Minor departures from the above filing system occur, of course. The Gainesville service uses small envelope pockets on a wall for follow-up. Gastonia, N.C. has weekly, rather than daily, meetings to review all calls. The service in Cheverly, Md. gives code names to unidentified callers in case they call back. Dallas, Texas files the anonymous case reports according to type or category of problem, suggesting this as an easier method of detection when the caller calls back. They have very well thought out recording forms including detailed instructions.

A method of indicating a high risk caller, or one who was a suicide attempter at some time, is to place a red mark, star, or dot on the Roladex card and on the file folder. The red mark enables the worker to know immediately that he is handling a high risk, repeat caller. (Jacksonville, Fla.; Stark County, Ohio; Manhasset, L.I.) An excellent system of closing a case is used by the service in Gainesville, Floria. In effect, they make a follow-up call to the caller to determine whether the crisis has been resolved; if so, they pull the file and place it in an inactive file; it can be reactivated if the need arises. The closing of the file is indicated on the Roladex file card also.

Follow-up

Responses to the questionnaire indicated that 55% of the services follow-up callers "as necessary," in other words they usually follow-up only when a very serious call has been taken. Some of the 31% who specified that they follow up all possible cases include services that do not often bother with names; the lack of names raises a question about how or whether they do follow up.

During some of the interviews it became obvious that some services would like to do follow ups more systematically and consistently but are concerned about the response they might receive. The services actually engaged in follow-up procedures seem to regard such concern as ill-founded. The Research Service (Gainesville, Fla.) is conducting a project of follow-up at specified times over the course of a year. Other services are doing less structured follow-up and they suggest that at least eight out of ten callers will be delighted that the service still is concerned about them. If the stress or crisis has been resolved, then the service can recognize the part they played in effecting this resolve, but if it has not been taken care of, it provides the service with the opportunity to become re-involved. The concensus is that services should follow up wherever possible.

The whole area of data collection and record keeping is intimately involved with evaluation. It provides the opportunity to evaluate the handling of the call by the worker, to evaluate the impact the service has on the caller and community, and to determine the population of people that is being served. If it is the desired one, data and records will make that fact evident; if records reveal the lethal population or particular section is not reached, they will serve as an impetus to re-direct publicity and appeal.

Lack of response to Questions 15, 18, 19 and 20 would appear to indicate that data collection is not a primary function of the services. One questionnaire respondent submitted that data collections do not demonstrate anything worthwhile and that he has no interest in receiving any results from the survey. Although there is evidence that not much data is being collected, a great many services commented that they are planning to do some collection of data in the future; they cite the lack of staff and funds as the intervening variables.

Problem Areas

Both the SPC and Youth services indicated that their major problem areas concern the (a) chronic (or repeater) callers (41%) and (f) funding (46%). Funding seems to be a more critical area for Youth services (57%). Volunteer drop out (c) (25%) and (g) staffing (12%) are also important problem areas. The next areas of concern, between 13%-17%, are (d) telephone hang-ups, (e) liaison with police or other services and (b) transfer or referral of callers. Areas (i) liaison with police and agencies and (h) transfer or referral of calls, may be somewhat related. It is interesting to note that very few indicated that (b) crank calls (7%), (c) obscene calls and (j) publicity are problems of major concern.

Chronic or Repeat Callers

This group of callers, variously described as "chronic" or "repeaters" by a great many services, has been referred to by the Jacksonville, Fla. service as the "charter members." The "chronic" caller to a SPC/Youth service can be typically described as one who calls the service consistently over a period of several weeks, months or even longer, with anywhere from 3-25 or more calls per week. One service noted 18 calls in one day (Stark County, Ohio) and another, 173 from the same caller in less than a year (Erie County, N.Y. Lester and Brockopp, 1970). Lester and Brockopp (1970) have concerned themselves with this problem area and conducted a study about chronic callers (those who called 10 times or more) to the Suicide Prevention and Crisis Service in Erie County. Lester and Brockopp suggest that the chronic caller "did not differ in general characteristics from the individual who only called once." (p. 247) They categorized the chronic callers according to their treatment status into four areas: the callers who were involved in therapy, those looking to the center to help them find treatment (therapy), some who had not been and were not presently in therapy but wished to "ventilate" their feelings, and, finally, the callers who had previously been in treatment. Lester and Brockopp imply that the chronic callers appeared to be as suicidal as the callers who were not considered chronic.

There appears to be some controversy about the therapeutic management of these calls, with some stating the necessity to eliminate the problem by limiting the time of the call and number of calls, and others allowing them to call whenever they feel the need but explaining that they must respond to others as well. Other problems with repeat or chronic callers arise when the call is taken at night or at home when only one phone line is available; some callers form an attachment to a specific telephone worker. Staff become very frustrated also when a chronic caller will not accept referrals or seek appropriate help. The staff's feeling of impotence with such a caller may result in some feelings of anger and hostility. Some approaches that have been used by different services are:

1. Limiting the time a call can last (5 to 30 min) but respond with warmth, empathy and concern. (Jacksonville, Fla., Stark County, Ohio, Orlando, Fla.)
2. Limiting the number of calls they will accept in a day or week.
3. Psychiatric reviewing of the case file to define a response that all workers should follow. (Stark County, Ohio; Berkeley, Calif.)
4. Not allowing caller to request and get one **specific** worker (Amarillo, Texas)
5. Encouraging caller to call a particular worker (Dallas, Texas, Erie County) but if the caller does not seek help then move toward termination in an attempt to motivate the caller to action.
6. Allowing them to call and talk as often or as long as desired as long as it doesn't interfere with other calls. (Cincinnati, Ohio)
7. Worker focussing on a particular problem area and attempting to have caller understand it.
8. A hostile and angry reaction (Blum and Lester, 1970)
9. Confrontation with callers behavior (Blum and Lester, 1970)

The above responses indicate some contrasting approaches; none of them have been consistently studied and researched in order to define a preferred effective method. The approach used will depend upon the goals and purposes of the service and the feelings of the telephone workers. There is some evidence of disparity between defined purposes and actual response. For example, one Youth service alluded to excessive frustration and anger at the chronic girl callers who "whine" on the phone, although the stated purpose of that service is to appeal to those who are "lonely, depressed, frustrated or non-communicative . . . who seek out peer understanding and mutual concern for problems."

Several services have indicated that the professionals tend to get more frustrated and angry with the chronic caller; others say it is the non-professional worker who becomes more frustrated. Lester (1971) suggests that a service can possibly be responsible for "maintaining and rewarding the dependency of chronic callers through insufficient supervision and coordination of the volunteer counselors who work as telephone counselors." (p. 65) Brockopp (1970) suggests some other responses to the chronic caller such as:

1. "Trying to find out if the chronic caller is seeing a therapist or calling other services and then attempting to work with the others to define a consistent approach." (p. 25)
2. Not underestimating the seriousness of suicidal behavior.
3. Recognizing the need for establishing a trusting and supporting relationship that is probably missing in his life because of exhausted family and friends.
4. Emphasizing self-support and mobilization of his own resources.
5. Focussing on a specific problem is a type of crisis therapy that makes the total overwhelming problem manageable.
6. Brockopp also suggests that it is important to try "arranging a liaison between the chronic caller and other lonely people in the community."
7. Enlisting the aid of former telephone therapists at the Center who have dropped out of scheduled work at the center and who might be willing to have their name and their number given out to a number of chronic callers. The chronic callers could then call them rather than the Center for ongoing support.
8. Since chronic callers tend to be older individuals, or individuals who demand a great deal of support and succor, Golden Age Club members could be talking with these individuals via the telephone.
9. Attempting to form group therapy approaches with these individuals through bringing together a group of chronic callers, for a period of time each week, and allowing them to interact with other people having problems similar to theirs. This minimizes the phone contact with the center and increases the interpersonal contact they may have with individuals who have similar problems.
10. Permitting the individual and the center to correspond by mail rather than telephone. Written correspondence allows both parties to give a more thoughtful type of response to each other and allows the service to deal with the problem through a less time-consuming method leaving telephone lines clear for others.
11. It appears that sometimes one can help the chronic callers best through showing interest and concern by calling them, rather than waiting for them to call the Center. This way, the telephone therapist also has more control over the conversation, may direct it without causing the caller to feel hurt. The center's initiating the call reassures the repeat caller that the agency is concerned; moreover, it diminishes the person's need to call for reassurance and acknowledges that the service is still concerned and available. (p. 26)

There is only anecdotal endorsement of the above approaches, although aspects of all of them have been employed by different services. The alternatives have been presented here to stimulate a review on an intelligent selection of alternatives by each service. There is little doubt that the problem of the chronic caller is to remain a frustrating challenge until some concrete evidence is discovered about the efficacy of the methods chosen to handle these callers.

Other callers that present similar problems are the obscene caller, the alcoholic and prank caller. In most cases each call is responded to in a serious way; only one service indicates that they hang up on an obscene call. The majority feel that these calls represent "surface" symptoms of more significant problems.

Funding

This category has been discussed in detail previously but since it was acknowledged as a primary problem area it is also noted here. Since most of the area has been thoroughly discussed in another section it will not be duplicated. Those who made comments on the questionnaire about this area suggested that the lack of funds interfered seriously with proper staffing, research, and evaluation.

Relationships with Police, Agencies and Referral

This particular area was also thoroughly discussed in the section on community involvement and will not be repeated here. The comments on the questionnaire imply that there are more problems with referrals and relationships with helping community agencies and emergency rooms than with the police. Lack of appropriate community resources was also cited as a problem.

Staffing

Problems concerning volunteer drop out and/or staff turnover appear to be of major concern. One service indicates that its staff remains in service 6-8 months (Manhasset, L.I.), another **expects** and requires its staff to leave after one year of service (Columbus, Ohio); Akron, Ohio reveals that it has staff who have been functioning for almost two years. Graduate or university students can be extremely helpful, especially on "night" duty, but their graduation and/or vacations play havoc with scheduling. Other staffing problems mentioned include problems with worker's not coming on duty on time (Palm Springs, Calif.), maintaining worker interest when there are few calls (Springfield, Ill.) not having enough staff at initial opening, dealing with inefficient staff, lacking role definition for staff, and recruiting and maintaining dedicated staff over a period of time. These problems and others are discussed and commented on in the category of Recruiting and Staffing.

Characteristics of Callers

The persons who call the SPC/Youth services use the service to answer some need, whether it is appropriate to the stated objectives of the services or not.

Response to Questions 15, 18 and 19 suggests the possibility of some general or common characteristics of the calling population. Response to these questions was hampered by several problems; hence the following discussion will incorporate experience at centers as well as available literature.

The age of the callers differs, of course, for the SPC and Youth services. Since the youth services focus their appeal to that age group, the majority of the callers to their services are between 10-20 years old with about 10-15% falling in the 20-30 year old category. On the other hand, since the SPC's appeal to a broad range of age groups (Stark County, Ohio shows age range from 7-89 years), callers of many ages call these services. The majority of callers (61%) are between the ages of 21-30 years. The second age category of callers to the SPC's is the 31-40 year range. Although all ages are represented among the callers, the number of calls decreases as the age increases. Seventy-five per cent (75%) of the respondents indicated that only 1-10% of their calls were from people of 51 years of age and over.

The implications of this response lie in the suicide statistics **currently** available. The completed suicide is most often a male of forty or above; the rate of suicides increases as the age increases. The services in general therefore are attracting a somewhat younger age group, although males are the most lethal population.*

The data also suggest that the older the male becomes, the less likely he is to call for help. The percentage of male callers to the services begins at 40% for the 10-20 year old and gradually decreases to 32% for the 61-70 year old male caller.

Comparing the response data to the suicide statistics a rather interesting phenomenon is observed. The male, as he ages, commits suicide three times more often than the female, yet his calls comprise only one third of the total calls received. This result of course has implications that will be more thoroughly discussed below.

Response to Question 18, concerning general categories of calls yields the following information: 73% of the respondents specified that 1-10% of their calls concern people who are in the midst of a suicide attempt; 58% note that 1-10% of their callers have a specific suicide plan; and 20% indicate that suicide attempts are reported in 11-20% of their calls; 55% of the respondents specify that crisis calls (not suicide) comprise from 41-100% of their calls; 63% state that 1-10% of their calls concern information gathering. Calls from a third party, not the person in crisis himself, constitute 1-10% of the calls received. The above pattern is similar for the Youth service, although they receive many fewer calls concerning suicide. Of the Youth, 50% suggest they receive 1-5% of their calls in the suicidal categories. By far the majority of their calls are crisis or problem calls, excluding suicidal crises. The Youth services appear to receive very few, if any, third party calls.

Question 19 attempted to define the primary reason for calling the SPC/Youth services. Response of the SPC group was based on answers from one hundred and seven rather than the full sample, some of whom answered only partially. The collected and tabulated data designate that marital conflict is the primary problem the majority of persons call about. This statement is made with the full recognition that the marital situation is very complex and that many other problems, like alcohol, drugs, employment, finances and sexual difficulties may contribute to the problem. Response to the questionnaire and personal experience indicate however that jeopardy of the interpersonal relationship within the marriage is the primary problem. Drugs constitute the second largest category: 86% indicated that 1-20% of the calls involved drug problems. Caution must be utilized when reacting to this figure because of the societal concern with the Youth drug culture. It is possible that the burgeoning drug problem prevalent in persons outside the youth culture is being neglected. This high percentage concerns abuse of prescribed psychoactive drugs by adults. Following in order of importance are alcohol (drug) problems, general multifactor problems, sexual problems, job difficulties and child management problems. Depression as a separate category was not significant, probably because depression often accompanies the above stresses. In terms of percentages of calls, hangups and prank calls are almost insignificant categories.

*Note: Recent research suggests that previous statistics concerning age and characteristics of callers may be changing. Reports show young (15-30 yr) suicides are increasing in the Los Angeles area.

For the youth groups, the major concerns of the callers involve problems with drugs, boy/girl relationships (marital), and sexual adjustments or difficulties. Another specific area of concern revolved around the child-parent relationship.

The above data indicate some general trends. The citizens young and old are defining the service according to their need, not necessarily as the service has defined its goals or purposes. It appears that some presently suicidal people are definitely calling the SPC's but very few call the Youth service. In fact, approximately 30% of the calls received by the services do concern a suicide attempt or suicidal plan. The data also tell us that the majority of calls from people in their 20's and 30's to the SPC concern marital crisis rather than specifically suicidal crisis.

Similar findings by Anderson and McLean (1969) Resnik (1969) Moyer (1970) Whittemore (1970) Erie County, N.Y. SPC, Stark County, Ohio, SPC and many others substantiate the fact that the SPC/Youth services are attracting as self-callers people who are experiencing some type of conflict, depression, or crisis concerning marital relationships, but are not, in most cases, planning suicide at that moment.

In a study of 55 self-callers, Murphey, Wetzel, Swallow and McLure (1969) suggest that the majority of those callers were calling about an affective state and appeared to be "chronically psychiatrically ill people with a minority of the acutely ill." (p. 324). Resnik (1969) noted also that fewer calls were received from aged white males, who have a high risk lethality rating. It is felt that this population should be particularly sought out because of the increasing number of elderly, idle people who are experiencing poor health, financial difficulties, and a sense of worthlessness.

The tabulated data for Question 13 describe some characteristics of the calls that are presenting problems. Both the SPC and Youth services disclose that they have a rather significant problem with the chronic or repeat caller; yet neither service is being significantly bothered with crank, hangup or obscene calls. Problems do appear to exist with the alcoholic caller and the chronic repeat caller as well.

Viewing the characteristics of the callers to the SPC/Youth services permits some tentative conclusions and suggestions. Primarily the callers are defining the purpose of the service by using it as they define their need and state of crisis. Recognizing, from the data, that there are many age groups not represented in the callers, a service can do much to make certain the channel is open. Publicity is a primary factor and it must be directed at specific populations that are underrepresented, such as the elderly, college students, blacks, and the welfare poor. Training for the telephone workers must include proper handling of the repeat callers and the problem alcoholic.

There appears to be some danger in accepting the existing suicide statistics concerning certain populations of people, for the data are in a state of flux. Recent research suggests that what was accepted as fact has now been proven to be erroneous because of lack of knowledge and research. For example, very recent research has demonstrated that black people and those persons from rural areas do in fact have much higher suicide rates than previously expected. Prior to this research, many suggested that if one was black or from the country then suicide would not likely be a problem. These assumptions are now known to be fallacious.

Recognition by Farberow (1970) Lester (1971) Litman (1969) McGee (1966) Motto (1969) Kiev (1969) Shneidman (1970) and others concerning the need for accountability and for evaluation of effectiveness and impact on the community has provided the needed impetus for more research. Criticism by Weiner (1969) and Maris (1969) about the lack of effectiveness of the centers also has spurred this needed research.

64

Research by Bagley (1968), Orlando, Fla. (1971) San Antonio, Texas (1971) Amarillo, Texas (1971) Boston (1970) and Sacramento (1971) reveals that suicide statistics lowered when the SPC was in existence. San Antonio and Boston mentioned a drop of 50%, and Amarillo stated that where the rate rose the first year, it dropped the next two years. These statements contradict the findings of a study completed by Weiner (1969) demonstrating that the rate of suicide increased in Los Angeles and remained stable in San Francisco. Using the suicide rate as the sole criteria for evaluation of the effectiveness of the SPC/Youth services appears to be much too limited. Weiner acknowledges that these services "are only in the initial stages of developing effective programs of suicide prevention--an exceedingly difficult and complex undertaking. This study raises some doubts and question about the effectiveness of present suicide prevention programs and points to the primary necessity of further research on, and examination of existing programs before they are expanded." (p. 363)

Responding to the task, many research studies are being conducted where funding and personnel are available. Response to the questionnaire indicates that few (23%) SPC/Youth services are truly evaluating their effectiveness or impact, although a great many commented that they hope to do so in the near future. Most cited lack of funding and staffing as primary problems preventing this type of evaluation. A great many respondents implied that they received calls, cards, and letters from callers attesting to help received.

Some recent research studies that have been completed or that are ongoing include a study in Orlando, Florida suggesting that 41% of those citizens who were called at random knew about the We Care Service. The service in Pittsburgh, Pennsylvania is following up those patients who are brought into the hospital for attempted suicide. Greer & Bagley (1971) compared untreated suicide attempters to treated (brief or prolonged) attempters and concluded that "subsequent suicidal attempts occurred significantly more often among **untreated** than among treated patients, prolonged treatment being associated with the best prognosis." (p. 310) Lester (1971) reported that 29-50% of the referred callers show up at the Erie County Service. Most of the "shows" are older, married; they themselves often suggested the referral.

Motto (1971) found that 80% of a group of depressed and suicidal persons heard of the Suicide Prevention Service, but only 11% used it. Weiner (1969) reported that only 2% of a group of completed suicides had called the service. Maris (1969) determined that four out of five completed suicides had made prior suicide attempts. Litman (1969) suggested that Suicide Prevention Services can be more effective with the "situational suicide" who has had a previous stable adjustment and life style than with the chronic suicidals. Quincy, Ill. SPC contacted callers, 80% of whom stated they felt the contact with the service was beneficial. Selkin and Morris (1971) in a study of suicide attempters have reported that the results imply that the suicide crisis is transient. The Gainesville and Los Angeles centers are conducting many important research studies too numerous to mention here. The above research projects are just a small sample of the kind of research and evaluation being attempted.

In summary, there appears to be very general agreement concerning the **absolute necessity** for recognizing the responsibility of the services to maintain certain standards (Motto 1969) of service and to evaluate, where possible, their impact on the community and the effectiveness of their services. The problem of criteria for evaluation remains a difficult and complex one, and, of course the lack of funds and personnel will prevent some services from conducting much meaningful evaluation.

These services can nevertheless evaluate themselves internally in terms of objectives, the quality of performance of the workers, their training, efficiency, and populations served.

There does exist much controversy concerning the definition of the services. Resnik (1971) recently suggested that a "credibility gap" exists concerning the field of suicide prevention; the services are and probably always were "crisis intervention" services. He suggests that it is not possible to prevent all suicides and implies, as do Kiev (1969) Anderson and McLean (1969), Maris (1969), and others that suicide prevention is a misnomer, requiring a person to be suicidal in order to call. Resnik states also that the majority of calls do not come from suicidal people, but rather from people facing crises resulting from problems of living. This fact was substantiated in the data from the present study.

Nevertheless, there are others including Farberow, Litman, Lester, Canan and McGee, who feel that the Suicide Prevention label is an appropriate focus, that lives are being saved, and that early intervention in minor crisis states may truly be Suicide Prevention. Incorporating the word "suicide" in the name of the service often makes it easier to discuss suicidal feelings and expands the repertoire of problem solving techniques. Cavan (1965) specifies the need for intervention in any crisis before suicide becomes the solution to the presenting problems. McGee (1966) also points out that providing help at an **early** stage in the crisis or problem will expand the problem solving repertoire and prevent suicide from becoming the only answer. The author submits that this early provision of help might be **ultimate** suicide prevention; this will be difficult to document for some years to come. Provision of early education to obliterate the taboos and stigma of receiving or seeking help for emotional problems and intervening in mild states may be the ways for the SPC's to prevent suicide. The low risk caller to the SPC/Youth services may, in fact, be the future high risk suicidal caller or completer if suicide prevention services are not available.

This controversy will linger for some time to come, at least until some concrete research and evaluation can demonstrate which name is more appropriate and effective. In the meantime, the need for self-evaluation concerning community impact remains a primary responsibility of all existing services.

CHAPTER VI
SUMMARY AND CONCLUSIONS

The purpose of this survey and descriptive study was to provide a synthesis of the variety of models of operational techniques and methods used by the Suicide Prevention and/or Crisis Intervention services throughout the country. Furthermore, a secondary purpose was to make this information available in a single volume to those people who wish to begin a service and also to those who wish to learn alternative techniques and ideas. In this study, designed for ease of use, separate categories of methods have been defined.

Summary

A national survey of Suicide Prevention and/or Crisis Intervention services was conducted through use of a questionnaire sent to a three way cross indexed list of known services. Respondents to the questionnaire were divided according to the focus of their service and data was compiled and tabulated for 142 SPC services and 50 Youth services resulting in a total tabulated sample of 192 services. Twenty questions within the questionnaire elicited defined information; opportunity was provided for additional comments; finally, reports and descriptive materials from the agencies surveyed made available still more detailed information.

Discussion of Results

Suicide Prevention (84%) and Crisis Intervention (94%) were depicted as the two major goals of the services with Referral following closely as a third goal. One significant discrepancy (24%) concerned the goal of Suicide Prevention: for 90% of the SPC's, but for only 66% of the Youth services, Suicide Prevention was the primary goal.

Funding often came from more than one source. Thirty-two per cent of the agencies funding came from three or more sources, with the majority of services, particularly the Youth services, receiving funds from community organizations or private donations.

The location of the services was usually in a separate office facility but the data also indicate that 19% use both an office and the home in combination; 12% use homes only; resulting in a combined total of 29% using homes either partially or totally.

Paid staff consists most often of one to two persons (31%) with 34% indicating they employ no paid staff. A vast majority (86%) use both professional and non-professional volunteers to provide service to the community. The majority of services indicate having a staff consisting of from 11-30 persons. More descriptive of the Youth services is the range of 11-50; the SPC's often have a much larger staff.

The recent proliferation of both SPC and Youth services is clearly documented: 42% of the SPC's and 86% of the Youth services have been in existence for less than three years.

Response to the caller is facilitated by the majority of the services through a direct telephone line most of the time; 45% use it exclusively. A rather substantial number of SPC's suggest that an answering service and/or patch system is also used.

Twenty-four hour availability was indicated by 93% of the SPC's; whereas only 50% of the Youth services have this provision. The remaining 50% of the Youth services seem to be available most evenings.

Both the SPC and Youth services using "telephone-contact-only" constitute 44% of the services. The remaining 56% suggest an outreach and/or personal contact operation of which more SPC's than Youth services use professionals for face to face contact.

Although simple recording or logging of calls is done by over 90% of both services, a great difference in their case files and their attempts to get all names and information can be noted. The Youth services most often do not bother with names and, thus, do very little follow-up. Follow-up is done in most cases for clinical reasons, although 16% of the SPC's suggest research as another reason.

Responses to Pre-service Training hours of telephone workers indicate that an equal number of services train for 1-10 hours, 10-20 and 20-30 hours; in the majority (over 70%), training consists of 30 or less hours. In-service training most often involves a once a month training meeting.

The four methods of publicity utilized equally by both types of services are newspaper, radio, lectures and speeches, and posters and brochures. Though television is next in popularity, Youth services (40%) seem to have this method available less than do the SPC services (65%).

Problem areas encountered are similar for both services: funding (a greater problem for Youth), volunteer drop out, and the chronic caller constitute the major problem areas.

Research concerning the degree of impact of services on the community is being minimally conducted by either the SPC or Youth services. Interestingly, the Youth services seem to be doing more research in this area. There is some concern that the research may be a simple tabulation of calls received rather than true evaluation of impact.

Although middle-aged and aged males successfully complete suicide more often than do women of any age, callers to the SPC and Youth services are more often female, especially with increasing age, and they tend to be in the 20-40 year age bracket.

Approximately 1-20% of the calls involve suicide attempts in progress or specific suicidal plans, while other crisis situations (not suicidal) are reported by the majority of the callers. Information requests usually constitute up to 20-25%, with third party calls comprising about 10% of the calls. Marital conflict and boy/girl relationships are the single primary concern for most of the callers. Drugs, including alcohol, are the second single major problem; sexual problems follow. The multifactor problem area is, of course, a catch-all which includes many of the above problems, and is a significant category. There appear to be a great many persons experiencing stressful situations and wishing someone to respond to them.

The number of calls received per month by slightly over 50% of the SPC and Youth services ranges between 1-300; the Youth services receive from 101-300 calls. Over 40% receive over 300 calls per month. There is no doubt that many thousands of persons do call the SPC/Youth services.

A significant majority of the calls to the services (73%) are received during the hours from 4 p.m. to 1 a.m. when traditional helping services are usually closed! The response to this question demonstrates the need for a 24-hour service to be available for the citizens when they are in crisis.

Response to the question concerning the number who committed suicide after contacting the SPC/Youth services demonstrates that few SPC services (35%) and only 10% of the Youth services indicated that some persons had taken their lives after contact. Nevertheless, attempting to evaluate impact through this criteria presents enormous problems. First, if the service stresses anonymity (as many Youth services do) it is impossible to verify the statistics, or if a person calling the SPC refuses to identify himself then no research follow-up can occur. Secondly, one may wonder, how long is the committed suicide statistic the responsibility of the SPC/Youth services? If the person received help and sought the referral and professional help, but, nevertheless, completed the act of suicide, does the responsibility for it still belong to the SPC/Youth Services? The data recorded in Table 29 of this study should be evaluated with these limitations and questions in mind.

The most significant conclusion of this study is that the SPC/Youth services are responding to an over-whelming number of persons in distress and crisis situations as the callers perceive themselves. What the citizens did before the services were available is hard to determine; determining the full impact of these services on the community will most likely take from ten to twenty years.

This study dealt primarily with the technical aspects of providing service to the callers. The operational techniques and methods were discussed and synthesized to share creative ideas as well as the problems involved in operation.

The intent of the present study was not to be evaluative, but to gather and collect the appropriate information and then present it with brief allusions to advantages and disadvantages of particular methods.

The SPC/Youth services exhibit the efficacy of the volunteer, non-professional and professional, in the meaningful role of a mental health agent. Although the use of volunteer staff members began because of the serious lack of funding, the volunteer must now be recognized as a viable force in the community. The volunteers are filling successfully the great void of mental health professionals and seem to be demonstrating their competence. Research by Knickerbocker and Fowler (1971) has demonstrated that in certain roles the non-professional volunteer provided with the appropriate training has been found to be more empathic and accepting, when responding to callers, than mental health professionals.

Recommendations

The very recent and rapid proliferation of services was somewhat overwhelming. Now it is time to pause and recognize the need for accountability and self-evaluation. It is time also to review purposes and goals, to research and evaluate impact on individuals, the community, and the nation. That the SPC/Youth movement has come "of age" and must impose upon itself high standards and quality of service is presently being documented by Motto (1971) and the N.I.M.H. evaluation of the training programs and their adequacy and effectiveness should also be investigated through response by the telephone workers themselves. It would be wise to question the workers, after they have been working for a few weeks, about the effectiveness of the training they received in preparing them appropriately and adequately.

Constant research should be encouraged and continued through standardization of report forms. The collection of data, with certain services functioning as central research facilities, should be effectively coordinated, for the lack of adequate funds and staff make it impossible for most services to conduct needed research; hence, central repositories could be utilized.

Although operation of the services should probably remain autonomous and unique to each community, there needs to be a vast communication network permitting **immediate** dissemination of new research results, techniques of operation, and creative publicity ideas.

Regional and state organizations could be initiated to share funds for workshops, in which new information could be disseminated to volunteers. The workshops could serve also to reward the volunteer worker with recognition of their worth and ability; moreover, the workshops should allow some meaningful interchange with other telephone workers.

An attempt should be made to recruit telephone worker volunteers from all economic classes and races, including indigenous workers, who can be a tremendous asset to the program.

Finally the SPC/Youth services should attempt to gain enough power and credibility to enable them to function as omsbudsmen responding to the needs of the citizens and, in turn, defining the **gaps** in community services. It is important also to recognize the value of the educational role of the services. The services can act as intermediaries between citizens of the community and the network of mental health agencies by maximizing the use of the agencies through helping the persons in distress to arrive at the **appropriate** agency. A follow-up and feed back procedure could provide both the agencies and the citizens with response data concerning expectations of and reactions to services provided.

One cannot help being amazed at the vibrancy and enthusiasm surrounding these services. Personnel are committed to actively caring about and being concerned for people. Now is the appropriate time to identify the role of the services, to recognize the need for responsibility and accountability, and to define future goals. The Suicide Prevention and/or Crisis services must decide whether they will expand and broaden their scope of services, focus on limited and defined goals, or become an integral facet of an existing comprehensive mental health clinic. Whichever role is decided upon, it is crucial to provide an immediate empathic and concerned response to every caller by trained people who care.

It has been adequately documented that people do **call for help** if these services are available and that it is vital to provide a significant response twenty-four hours a day, every day.

The following poem was written by a "caller" to a Suicide Prevention Service who had been responded to in a meaningful and helpful way after attempting suicide.

70

A FRIEND IN NEED

Did you ever need someone to talk to,
Whether the problem be large or small?
But you thought there was no one who would listen
And you didn't think anyone would care at all.

Well I have had times like that.
And a few times I wanted to die.
I thought I wanted to kill myself,
But I knew I was too scared to try.

Well tonight I talked to Nancy.
She's a girl I have never met,
But she changed my way of thinking,
And she's one girl I'll never forget.

I often feel down-hearted
And think there's no one who cares,
So I pick up the phone and dial a number,
And I can be sure there's someone there.

Someone who wants to listen,
And do whatever they can
To help to solve my problem,
And lend a helping hand.

It makes life a lot more worth living
When you know they really care.
And no matter what time of day or night,
You can be sure they'll always be there.

The Suicide and Crisis Prevention
Was the best thing that ever happened to me.
They gave me a reason to go on living,
And they can do the same for you
Please Believe Me.

So why don't you call their number
If you feel the way I do.
They sure helped to save my life,
And they'll do the same thing for you.

APPENDICES

APPENDIX A

Results of General Survey Form

QUESTION 1: GOALS AND PURPOSE

___ (a) Suicide Prevention
___ (b) Crisis Intervention
___ (c) Community Education
___ (d) Referral

___ (e) Research
___ (f) Comment:
*___ (g) Religious Message

TABLE 1

Group	A	B	C	D	E	F	G
SPC (N = 142)	90% **(128)	92% (131)	51% (73)	83% (118)	35% (49)	12% (17)	2% (3)
YOUTH (N = 50)	66% (33)	98% (49)	54% (27)	82% (41)	24% (12)	22% (11)	6% (3)
TOTAL (N = 192)	84% (161)	94% (180)	52% (100)	83% (159)	32% (61)	15% (28)	3% (6)

*Denotes added category
**Number appears in brackets.

QUESTION 2: SPONSORS AND FUNDING

___ (a) United Fund
___ (b) Mental Health Association
___ (c) Mental Health and Mental
       Retardation County Board
___ (d) Private
___ (e) Grants or Contracts from government
___ (f) Grants or Contracts from private
       foundations

*___ (g) Community
       Organizations
*___ (h) Health Depts.
*___ (i) University
*___ (j) Mental Health Center
*___ (k) City and/or County

TABLE 2

Group	A	B	C	D	E	F
SPC (N = 142)	25% (36)	27% (38)	25% (35)	43% (61)	35% (50)	17% (24)
YOUTH (N = 49)	16% (8)	8% (4)	6% (3)	71% (35)	18% (9)	27% (13)
TOTAL (N = 191)	23% (44)	22% (42)	20% (38)	50% (96)	31% (59)	19% (37)

	G	H	I	J	K
SPC (N = 142)	27% (38)	3% (4)	1% (1)	6% (9)	4% (6)
YOUTH (N = 49)	53% (26)	- - - -	6% (3)	2% (1)	2% (1)
TOTAL (N = 191)	34% (64)	2% (4)	2% (4)	5% (10)	4% (7)

QUESTION 3: SETTING OR LOCATION

_____ (a) Community Comprehensive
　　　　　 Center
_____ (b) Separate Office Facility
_____ (c) Attached to University
_____ (d) Attached to Hospital or Clinic

_____ (e) Use of homes
*_____ (f) Church-affiliated
*_____ (g) Church-Not
　　　　　 affiliated
_____ (h) Other

TABLE 3

Group	A	B	C	D	E	F	G	H
SPC (N = 141)	26% (37)	38% (54)	2% (3)	23% (33)	35% (50)	6% (9)	7% (10)	6% (9)
YOUTH (N = 50)	10% (5)	50% (25)	20% (10)	6% (3)	12% (6)	10% (5)	8% (4)	8% (4)
TOTAL (N = 191)	22% (42)	41% (79)	7% (13)	19% (36)	29% (56)	7% (14)	7% (14)	7% (13)

QUESTION 4: STAFFING

Paid Staff

_____ (a) 1-2
_____ (b) 3-5

_____ (c) More than 5
*_____ (d) No paid staff

TABLE 4

Group	A	B	C	D
SPC (N = 142)	30% (42)	16% (23)	22% (31)	32% (46)
YOUTH (N = 50)	34% (17)	16% (8)	12% (6)	38% (19)
TOTAL (N = 192)	31% (59)	16% (31)	19% (37)	34% (65)

_____ (e) Volunteer Staff

_____ (f) Professional Volunteer
_____ (g) Non-professional Volunteer

77

TABLE 5

Group	E	F	G
SPC (N = 142)	85% (120)	50% (71)	51% (73)
YOUTH (N = 50)	90% (45)	46% (23)	58% (29)
TOTAL (N = 192)	86% (165)	49% (94)	53% (102)

TOTAL NUMBER OF STAFF

TABLE 6

Group	1 - 10	11 - 30	31 - 50	51 - 100	101 - 200
SPC (N = 121)	11% (13)	31% (37)	22% (27)	24% (29)	12% (15)
YOUTH (N = 39)	1% (1)	46% (18)	31% (12)	26% (10)	8% (3)
TOTAL (N = 160)	9% (14)	34% (55)	24% (39)	24% (39)	11% (18)

QUESTION 5: LENGTH OF TIME CENTER HAS BEEN IN OPERATION

_____ (a) 1 year or less   _____ (d) 4 years
_____ (b) 2 years   _____ (e) 5-10 years
_____ (c) 3 years   _____ (f) Over 10 years

TABLE 7

Group	A	B	C	D	E	F
SPC (N = 142)	18% (26)	24% (34)	17% (24)	14% (20)	23% (32)	4% (6)
YOUTH (N = 50)	52% (26)	34% (17)	8% (4)	6% (3)	- - - -	- - - -
TOTAL (N = 192)	27% (52)	27% (51)	15% (28)	12% (23)	17% (32)	3% (6)

QUESTION 6: TELEPHONE METHOD

_____ (a) Direct   *_____ (d) Diverter
_____ (b) Patch   _____ (e) Other
_____ (c) Answering Service

TABLE 8

Group	A	B	C	D	E
SPC (N = 142)	74% (105)	20% (28)	44% (63)	6% (9)	- - - -
YOUTH (N = 50)	90% (45)	6% (3)	30% (15)	- - - -	2% (1)
TOTAL (N = 192)	78% (150)	16% (31)	41% (78)	6% (9)	2% (1)

TABLE 9

Group	Using Answering Service Only	Using Answering Service or Patch
SPC (N = 142)	16% (23)	28% (40)
YOUTH (N = 50)	6% (3)	24% (12)
TOTAL (N = 192)	14% (26)	27% (52)

QUESTION 7: TELEPHONE COVERAGE

_____ (a) 24 Hour   *_____ (d) Weekends
_____ (b) Less than 24 Hours   _____ (e) Other
*_____ (c) Evenings

TABLE 10

Group	A	B	C	D	E
SPC (N = 142)	93% (132)	7% (10)	1% (2)	1% (1)	2% (3)
YOUTH (N = 50)	50% (25)	50% (25)	32% (16)	10% (5)	6% (3)
TOTAL (N = 192)	82% (157)	18% (35)	9% (18)	3% (6)	3% (6)

QUESTION 8: CONTACT WITH CALLERS

_____ (a) Telephone Only

_____ (b) Telephone & Direct Contact

Outreach

_____ (c) Professional

_____ (d) Non-professional

TABLE 11

Group	A	B	C	D
SPC (N = 142)	50% (71)	56% (79)	27% (38)	21% (30)
YOUTH (N = 50)	50% (25)	56% (28)	20% (10)	34% (17)
TOTAL (N = 192)	50% (96)	56% (107)	25% (48)	24% (47)

QUESTION 9: RECORD KEEPING

_____ (a) Record of Calls

_____ (b) Case files for all

_____ (c) Attempt to get all names and other identifying information

_____ (d) Don't bother with names

_____ (e) Tape Recording

* _____ (f) Names only for referral or action

TABLE 12

Group	A	B	C	D	E	F
SPC (N = 141)	93% (131)	51% (72)	67% (94)	10% (14)	9% (13)	4% (6)
YOUTH (N = 50)	92% (46)	34% (17)	18% (9)	46% (23)	4% (2)	14% (7)
TOTAL (N = 191)	93% (177)	47% (89)	54% (103)	19% (37)	8% (15)	7% (13)

QUESTION 10:   FOLLOW-UP OF CALLERS

_____ (a) We follow up all
            possible cases
_____ (b) We follow up some
            possible cases
_____ (c) Follow up within 1 week
_____ (d) Follow up within 1 month

_____ (e) Follow up within 6 months
_____ (f) Follow up one or more
            years later
_____ (g) Follow up as necessary
*_____ (h) No follow up

COMMENT: (Kind of follow up)
            _____ (j)   Research

_____ (i)   Clinical
_____ (k)   Other

TABLE 13

Group	A	B	C	D	E	F	G	H	I	J	K
SPC	34%	30%	29%	6%	5%	3%	56%	12%	48%	16%	22%
(N = 140)	(47)	(42)	(41)	(9)	(7)	(4)	(79)	(17)	(67)	(23)	(31)
YOUTH	23%	38%	8%	4%	4%	- -	50%	21%	31%	8%	38%
(N = 48)	(11)	(18)	(4)	(2)	(2)	- -	(24)	(10)	(15)	(4)	(18)
TOTAL	31%	32%	24%	6%	5%	2%	55%	14%	44%	14%	26%
(N = 188)	(58)	(60)	(45)	(11)	(9)	(4)	(103)	(27)	(82)	(27)	(49)

QUESTION 11:   TELEPHONE WORKER TRAINING HOURS

Preservice
_____ (a) 1-10
_____ (b) 10-20
_____ (c) 20-30
_____ (d) 30-40
_____ (e) Over 40
*_____ (f) None

Inservice Training
_____ (g) 1 meeting a month
_____ (h) 2 meetings a month
_____ (i) Every week
*_____ (j) Less than all above

TABLE 14

Group	A	B	C	D	E	F	G	H	I	J
SPC	22%	24%	22%	14%	12%	5%	58%	13%	13%	1%
(N = 138)	(31)	(33)	(31)	(20)	(17)	(7)	(80)	(18)	(18)	(1)
YOUTH	30%	32%	20%	4%	8%	2%	36%	12%	44%	- -
(N = 50)	(15)	(16)	(10)	(2)	(4)	(1)	(18)	(6)	(22)	- -
TOTAL	24%	26%	22%	12%	11%	4%	52%	13%	21%	1%
(N = 188)	(46)	(49)	(41)	(22)	(21)	(8)	(98)	(24)	(40)	(1)

QUESTION 12: PUBLICITY

_____ (a) Newspaper   _____ (e) Lectures, speeches
_____ (b) Radio   *_____ (f) Billboards
_____ (c) T.V.   *_____ (g) Cards
_____ (d) Posters, pamphlets   _____ (h) Other

TABLE 15

Group	A	B	C	D	E	F	G	H
SPC (N = 142)	94%	85%	65%	69%	88%	14%	6%	7%
	(134)	(120)	(92)	(98)	(125)	(20)	(8)	(10)
YOUTH	88%	80%	40%	88%	72%	14%	8%	14%
(N = 50)	(44)	(40)	(20)	(44)	(36)	(7)	(4)	(7)
TOTAL	93%	83%	58%	74%	84%	14%	6%	9%
(N = 192)	(178)	(160)	(112)	(142)	(161)	(27)	(12)	(17)

QUESTION 13: BIGGEST PROBLEM AREA

_____ (a) Chronic Caller   _____ (h) Transfer or referral of callers
_____ (b) Crank Calls   _____ (i) Liaison with police or other services
_____ (c) Obscene Calls   *_____ (j) Publicity
_____ (d) Hangups   _____ (k) Other
_____ (e) Volunteer drop out
_____ (f) Funding
_____ (g) Staff

TABLE 16

Group	A	B	C	D	E	F	G	H	I	J	K
SPC	42%	8%	5%	18%	22%	42%	16%	13%	14%	5%	11%
(N = 132)	(56)	(10)	(7)	(24)	(29)	(55)	(21)	(17)	(19)	(6)	(14)
YOUTH	36%	6%	- -	15%	34%	57%	19%	15%	13%	6%	15%
(N = 47)	(17)	(3)	- -	(7)	(16)	(27)	(9)	(7)	(6)	(3)	(7)
TOTAL	41%	7%	4%	17%	25%	46%	17%	13%	14%	5%	12%
(N = 179)	(73)	(13)	(7)	(31)	(45)	(82)	(30)	(24)	(25)	(9)	(21)

QUESTION 14:   RESEARCH OF IMPACT ON COMMUNITY

Research efforts concerning degree of impact of centers upon the community. Please comment.

_____ (a)   No   _____ (b)   Yes

TABLE 17

Group	A	B
SPC (N = 142)	80% (113)	20% (29)
YOUTH (N = 50)	68% (34)	32% (16)
TOTAL (N = 192)	77% (147)	23% (45)

QUESTION 15:   CHARACTERISTIC OF CALLERS

	Age	Total	Male	Female
A.	10-20 yrs	_____ %	_____ %	_____ %
B.	20-30 yrs	_____ %	_____ %	_____ %
C.	30-40 yrs	_____ %	_____ %	_____ %
D.	40-50 yrs	_____ %	_____ %	_____ %
E.	50-60 yrs	_____ %	_____ %	_____ %
F.	60-80 yrs	_____ %	_____ %	_____ %

TABLE 18

Group	N Who Didn't Answer Question	N Who Answered Only Totals	N Who Answered Both Total + Male and Female
SPC (N = 142)	48% (69)	33% (47)	19% (27)
YOUTH (N = 50)	38% (19)	22% (11)	40% (20)
TOTAL (N = 192)	46% (88)	30% (58)	24% (47)

QUESTION 15: CHARACTERISTIC OF CALLERS (Cont.)

Services Who Answered Totals Completely - SPC Only

TABLE 19

(N = 80)	1 - 10%	11 - 20%	21 - 30%	31 - 40%	41 - 50%	51 - 80%
A-10-20 yrs	26% (21)	24% (19)	20% (16)	8% (6)	5% (4)	9% (7)
B-21-30 yrs	4% (3)	24% (19)	38% (30)	23% (18)	1% (1)	5% (4)
C-31-40 yrs	15% (12)	43% (34)	20% (16)	13% (10)	3% (2)	- - - -
D-41-50 yrs	33% (26)	44% (35)	15% (12)	3% (2)	- - - -	1% (1)
E-51-60 yrs	75% (60)	8% (6)	1% (2)	3% (1)	- - - -	1% (1)
F-61-70 yrs	70% (56)	5% (4)	- - - -	1% (1)	- - - -	1% (1)

Services Who Answered Totals Completely - Youth

TABLE 19(b)

(N = 27)	1 - 10%	11 - 20%	21 - 30%	31 - 40%	41 - 50%	51 - 80%	81 - 99%
A 10-20 yrs	- - - -	- - - -	- - - -	15% (4)	7% (2)	44% (12)	33% (9)
B 21-30 yrs	41% (11)	19% (5)	7% (2)	15% (4)	11% (3)	4% (1)	- -
C 31-40 yrs	66% (18)	- - - -	- -	- -	- -	- -	- -
D 41-50 yrs	41% (11)	4% (1)	- - - -	- -	- -	- -	- -
E 51-60 yrs	11% (3)	- - - -	- -	- -	- -	- -	- -
F 61-70 yrs	11% (3)	- - - -	- -	- -	- -	- -	- -

QUESTION 15: CHARACTERISTIC OF CALLERS (Cont.)

Average Percent Answered by Services Who Answered.
Male and Female Percent.

TABLE 20

	SPC Male	SPC Female	YOUTH Male	YOUTH Female	TOTAL Male	TOTAL Female
A-20-20 yrs	40%	60%	40%	60%	40%	60%
B-21-30 yrs	33%	67%	42%	58%	38%	62%
C-31-40 yrs	36%	64%	35%	65%	36%	64%
D-41-50 yrs	33%	67%	34%	66%	34%	66%
E-51-60 yrs	32%	68%	- -	- -	32%	68%
F-61-70 yrs	32%	68%	- -	- -	32%	68%

QUESTION 16: FREQUENCY OF CALLS

Number of Calls Per Month

TABLE 21

Group	1-100	101-300	301-500	501-1000	1001-Up
SPC (N = 131)	33% ((44)	23% (29)	15% (19)	16% (21)	13% (18)
YOUTH (N = 46)	13% (6)	41% (19)	13% (6)	13% (6)	19% (9)
TOTAL (N = 177)	28% (50)	27% (48)	14% (25)	15% (27)	15% (27)

QUESTION 17: HIGHEST FREQUENCY OF CALLS TIME OF DAY

_____ (a) 1 am - 4 am   _____ (d) 12 pm - 4 pm
_____ (b) 4 am - 8 am   _____ (e) 4 pm - 8 pm
_____ (c) 8 am - 12 am   _____ (f) 8 pm - 1 am

TABLE 22

Group	A	B	C	D	E	F
SPC (N = 121)	5%	2%	9%	15%	25%	44%
	(6)	(3)	(11)	(18)	(30)	(53)
YOUTH (N = 44)	- -	5%	5%	7%	36%	48%
	- -	(2)	(2)	(3)	(16)	(21)
TOTAL (N = 165)	3%	3%	8%	13%	28%	45%
	(6)	(5)	(13)	(21)	(46)	(74)

QUESTION 18: APPROXIMATE GENERAL CATEGORY OF CALLS

_____ (a) % Actual Suicide Attempt in Progress   _____ (d) % Information
_____ (b) % Specific Suicide Plan   _____ (e) % Third Party Calls
_____ (c) % Crisis Situation (not suicide) (not suicide)

TABLE 23

SPC (N = 117)	1-5%	6-10%	11-20%	21-40%	41-60%	61-100%
A	62%	11%	8%	4%	- -	- -
	(72)	(13)	(9)	(5)	- -	- -
B	38%	11%	20%	10%	2%	- -
	(45)	(13)	(23)	(12)	(2)	- -
C	3%	6%	6%	21%	20%	33%
	(3)	(7)	(7)	(24)	(23)	(39)
D	25%	19%	19%	16%	4%	3%
	(29)	(22)	(22)	(19)	(5)	(3)
E	26%	17%	7%	12%	1%	- -
	(31)	(20)	(8)	(14)	(1)	- -

QUESTION 18: APPROXIMATE GENERAL CATEGORY OF CALLS (Cont.)

TABLE 24

YOUTH (N = 42)	1-5%	6-10%	11-20%	21-40%	41-60%	61-100%
A	52% (22)	2% (1)	- - - -	- - - -	- - - -	- - - -
B	52% (22)	10% (4)	2% (1)	2% (1)	- - - -	2% (1)
C	7% (3)	5% (2)	16% (7)	1% (2)	26% (11)	26% (11)
D	10% (4)	10% (4)	16% (7)	43% (18)	5% (2)	12% (5)
E	19% (8)	26% (11)	10% (4)	7% (3)	- - - -	- - - -
F	- - - -	- - - -	5% (2)	- - - -	2% (1)	- - - -

TABLE 25

Total (N = 159)	1-5%	6-10%	11-20%	21-40%	41-60%	61-100%
A	59% (94)	9% (14)	6% (9)	3% (5)	- - - -	- - - -
B	42% (67)	11% (17)	15% (24)	8% (13)	1% (2)	1% (1)
C	4% (6)	6% (9)	9% (14)	16% (26)	21% (34)	31% (50)
D	20% (32)	16% (25)	18% (29)	23% (36)	4% (7)	4% (7)
E	25% (39)	19% (31)	8% (12)	11% (17)	1% (1)	- - - -
F	1% (1)	1% (1)	1% (2)	1% (1)	1% (1)	1% (1)

QUESTION 19: APPROXIMATE PERCENT OF
THE PRIMARY CONTACT

_____ (a) % Marital
_____ (b) % Drugs
_____ (c) % Sex
_____ (d) % Child Management
_____ (e) % Job
_____ (f) % Alcohol

_____ (g) % Multi-factor Problems
_____ (h) % Other (specify)
              Depression/Anxiety
* _____ (i) % Hangups
* _____ (j) % Info
* _____ (k) % Legal

TABLE 26

SPC (N = 107)	1-10%	11-20%	21-30%	31-40%	41-50%	51-70%	71-90%
A	31% (33)	27% (29)	14% (15)	5% (5)	6% (6)	2% (2)	3% (3)
B	64% (68)	22% (24)	5% (5)	2% (2)	1% (1)	- - - -	- - - -
C	60% (64)	14% (15)	4% (4)	- - - -	2% (2)	- - - -	- - - -
D	50% (54)	7% (8)	4% (4)	1% (1)	- - - -	- - - -	- - - -
E	68% (73)	7% (8)	1% (1)	- - - -	- - - -	- - - -	- - - -
F	55% (59)	23% (25)	10% (11)	- - - - .	3% (3)	- - - -	- - - -
G	21% (23)	18% (19)	11% (12)	11% (12)	2% (2)	10% (11)	7% (7)
H	12% (13)	7% (7)	5% (5)	1% (1)	4% (4)	- - - -	- - - -
I	1% (1)	1% (1)	1% (1)	- - - -	- - - -	- - - -	- - - -
J	2% (2)	1% (1)	- - - -	- - - -	- - - -	- - - -	1% (1)
K	2% (2)	- - - -	- - - -	- - - -	- - - -	- - - -	- - - -

QUESTION 19: APPROXIMATE PERCENT OF THE PRIMARY CONTACT (Cont.)

TABLE 27

YOUTH (N = 45)	1-10%	11-20%	21-30%	31-40%	41-50%	51-70%	71-90%
A	51% (23)	20% (9)	6% (3)	4% (2)	- - - -	- - - -	- - - -
B	29% (13)	31% (14)	16% (7)	7% (3)	9% (4)	7% (3)	1% (1)
C	36% (16)	38% (17)	7% (3)	- - - -	1% (1)	4% (2)	- - - -
D	36% (16)	16% (7)	1% (1)	1% (1)	- - - -	1% (1)	- - - -
E	42% (19)	4% (2)	1% (1)	- - - -	- - - -	- - - -	- - - -
F	36% (16)	9% (4)	- - - -	- - - -	- - - -	1% (1)	- - - -
G	11% (5)	22% (10)	7% (3)	9% (4)	7% (3)	7% (3)	- - - -
H	9% (4)	1% (1)	4% (2)	1% (1)	- - - -	- - - -	1% (1)
I	- - - -	- - - -	- - - -	- - - -	- - - -	- - - -	- - - -
J	- - - -	- - - -	- - - -	- - - -	- - - -	- - - -	- - - -
K	1% (1)	- - - -	- - - -	- - - -	- - - -	1% (1)	- - - -

QUESTION 19: APPROXIMATE PERCENT OF THE PRIMARY CONTACT (Cont.)

TABLE 28

TOTAL (N = 162)	1-10%	11-20%	21-30%	31-40%	41-50%	51-70%	71-90%
A	35% (56)	23% (38)	11% (18)	4% (7)	4% (6)	1% (2)	2% (3)
B	50% (81)	23% (38)	7% (12)	3% (5)	3% (5)	2% (3)	1% (1)
C	49% (80)	20% (32)	4% (7)	- - - -	2% (3)	1% (2)	- - - -
D	43% (70)	9% (15)	3% (5)	1% (2)	- - - -	1% (1)	- - - -
E	57% (92)	6% (10)	1% (2)	- - - -	- - - -	- - - -	- - - -
F	46% (75)	18% (29)	7% (11)	- - - -	2% (3)	1% (1)	- - - -
G	17% (28)	18% (29)	9% (15)	10% (16)	3% (5)	9% (14)	4% (7)
H	10% (17)	5% (8)	4% (7)	1% (2)	2% (4)	- - - -	1% (1)
I	1% (1)	1% (1)	1% (1)	- - - -	- - - -	- - - -	- - - -
J	1% (2)	1% (1)	- - - -	- - - -	- - - -	- - - -	1% (1)
K	2% (3)	- - - -	- - - -	- - - -	- - - -	1% (1)	- - - -

QUESTION 20: NUMBER WHO COMMITTED SUICIDE AFTER CONTACT

*____ (a) No Answer
*____ (b) Question Mark
*____ (c) Zero

____ (d) Number of Suicides
         After Contact
____ (e) Number

TABLE 29

Group	A	B	C	D	E
SPC (N = 142)	16% (23)	18% (26)	30% (42)	35% (49)	(202)
YOUTH (N = 50)	16% (8)	32% (16)	42% (21)	10% (5)	(6)
TOTAL (N = 192)	16% (31)	22% (42)	33% (63)	28% (54)	(208)

Range of Number of Committed Suicides After Contact

	1-2	3-5	6-10	11-20	21-up
SPC	27	13	6	1	1
YOUTH	5	- -	- -	- -	- -
TOTAL	32	13	6	1	1

91

APPENDIX B
Detailed List of Associations
and Publications

Associations and Publications

The Center for Studies of Suicide Prevention (CSSP) established in 1956, is an arm of the National Institute of Mental Health. The specified purposes of the creation of this center are: 1. The center coordinates and directs research that increases knowledge of the growing problem of suicide and suicide attempts. 2. Such knowledge enables the development of techniques to help prevent suicide. 3. The center compiles and disseminates information and training materials to help understand suicidal activity. 4. The development of suicide prevention services is assisted by the center which continues the effort to maintain a liaison with suicide studies and programs being developed. 5. Furthermore, the center fosters and promotes research studies throughout the nation and attempts to apply the findings (Yolles 1967).

The CSSP publishes the Bulletins of Suicidology which come on the scene rather irregularly. They also sponsor two, one-week Institutes on Suicidology, one in the summer and the other in January. A Training Record and several films are also available. Audio tapes and a series of training films are to be completed and available sometime in 1972. One year fellowships in Suicidology are available through the center in cooperation with St. Elizabeth's hospital in Washington, D.C.

The Center for Studies of Suicide Prevention may possibly be discontinued as a separate entity by July 1972. Dr. B. Brown, Director of the National Institute of Mental Health states in Behavior Today (1972) that "his decision to phase out the Center for Studies of Suicide Prevention is a broadening of the program, not its end. Focus will spread to Crisis Intervention in general with emphasis on direct services." (p. 1) For information and input on new program contact Dr. James Goodman, Division of Special Mental Health Programs, National Institute of Mental Health 5600 Fishers Lane, Rockville, Md., 20852.

The American Association of Suicidology (established in 1968) Dr. Robert Kastenbaum is President. The objectives of the AAS are to advance suicidology as a science and to encourage the initiation of life-saving services by stimulating research, education, and training in suicidology, disseminating knowledge through programs and publications, and encouraging the application of research to the understanding and reduction of self-destruction in man.

Membership in the AAS is open to both professionals and non-professionals who are concerned with suicide or suicide prevention. Dues: Ten ($10) dollars per annum for all classes of membership except Student Associate, for whom per annum dues will be five ($5) dollars. Membership application forms may be obtained by writing to Nancy Allen, M.P.H., State of California, Dept. of Public Health, 2151 Berkeley Way, Berkeley, California 94704. The American Association of Suicidology has an annual meeting in March which includes lectures and workshops. The official journal of the A.A.S. is **Life-Threatening Behaviors**. Proceedings of National meetings are published.

Erwin Stengel, M.D. (England) is President of the International Association of Suicide Prevention. International meetings are held every second year. The next one will be in Holland in August, 1973. **Vita** is the official newsletter. Information concerning membership or the receiving of the newsletter or published proceedings of meetings can be obtained by writing to Robert Litman, M.D. c/o Suicide Prevention Center, 2521 W. Pico Blvd., Los Angeles, Cal. 90006.

The Exchange is an international information center that provides a National Youth Hotline Directory and a Newsletter, edited by Ken Beitler. Cost: Directory $2.00; Monthly Newsletter, $6. Write to: The Exchange, 311 Cedar Ave. So., Minneapolis, Minn. 55404.

Northeast Region News Exchange edited by Gus Potter tells about conferences and meetings. Write to: Hotline, 1355 Northern Blvd., Manhasset, N.Y. 11030.

Bulletin of Suicidology issued from the Center for Studies of Suicide Prevention is sponsored by the National Institute of Mental Health (no longer being published).

Life-Threatening Behavior, edited by Dr. Edwin Shneidman, is the official journal of the American Association of Suicidology. Cost: Members $7.00; non-members $10.00; Libraries or Institutions, $20.00. Write to: Behavioral Publications, Subscriptional Department,2852 Broadway-Morningside Heights, New York City, N.Y. 10025

Vita is the official newsletter of the International Association of Suicide Prevention. Members, no charge; non-members, $1.00. Contact Dr. Robert Litman, c/o Los Angeles Suicide Prevention Center, 2521 W. Pico Blvd., Los Angeles, Cal. 90006.

Crisis Intervention is a Journal distributed by the Erie County Suicide Prevention Center. Cost: Was free--probably will charge $4-10. Its articles by people in the field are usually very relevant to operation and problems of Suicide Prevention and/or Crisis Centers. Write to Dr. Gene Brockopp, c/o Suicide Prevention and Crisis Service, 560 Main St. (Suite 405), Buffalo, N.Y. 14202.

716- 834-3131

APPENDIX C

Survey Questionnaire Plus

Four cover Letters

GENERAL SURVEY FORM

Please check ONE or MORE appropriate to your service.

NAME OF SERVICE _____

METHOD OF OPERATION:

1. GOALS AND PURPOSE

_____ (a) Suicide Prevention

_____ (b) Crisis Intervention

_____ (c) Community Education

_____ (d) Referral

_____ (e) Research

_____ (f) Comment: _____

2. SPONSORS AND FUNDING

_____ (a) United Fund

_____ (b) Mental Health Association

_____ (c) Mental Health & Mental Retardation County Board

_____ (d) Private

_____ (e) Grants or Contracts from government

_____ (f) Grants or Contracts from private foundations

_____ (g) Other _____

3. SETTING (PHYSICAL)

_____ (a) Community Comprehensive Center

_____ (b) Separate Office Facility

_____ (c) Attached to University

_____ (d) Attached to Hospital or Clinic

_____ (e) Use of homes

_____ (f) Other

Comments: _____

_____

4. STAFFING

___ (a) Paid (Professional)   ___ (b) Volunteers

      ___ 1-2   ___ (c) Professional

      ___ 2-5   ___ (d) Non-professional

      ___ More than 5   ___ (e) Total Staff Number

5. LENGTH OF TIME CENTER HAS BEEN IN OPERATION

___ (a) 1 year or less   ___ (d) 4 years

___ (b) 2 years   ___ (e) 5-10 years

___ (c) 3 years   ___ (f) Over 10 years

6. TELEPHONE METHOD

___ (a) Direct   ___ (c) Answering Service

___ (b) Patch   ___ (d) Other _____

7. TELEPHONE COVERAGE

___ (a) 24 Hour   ___ (b) Less than 24 Hours

If less, what hours? _____

8. CONTACT WITH CALLERS

___ (a) Telephone Only   ___ (c) Out reach team

___ (b) Telephone & direct contact   ___ 1. Professional

                                      ___ 2. Non-professional

COMMENTS: _____

_____

9. RECORD KEEPING

___ (a) Record of Calls   ___ (d) Don't bother with names

___ (b) Case files for all   ___ (e) Tape Recording

___ (c) Attempt to get all names and ___ (f) Other _____
      other identifying information

COMMENTS: _____

_____

10. FOLLOW UP OF CALLERS

_____ We follow up all possible cases   _____ Follow up within 6 months

_____ We follow up some possible cases   _____ Follow up one or more years later

_____ Follow up within 1 week

_____ Follow up as necessary

_____ Follow up within 1 month

COMMENT: (Kind of follow up) _____ Clinical _____ Research _____ Other

11. TELEPHONE WORKER TRAINING HOURS

(A)   Preservice   (B)   Inservice Training

     _____ (a)   1-10   _____ 1 meeting a month

     _____ (b)   10-20   _____ 2 meetings a month

     _____ (c)   20-30   _____ Every week

     _____ (d)   30-40

     _____ (e)   Over 40

COMMENTS: _____

12. PUBLICITY

     _____ (a)   Newspaper   _____ (d)   Posters, pamphlets

     _____ (b)   Radio   _____ (e)   Lectures, speeches

     _____ (c)   T.V.   _____ (f)   Other

13. BIGGEST PROBLEM AREAS

     _____ (a)   Chronic Callers   _____ (f)   Funding

     _____ (b)   Crank Calls   _____ (g)   Staff

     _____ (c)   Obscene Calls   _____ (h)   Transfer or referral of callers

     _____ (d)   Hangups   _____ (i)   Liason with police or other services

     _____ (e)   Volunteer drop out   _____ (j)   Other

COMMENTS: _____

_____

_____

14. Research efforts concerning degree of impact of centers upon the community. Please comment.

_____

_____

_____

15. CHARACTERISTICS OF CALLERS

Age	Total	Male	Female
10-20 yrs.	_____ %	_____ %	_____ %
20-30 yrs.	_____ %	_____ %	_____ %
30-40 yrs.	_____ %	_____ %	_____ %
40-50 yrs.	_____ %	_____ %	_____ %
50-60 yrs.	_____ %	_____ %	_____ %
60-80 yrs.	_____ %	_____ %	_____ %

16. FREQUENCY OF CALLS - Number

_____ per day   _____ per month

_____ per week   _____ per year

17. HIGHEST FREQUENCY OF CALLS - TIME OF DAY

_____ 1 am - 4 am   _____ 12 pm - 4 pm

_____ 4 am - 8 am   _____ 4 pm - 8 pm

_____ 8 am -12 am   _____ 8 pm - 1 am

18. APPROXIMATE GENERAL CATEGORY OF CALLS

_____ % Actual Suicide Attempt in Progress

_____ % Specific Suicide Plan

_____ % Crisis Situation (not suicide)

_____ % Information

_____ % Third Party Calls

19. APPROXIMATE PERCENT OF THE PRIMARY CONTACT

_____ % Marital

_____ % Drugs

_____ % Sex

_____ % Child Management

_____ % Job

_____ % Alcohol

_____ % Multi-Factor Problems

_____ % Other (specify) _____

_____

20. NUMBER WHO COMMITTED SUICIDE AFTER CONTACT

_____ (number)

If you know of any new SP/CI Centers that may not be registered with NIMH or AAS, please list:

PLEASE SEND ANY INFORMATION YOU CAN! Thank you.
Samples of forms, publicity, year-end reports, etc.

Further Comments: _____

_____

_____

_____

_____

_____

Position of person filling out questionnaire _____

Name of Service _____

       Street _____

       City _____

Would you like a Summary of the Results?   ☐ Yes   ☐ No

If yes:

       Name _____

       Address _____

THANK YOU AGAIN
Sheila A. Fisher

SUICIDE PREVENTION AND CRISIS HELP
SERVICE OF STARK COUNTY

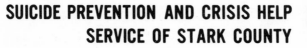

Dear Director,   May, 1971

Appreciating only too well the excessive demands of your time because of operating
an efficient and effective suicide prevention and/or crisis center, the enclosed questionnaire is nevertheless sent because of a feeling of extreme need. This questionnaire
is being used to collect data for a doctoral dissertation at Case Western Reserve University, and also to determine some basic facts about the operation of suicide prevention centers in the country. As all of you know, centers have proliferated in the past
few years; we now number over 200 suicide prevention centers and about 600 hotlines

It is my intention to gather basic and pertinent data about the establishment of these
centers and synthesize this knowledge so that it may be used by all who want and
need more information. The aim will be to establish a basic outline about our services
which can be used by those who are considering or are in the process of establishing
centers. It will be of "immense value" (Dr. Norman L. Farberow, March 1971) to
have information which is not fragmented or so extremely difficult to obtain in any
depth.

Filling out this form may possibly avoid numerous requests for information by others
in the future. Some of you will be personally contacted at a later date for a more
detailed interview, at your convenience.

Any information describing your center, forms used, publicity methods or year-end
reports would be most gratefully received and I will be happy to reimburse any cost
involved. Responding centers will be acknowledged in the dissertation.

Dr. Farberow and I estimated a 60% return of questionnaires but if each one takes a
few minutes of time to cooperate you could prove us completely wrong.

Again, I express my sincere appreciation for your response, cooperation and understanding. Any suggestions will be most welcome!

Sincerely,

Sheila A. Fisher, M.A.
President, Executive Board
The Suicide Prevention and Crisis Help
Service of Stark County

Enc.: Self-addressed Envelope

102

SUICIDE PREVENTION AND CRISIS HELP
SERVICE OF STARK COUNTY

June 17, 1971

Dear Director:

Your help is sincerely requested!

During the past five years there has been a phenomenal proliferation of Suicide
Prevention and/or Crisis services and Hot Lines. Because there has not been a
corresponding growth in desperately needed information about the services, both
Dr. Norman Farberow, L.A. S.P.C. and President of A.A.S., and Dr. Calvin
Frederick, NIMH, encouraged me to collect the relevant and pertinent data. The
resulting information can then be synthesized and made available for more effective service by Suicide Prevention Centers to the people. This would further eliminate many requests for information which can become very time-consuming.

Your service was one of 250 chosen from over 800 because it appeared to be a
more comprehensive and stable service and included features that would be beneficial to others.

Approximately one month ago you received the enclosed questionnaire, which
was designed so it could be answered with a minimum amount of effort and time.
Your cooperation is sincerely requested and is absolutely essential to the value of
the study in terms of depth and scope of coverage. We all can benefit from shared
experiences and problems.

Please respond at your earliest convenience and include year-end reports and forms!

Very sincerely,

Sheila A. Fisher
President · Executive Board

enc.

103

SUICIDE PREVENTION AND CRISIS HELP
SERVICE OF STARK COUNTY

September 14, 1971

Dear Director:

This truly is a plea for help!! In order to complete
my national survey of Suicide Prevention and/or Crisis
Services with depth and scope, it is crucial to have
your completed questionnaire.

If you did not receive either of the two previous
questionnaires or possibly mislaid them I will
certainly be happy to send you another.

If, on the other hand, you have been meaning to complete it but the work load has been too heavy, please
try NOW.

As you well know, providing an immediate and meaningful
response to those who 'cry for help' is critical in an
era when societal change and advancing technology is
making communication and relationships even more
difficult.

Because these services are attempting to fill the void
in community service it is even more important then,
for us to be able to share our successes, failures,
problems, and ideas with others in the field in order
that we may benefit from your knowledge, experience
and expertise.

Your cooperation and help will be most sincerely
appreciated.

Sincerely,

Sheila A. Fisher MA
President-Executive Board

104

SUICIDE PREVENTION AND CRISIS HELP
SERVICE OF STARK COUNTY

October 30, 1971

PLEASE HELP

Your "immediate and meaningful response" to this Call For Help will allow us all to share and learn from each other so we can all do a more effective job in our communities!

Please respond by completing and returning the enclosed. It won't take long.

We need your information and your ideas.

Thank you,

Sheila Fisher

*Sent to 22 centers and handwritten on personal stationery. Questionnaire was included with this last cover letter.

APPENDIX D

List of 192 SPC/Youth Services
Used for the Tabulation of Data
List of 25 Services Visited

Crisis Line
First Presbyterian Church
Thatch St.
Auburn, Alabama 36830

Muscle Shoals Mental Health Center
Suicide Prevention & Crisis Service
635 West College St.
Florence, Alabama 35630

Tellus Hotline
P.O. Box 64
Tempe, Ariz. 85281

Suicide Prevention Center
801 S. Prudence Rd.
Tucson, Ariz. 85716

Yuma Suicide & Crisis Intervention Center
1300 First St.
Yuma, Ariz. 85364

The Fayettville Free Switchboard
702 N. College
Fayetteville, Ark. 72701

Action Hotline
P.O. Box 6234
Anaheim, Calif. 92806

Crisis Center Hotline
P.O. Box 44
Bakersfield, Cal. 93302

Suicide Prevention of Alameda Inc.
P.O. Box 9102
Berkeley, Cal. 94709

Monterey County Suicide Prevention
P.O. Box 3241
Carmel, Cal. 93921

Helpline Inc.
Crisis Intervention
P.O. Box 5658
China Lake, Calif. 93555

Helpline-Saddleback Valley
El Toro, Calif. 92630

Dialogue
P.O. Box 772
Fairfield, Calif. 94533

Help for Emotional Trouble
1759 Fulton St.
Fresno, Calif. 93721

Gardena Hot Line
P.O. Box 2017
Gardena, Calif. 90247

Switchboard Teen Aid Line
6575 Seville
Goleta, Cal. 93017

Suicide Prevention Alameda County
P.O. Box 537
Hayward, Calif. 94543

Help Line Inc. & Free Help Clinic
222 5th St.
Huntington Beach, Calif. 92648

Crisis Clinic
150 Palm Ave.
Imperial Beach, Ca. 92032

Inglewood Hot Line
Morningside United Church of Christ
P.O. Box 5532
Inglewood, Cal. 90310

Agape Inn Coffee House Hot Line
1358 N. Hacienda
LaPuente, Cal.

Help Now Line
Memorial Hospital
2801 Atlantic Blvd.
Long Beach, Calif. 90801

Children's Hospital
Hot Line
Box 54700
Los Angeles, Cal. 90027

UCLA Hot Line
308 Westwood Plaza
Los Angeles, Cal. 90024

Help Line Telephone Clinic
427 W. 5th St. Suite 524
Los Angeles, Cal. 90013

*Suicide Prevention Center
2421 W. Pico Blvd.
Los Angeles, Cal. 90006

*Denotes Centers Visited and/or interviewed 1970/1971.

Help Line
Agape Inn
5609 York Blvd.
Los Angeles, Cal. 90042

Suicide Prevention & Crisis Intervention Center
101 S. Manchester Ave.
Orange, Cal. 92668

Hotline & Suicide Crisis Intervention Service
of Palm Springs
161 Civic Dr. #8
Palm Springs, Cal. 92262

Hot Line
Pasadena Suicide Prevention Center
1815 N. Fair Oaks Ave.
Pasadena, Cal. 91103

Crisis Line
6000 Jay St.
Sacramento, Cal. 95819

Suicide Prevention Service
P.O. Box 4463
Sacramento, Cal. 95825

Suicide Prevention Center
S.B.A. Mental Health Association
1999 North "D" St.
San Bernardino, Cal. 92485

Help Center-State College
5812 Lindo Paseo
San Diego, Calif.

Fort Help
199 - 10th St.
San Francisco, Calif.

San Francisco Suicide Prevention
207 - 12th Ave.
San Francisco, Cal. 94118

Suicide & Crisis Service
645 S. Bascom Ave.
San Jose, Cal. 95128

Marin Suicide Prevention
P.O. Box 4212
San Raphael, Cal. 94903

Human Outreach Counsel
211 N. Broadway
Santa Ana, Calif.
Att: Mrs. Duncan

Teen-Aid Line
36 Hitchcock Way
Santa Barbara, Calif. 93105

Suicide Prevention Service
350 Mission St.
Santa Cruz, Ca. 95060

I Care Agency
Box 1380
Santa Maria, Cal. 93454

Helpline Santa Paula
606 W. Howard St.
Santa Paula, Calif. 93060

Help Line
Box 441
Santa Ynez, Calif.

Sunland Helpline
P.O. Box 102
Sunland, Cal. 91040

Action Life Hot Line
Van Nuys, Calif.

Ventura Suicide Prevention Center
881 E. Main
Ventura, Cal.

Ventura Hot Line
c/o Mrs. Robert Elden
4509 Westmont
Ventura, Cal. 93003

Contra Costs SPS
Box 4852
Walnut Creek, Ca. 94596

Suicide Referral Service
P.O. Box 1351
Colorado Springs, Col. 80901

Psychological Emergency Service
W. 6th Ave. & Cherokee St.
Denver, Col. 80204

Suicide Prevention Clinic
2459 S. Ash
Denver, Col. 80222

Arapahoe Crisis Service
Arapahoe Mental Health Center
4857 S. Broadway
Englewood, Col. 80110

Crisis Center & Suicide Prevention Service
c/o Crossroads Methodist Church
599 Thirty Rd.
Grand Junction, Col. 81501

Help Anonymous
So. Colorado State College
900 W. Ohman Ave.
Pueblo, Col. 81004

Pueblo Suicide Prevention Center
151 N. Central Main
Pueblo, Col. 81001

Bridgeport Suicide Prevention
Connecticut Mental Health Center
1862 E. Main
Bridgeport, Conn. 06610

Center Stone
1081 Post Rd.
Darien, Conn. 06820

Mental Health Emergency Service
Kent County Mental Hygiene Clinic
738 S. Governors Ave.
Dover, Del. 19901

Psychiatric Emergency Line
Sussex County Mental Health Clinic
Route #1, Box 31K
Georgetown, Del. 19947

Youth Inc. Help
420 Willa Rd.
Newark, Del. 19711

Psychological Emergency Service
Delaware State Hospital
New Castle, Del. 19720

*Suicide Prevention & Emergency Service
801 N. Capitol St. N.E.
Washington, D.C. 20002

The Bridge
221 Amelia N.
Deland, Fla. 32720

*Suicide & Crisis Intervention Service
808 SW 4th Ave.
Gainesville, Fla. 32601

Crisis Intervention Center Inc.
P.O. Box 651
Eustis, Florida

*Suicide Prevention Center
P.O. Box 6393
Jacksonville, Fla. 32205

*Personal Crisis Service
Mental Health Assn-Dade County
30 S.E. 8th St.
Miami, Fla. 33131

Switchboard
2175 NW 26th St.
Miami, Fla. 33142

*Director
We Care, Inc.
610 Mariposa Ave.
Orlando, Fla. 32801

Crisis & Suicide Intervention
Emergency Mental Health
1770 Cedar St.
Rockledge, Fla. 32955

*Crisis Line
Community Mental Health
1041 - 45th St.
West Palm Beach, Fla. 33407

*Community Crisis Center
1013 Peachtree St.
Atlanta, Ga. 30309

Fulton County Emergency Health
   Service
99 Butler St.
Atlanta, Ga. 30303

Health & Community Services
   Council of Hawaii
Information & Referral Crisis
   Intervention Center
Room 602, 200 N. Vineyard Blvd.
Honolulu, Hawaii 96817

Night Line
Office of Intercultural Affairs
University of Idaho
Moscow, Idaho 83843

Suicide Prevention & Crisis Service
1206 South Randall St.
Champaign, Ill. 61820

Crisis Intervention Program
4200 N. Oak Park Ave.
Chicago, Ill. 60634

*Path Crisis Center
c/o Illinois State University
Normal, Ill. 61761

*Call For Help
Illinois Valley Mental Center
320 E. Armstrong
Peoria, Ill. 61603

Suicide Prevention Service
520 S. Fourth St.
Quincy, Ill. 62301

Suicide Prevention Crisis
1300 S. 7th St.
Springfield, Ill. 62703

Suicide Prevention Service
1433 No. Meridian St.
Indianapolis, Ind. 46204

Crisis Intervention Center of Delaware County
P.O. Box 404
Muncie, Indiana 47304

Community Youth Line
c/o Y.M.C.A.
101-109 Locust
Des Moines, Iowa 50309

Teen Trouble Line
316 E. 5th St.
Suite 401
Waterloo, Iowa

Suicide Prevention Center
250 N. 17th St.
Kansas City, Kan. 66102

Can Help
Box 4253
Topeka, Kansas 66604

Suicide Prevention Service
1045 N. Minneapolis St.
Wichita, Kan. 67202

Dial Help
c/o The Counseling Center
43 Illinois Ave.
Bangor, Maine 04401

Rescue, Inc.
331 Cumberland Ave.
Portland, Maine 04111

Bath-Brunswick Rescue Inc.
Woolwick, Maine 04011

Inner City Community Mental Health
Center
25 South Calvert St.
Baltimore, Md. 21202

Crisis Service
Prince George's General Hospital
Cheverly, Md. 20785

Montgomery County Hot Line
c/o Mental Health Association
11141 Georgia Ave.
Wheaton, Md. 20902

Re-Place Inc.
Boxton Switchboard
45 Bowdoin St.
Boston, Mass.

*Rescue Inc.
115 S. Hampton St.
Boston, Mass. 02118

Help of Capecod
676 Main St.
Hyannis, Mass. 02601

Replace Inc.
1912 Massachusetts Ave.
Lexington, Mass. 02173

Newton Community Hotline
17 Trinity Terrace
Newton, Mass.

The Listening Ear of Westborough Inc.
44 Upton Rd.
Westboro, Mass. 01581

Crisis Walk In Clinic
208 N. 4th Ave.
Ann Arbor, Mich. 48108

Common Ground
279 S. Woodward Ave.
Birmingham, Mich. 48011

Suicide Prevention Center
1151 Taylor St.
Detroit, Mich. 48202

The Listening Ear Inc.
547½ E. Grand River
East Lansing, Mich. 48823

Flint Emergency Service Room 700
Metro Bldg.
Flint, Michigan 48502

The Establishment
30 Washington
Mt. Clemens, Mich. 48043

Brainerd Emergency Line
201 Parker Bldg.
Brainerd, Minn. 56401

Hotline of Minnesota
Box 193
Excelsior, Minn.

Y.E.S. Youth Emergency Service
1232 Highland Ave.
Mankato, Minn. 56001

Suicide Prevention Service
5th & Portland
Minneapolis, Minn. 55415

The Listening Post
Mississippi State Hospital
P.O. Box 2072
West Station
Meridian, Miss. 39301

Suicide Prevention Service & Crisis Intervention
P.O. Box 263
St. Joseph, Mo. 64502

Suicide Prevention Inc.
1118 Hampton Ave.
St. Louis, Mo. 63139

Youth Line
Box 158
801 DeMunn Ave.
St. Louis, Mo. 63105

Great Falls Crisis Center
39 Prospect Drive
Great Falls, Montana 59401

Guideline
Southern Medical Center
402 South 24th Ave.
Omaha, Nebraska

Suicide Prevention & Crisis Call Center
Room 206 Mac.
Social Science Bldg.
University of Nevada
Reno, Nev. 89507

North Country Mental Health Clinic
227 Main St.
Berlin, N.H. 03570

Ancora Suicide Prevention Service
Ancora Psychiatric Hospital
Hammonton, N.J. 08037

Middlesex County Mental Health
    Emergency Service
c/o Roosevelt Hospital
P.O. Box 151
37 Oakwood Rd.
Metuchen, N.J. 08840

Crisis Referral & Information Hot Line
232 E. Front St.
Plainfield, N.J. 07060

Friends Hot Line
1000 River Rd.
Student Union Bldg.
Fairleigh-Dickenson University
Teaneck, N.J. 07666

Suicide Prevention & Crisis
P.O. Box 727
1028 Solar Rd.
Albuquerque, N. Mex. 87101

Crisis Center
Box 4103
200 Boutz Rd.
Las Cruces, N.M. 88001

*Suicide Prevention Service
560 Main St. Suite 405
Buffalo, N.Y.

Lifeline
2201 Hempstead Turnpike
East Meadow, N.Y. 11554

Nassau Community College
Stewart Ave.
Garden City, N.Y.

Suicide Prevention Tompkins County
114 East Court St.
Ithaca, N.Y. 14850

*Hotline
1355 Northern Blvd.
Manhasset, N.Y. 11030

Help Line Telephone Center
One West 29th St.
New York, N.Y. 10001

*National Sav-A-Life League Inc.
20 W. 43rd St.
New York, N.Y. 10036

Operation Help
Gatt. County Guidance Center
265 N. Union St.
Olean, N.Y. 14760

Suicide Prevention Service
29 Sterling Ave.
White Plains, N.Y. 10606

Five Towns Hot Line
c/o Family Service Assn.
124 Franklin Place
Woodmere, N.Y. 11598

Switchboard
408 W. Rosemary
Chapel Hill, N. Carolina

Gaston County Suicide Prevention Service
817 W. Mauney Ave.
Gastonia, N. Carolina 28052

Crisis Control Center
P.O. Box 735
Greensboro, N.C. 27402

Care Line
Onslow County Mental Health Center
P.O. Box 547
Jacksonville, N.C.

Suicide Prevention & Crisis Service
Halifax County Mental Health Association
P.O. Box 577
Roanoke Rapids, N.C. 27870

Together
503 High St.
Winston-Salem, N.C. 27101

Suicide Prevention & Mental Health Center
Ward 2 East-Neuro Psychiatric Hospital
Fargo, N.D. 58102

Emergency Service
509 S. Third St.
Grand Forks, N.D. 58201

Suicide Prevention & Psychiatric Service
Memorial Mental Health &
   Retardation Center
1007 N.W.
Mandan, N. Dakota

*Support Inc.
1361 W. Market
Akron, Ohio 44313

Suicide Prevention & Crisis Intervention
Athens Mental Health Center
Athens, Ohio

Suicide Prevention & Crisis Help Service
2600 Sixth St. S.W.
Canton, Ohio 44710

*621 Care
2444 Vine St.
Cincinnati, Ohio 45219

Psychiatric Emergency Evaluation Referen
10539 Carnegie Ave.
Cleveland, Ohio 44106

Suicide Prevention Service
275 E. State
Columbus, Ohio 43215

Switchboard Inc.
P.O. Box 3062
University Station
Columbus, Ohio 43101

Suicide Prevention Service
Room 924 - 137 N. Main St.
Dayton, Ohio 45402

*Crisis Hotline
Muskingum Comprehensive Mental
   Health Clinic
2845 Bell St.
Zanesville, Ohio 43701

112

Crisis Service
Benton County Mental Health Clinic
127 N. 6th St.
Corvallis, Oregon 97330

Suicide & Personal Crisis Service
P.O. Box 4443
Portland, Oregon 97208

Lifeline
520 Broad
Bethlehem, Pa. 18016

Contact
900 S. Arlington Ave.
Harrisburg, Pa. 17109

Help Inc.
2310 Locust St.
Philadelphia, Pa. 19103

Suicide Prevention Center
Room 430 - City Hall Annex
Philadelphia, Pa. 19107

Information & Volunteer Service of
   Allegheny County
200 Ross St. Room 308
Pittsburgh, Pa. 15219

Teen Hot Line
1815 Washington Rd.
Pittsburgh, Pa. 15241

Butler County Helpline Inc.
R.D. #1
Renfrew, Pa. 16053

Crisis Intervention
Emergency Mental Health Service
715 Grove Rd.
Greenville, S. Carolina

Suicide Prevention Service
Mental Health Assn.
2400 Popular Ave.
Memphis, Tenn.

*Crisis Call Center
944 - 21st Ave. N.
Nashville, Tenn. 37208

*Abilene Suicide Prevention Service
P.O. Box 2707
Abilene, Texas 79604

*Suicide Prevention Crisis
   Intervention Center
Box 3044
Amarillo, Texas 79106

Telephone Counsel & Referral
University of Texas-Austin
Austin, Texas 78712

Suicide Prevention Crisis Service
P.O. Box 3075
Corpus Christi, Tex. 78404

*Suicide Prevention of Dallas Inc.
P.O. Box 19651
Dallas, Texas 75219

San Antonio Suicide Prevention Center
P.O. Box 10192
San Antonio, Texas 78210

Suicide Prevention Program
110 S. 12th St.
Waco, Texas 76705

Crisis Intervention Service
   Granite Community
156 Westminister Ave.
Salt Lake City, Utah 84101

Listening Post
P.O. Box 1727
Salt Lake City, Utah 84117

H.E.L.P.
Union Line-Student Activity Center
University of Utah
Salt Lake City, Utah 84112

Crisis Intervention & Suicide Prevention
Suite 3 1726 W. 7th Ave.
Vancouver, B.C. 9

Alexandria Mental Health Hotline
101 North Columbus St.
Alexandria, Va. 22314

Northern Virginia Hotline
1132 N. Ivanhoe St.
Arlington, Va. 22205

Suicide-Crisis Center of Portsmouth Va.
P.O. Box 6502
Portsmouth, Virginia 23703

Richmond Hot Line
Medical College of Virginia
Box 151
Richmond, Va. 23219

Crisis Clinic
3421 6th St. Room 109
Bremerton, Washington 98310

Emotional Crisis Service
Community Mental Health Center
1801 E. 4th Ave.
Olympia, Wash. 98501

Crisis Clinic Inc.
905 E. Columbia
Seattle, Wash. 98122

Community Mental Health Center
South 107 Division St.
Spokane, Wash. 99202

Suicide Prevention Center
310 Chestnut St.
Eau Claire, Wisc. 54701

Emergency Psychiatry
Box 290
Elk Horn, Wisc. 53121

People's Drug Abuse Center
423 E. Mason St.
Greenbay, Wisc. 54301

People's Office
1121 University Ave.
Madison, Wisc. 53705

Suicide Prevention Center-Mental
   Health Center
313 S. Mills St.
Madison, Wisc. 53715

"Concern Inc."
Pinkney Hall
South State University
1014 - 9th Ave.
Menomonie, Wisc. 54751

Psychiatric Emergency Service
8700 W. Wisconsin Ave.
Milwaukee, Wisc. 53226

*Denotes centers visited and/or interviewed 1970-1971

CENTERS VISITED AND/OR INTERVIEWED

1970

Dr. Norman Farberow
Suicide Prevention Center
Los Angeles, Calif.

Nancy Wylie
Personal Crisis Service
Miami, Florida

Father Cote
Rescue Inc.
Boston, Mass.

Rabbi Coplin
Support Inc.
Akron, Ohio

Mr. Stanley Hall
Psychiatric Emergency Referral Service
Cleveland, Ohio

1971

Dr. Wayne Richard
Suicide and Crisis Intervention
Gainesville, Florida

Mrs.Bonnie Jacob
Suicide Prevention Center
Jacksonville, Florida

Mrs. Nancy Grimm
We Care Inc.
Orlando, Florida

Dr. R.K. Alsofrom
Crisis Line
West Palm Beach, Florida

Vicki Powell et al
Community Crisis Center
Atlanta, Georgia

Dr. William Arnold
Path Crisis Center
Normal, Illinois

Call For Help
Peoria, Illinois

Dr. Gene W. Brockopp
Suicide Prevention & Crisis Service
Buffalo, New York

Mr. Gus Potter
Hotline
Manhasset, N.Y.

Mr. Harry M. Warren
National Sav-A-Life
New York, N.Y.

621-Care
Cincinnati, Ohio

Michael Donovan, MA
Suicide Prevention
Columbus, Ohio

Dr. Robert Birch
Crisis Hotline
Zanesville, Ohio

Secretary
Contact Teleministries
Nashville, Tenn.

Mrs. Pat Higgenbotham
Crisis Call Center
Nashville, Tenn.

Mrs. Chris Kyker
Abilene Suicide Prevention Service
Abilene, Texas

Mrs. Claire Rigler
Suicide Prevention Crisis Intervention
  Service
Amarillo, Texas

A. Gerald Spalding, ACSW
Suicide Prevention
Dallas, Texas

Phyllis Clemmons
Suicide Prevention & Emergency Service
Washington, D.C.

LIST OF SERVICES WHO RESPONDED TOO LATE

FOR TABULATION

Emergency Mental Health Service of Maricopa County
2214 N. Central Ave.
Phoenix, Ariz.

Desert Counseling Clinic
Box 5246
China Lake, Calif. 83555

Student Health Service
California State College at Los Angeles
5151 State College Drive
Los Angeles, Calif. 90032

Emergency Psychiatric Service
4200 East 9th Ave.
Denver, Col. 80220

Keokuk Mental Health Center
110 N. 8th Blondeau St.
Keokuk, Iowa 52632

Crisis Service
University of Maine at Presque Isle
181 Main St.
Presque Isle, Maine 04769

Homophile Community Health Service
112 Arlington St.
Boston, Mass.

Walk In Service - Emergency Psychiatric Service
Martland Medical Center-Dept. of Psychiatry
100 Bergan St.
Newark, N.J.

Contact Center
633 S.W. Montgomery
Portland, Oregon 97208

Suicide Prevention Association
1520 Cherokee Trail
Knoxville, Tenn. 37920

APPENDIX E

Facts and Fables

on Suicide

From Some Facts About Suicide, by E.S. Shneidman and N.L. Farberow, Washington, D.C., PHS Publication, No. 852, United States Government Printing Office. 1961

FACTS AND FABLES ON SUICIDE*

FABLE: People who talk about suicide don't commit suicide.

FACT: Of any ten persons who kill themselves, eight have given definite warnings of their suicidal intentions.

FABLE: Suicide happens without warning.

FACT: Studies reveal that the suicidal person gives many clues and warnings regarding his suicidal intentions.

FABLE: Suicidal people are fully intent on dying.

FACT: Most suicidal people are undecided about living or dying, and they "gamble with death," leaving it to others to save them. Almost no one commits suicide without letting others know how he is feeling.

FABLE: Once a person is suicidal, he is suicidal forever.

FACT: Individuals who wish to kill themselves are "suicidal" only for a limited period of time.

FABLE: Improvement following a suicidal crisis means that the suicidal risk is over.

FACT: Most suicides occur within about three months following the beginning of "improvement," when the individual has the energy to put his morbid thoughts and feelings into effect.

FABLE: Suicide strikes much more often among the rich--or, conversely, it occurs almost exclusively among the poor.

FACT: Suicide is neither a rich man's disease nor the poor man's curse. Suicide is very "democratic" and is represented proportionately among all levels of society.

FABLE: Suicide is inherited or "runs in the family."

FACT: Suicide does not run in families. It is an individual pattern.

FABLE: All suicidal individuals are mentally ill, and suicide always is the act of a psychotic person.

FACT: Studies of hundreds of genuine suicide notes indicate that although the suicidal person is extremely unhappy, he is not necessarily mentally ill.

*From SOME FACTS ABOUT SUICIDE, by E.S. Shneidman and N.L. Farberow, Washington, D.C., PHS Publication No. 852, U.S. Government Printing Office. 1961.

Please request permission from the services to use any of their materials found in the appendices.

APPENDIX F

Questionnaire Sent to Existing
Community Services to Determine
Type of Services Provided

SUICIDE PREVENTION AND CRISIS HELP SERVICE
OF STARK COUNTY, OHIO

Name of Fire Department _____

Location _____

Geographic Area Served _____

Emergency & First Aid Equipment _____

_____

Do you have an ambulance? _____

Types of emergencies you can handle _____

_____

Person and number to contact _____

_____

How should contact be made? - Direct? - Thru Police? -

Thru Sheriff's Office? - Others? _____

_____

Comments and Suggestions:

Name and address of Chief: _____

_____

_____

Date _____ Filled out by _____

SUICIDE PREVENTION AND CRISIS HELP SERVICE
OF STARK COUNTY, OHIO

Agency Name _____ Phone _____

Address _____

Geographic Area Served _____

Check types of   ( ) Male   ( ) Female   ( ) Families
people served: ( ) Youth   ( ) MiddleAge   ( ) Aged

Method of acceptance _____
Check types of   Comments on types of service:
Cases accepted:

( )   Social Problems--

( )   Spiritual Problems--

( )   Mental Problems--

( )   Emotional--

( )   Physical--

( )   Economic--

( )   Employment--

( )   Housing--

( )   Finances--

( )   Truancy--

( )   Delinquency--

( )   Pregnant girls--

( )   Unwed mothers--

( )   Planned parenthood--

( )   Family conflict--

( )   Marriage conflict--

( )   Alcoholism--

( )   Drugs--

( )   Sex Problems--

( )   Legal Problems--

Suicide Prevention of Dallas, Inc.
REFERRAL INFORMATION
Agency

Name _____

Address _____

Day Telephone Number _____ Night Telephone _____

Office Hours: From _____ To _____ Days: M Tu W Th F S Su

From _____ To _____ Days: M Tu W Th F S Su

(Please note if hours vary on different days.
Circle days service is open)

Do you accept emergency calls 24 hours a day? Yes _____ No _____

Note any comments _____

_____

_____

Fee Scale: Individual From $ _____ to $ _____ (If Categories to
Group $ _____ to $ _____ left do not fit,
Other: note below in
appropriate manner).
_____ $ _____ to $ _____
_____

Sliding Fee
Scale Yes _____ No _____
Free Yes _____ No _____

Services Available

(Please make note if these services are available only at certain times during the week
and names of any specific contact persons. Also note if fees vary on different services.)

Psychiatric Services: Contact Person_____

Position _____

Psychotherapy _____ Other services not listed to left:
Counseling _____
In-Patient
Hospital _____
Day Hospital _____

Referral Form 1 6/71

123

Dallas, Texas (Cont.)   (2)
Referral Information
Agency -- Psychiatric Services, cont.
Ages and Types serviced:

	Individually	Group
Children	_____	_____
Teenagers	_____	_____
Adults	_____	_____
Family	_____	_____
Marriage	_____	_____
Other:		
_____	_____	_____

Persons or types of problems they have special groups or services for:

Persons or types of problems they will not see:

Length of Waiting:

_____ Emergency calls 24 hours
_____ Walk-in service during office hours
_____ One to three days
_____ Three days to two weeks
_____ Other_____

Is there an appointment necessary? Yes _____ No _____

Physical Needs Served: (Use back if necessary)

_____ Financial Aid   Contact Person _____
Explain: Postition _____

_____ Medical   Contact Person _____
Explain: Position_____

_____ Vocational Rehab   Contact Person _____
Explain: Position _____

_____ Physical Rehab   Contact Person _____
Explain: Position _____

Physical Needs Served, cont.

_____ Homemaker Services   Contact Person: _____
Explain: Position _____

_____ Child Care   Contact Person: _____
Explain: Position _____

_____ Other: _____   Contact Person: _____
Explain: Position _____

Social Needs Served: Contact Person _____
                                    Position _____

_____ Interest Groups   Note type of topics:

_____ Recreation   Note types of sports and games:

_____ Other: Explain:

Are these activities supervised?   Yes_____   No _____

Who supervises them? Note qualifications for supervisors if any.

Persons on Staff:

		Number	
Psychiatrists	_____		_____
Residents	_____		_____
Psychologists	_____		_____
Internships	_____		_____
Social Workers	_____		_____
Internships	_____		_____
Ministers	_____		_____
In-training	_____		_____
Doctors	_____		_____
Residents	_____		_____
Interns	_____		_____
Nurses	_____		_____
In-training	_____		_____

Volunteers　　_____　　　　　_____

　　Note in what capacity volunteers are used. If they are
　　involved in direct client work, note their training:

Other:　　_____　　　　　_____
　　Describe:

Can you furnish transportation for persons needing your services but have no means of
transportation? Yes _____ No _____

Is there a bus line which runs near your office? Yes _____ No _____ Do you know
the name of the line?

Do you have child care available for mothers while receiving your services? Yes _____
No _____

　　Is there a cost? Yes _____ No _____ If Yes, list:

　　Is child care available at all hours that your service
　　is open? Yes _____ No _____ If no, list hours and days available:

APPENDIX G

Authority Structures of
Suicide Prevention Services

Dallas, Texas

SUICIDE PREVENTION OF DALLAS, INC.
Organizational Chart

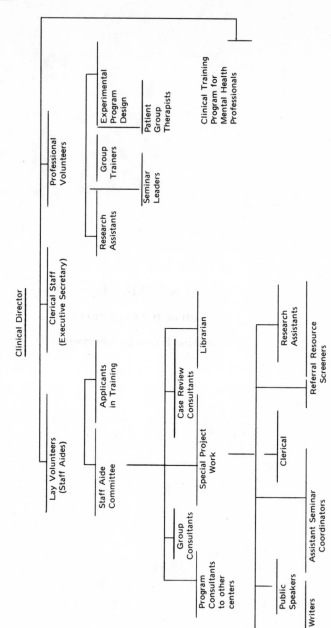

128

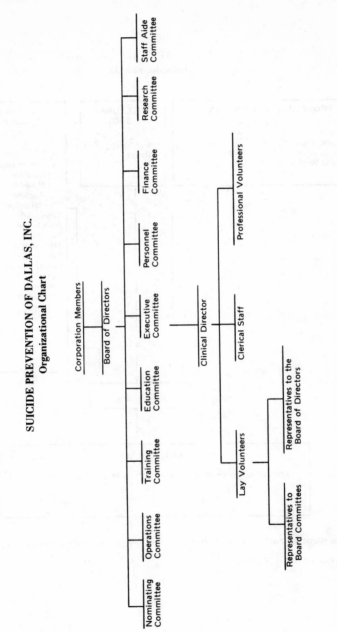

SUICIDE PREVENTION OF DALLAS, INC.
Organizational Chart

WE CARE
Orlando, Florida

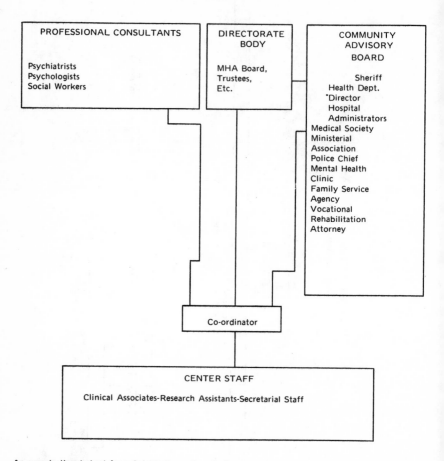

An organizational chart for a Suicide Prevention Center according to the design utilized in Orlando and Brevard Counties, Florida.

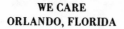

WE CARE
ORLANDO, FLORIDA

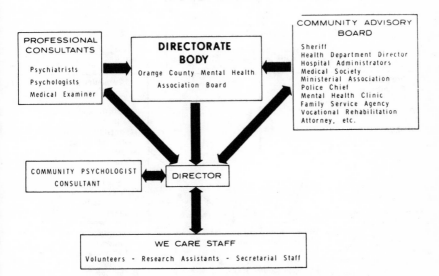

FIG. 1. The Organizational Structure of WE CARE, Showing the Relationship of the Advisory Board to the Other Elements of the Total Program.

SUICIDE PREVENTION AND CRISIS HELP SERVICE
CANTON, OHIO

TABLE OF ORGANIZATION

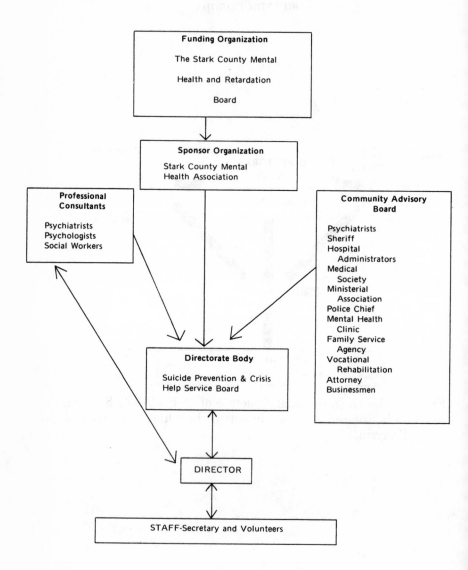

APPENDIX H

Examples of Referral Forms

MARION COUNTY ASSOCIATION FOR MENTAL HEALTH
1433 North Meridian   Indianapolis, Indiana 46202
Phone: 636-2491

SUICIDE PREVENTION SERVICE
REFERRAL FORM

_____ 197 ____

TO: _____

_____

_____

Dear Sir:

NAME: _____ AGE _____

ADDRESS _____ PHONE _____

CITY _____

was referred to you by the Suicide Prevention Service of the Marion County Association for Mental Health on _____ 197 ____

Risk of Suicide, as evaluated by the Clinical Associate, was:

_____ High Medium _____ Low _____ None _____ Undetermined

We received our call from _____

REMARKS: _____

We would appreciate it very much if you would complete the information on the reverse side of this letter and return this copy to us. The blue duplicate referral form attached is for your files.

The information requested is vital for evaluating our performance in assisting potential suicides. Thank you.

Sincerely yours,

Clinical Associate
Suicide Prevention Service

SUICIDE PREVENTION SERVICE REFERRAL VERIFICATION

DATE _____ 197 _____

Dear Sir:

NAME _____ AGE _____

ADDRESS _____

CITY _____

who was referred by the Suicide Prevention Service of the Marion County Association
for Mental Health:

(A) _____ has not contacted us.

(B) _____ has contacted us indirectly through _____

_____

(specify- wife, sister, etc.)

(C) _____ has contacted us _____ in person _____ by telephone.

    1. _____ was given an appointment but did not keep it.

    2. _____ has been seen and does not need additional appointments.

    3. _____ has been seen and will be given additional appointments.

    4. _____ has been referred to _____

Referral to us was:

(D) _____ appropriate.

(E) _____ inappropriate.

(F) _____ Remarks: _____

_____

NAME _____

TITLE _____

AGENCY _____

135

APPENDIX I

Publicity: Brochures, Cards, Stickers

Permission for use granted by:

Suicide Prevention Center, Detroit, Michigan

Suicide Prevention & Crisis Help Service, Stark County, Ohio

Suicide Prevention-Crisis Intervention, Amarillo, Texas

We Care, Orlando, Florida

Crisis Hotline of Muskingum County, Zanesville, Ohio

Suicide & Crisis Intervention Service, Gainesville, Florida

Suicide Prevention Center, Jacksonville, Florida

Teenage Hotline, Pittsburgh, Pennsylvania

Crisis Service, Prince George Hospital, Cheverly, Maryland

Crisis Line of Palm Beach County, Florida

SUICIDE PREVENTION CRISIS INTERVENTION

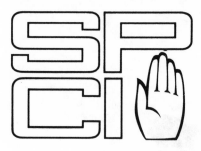

"OUR GOAL IS TO
SHORTEN THE DISTANCE
ONE HAS TO TRAVEL
TO THE NEAREST HEART"

MAY WE HELP YOU?
...CALL 376-4251...
24 HOURS A DAY

A service of the
AMARILLO COMMUNITY HEALTH CENTER

CRISIS HOTLINE
ZANESVILLE, OHIO

HELP WHEN
YOU NEED IT!

CRISIS HOTLINE

**THE SHORTEST DISTANCE
TO A HELPING HAND
DURING EMOTIONAL CRISIS**

CALL

452-8403
-24 HOURS A DAY-

**A SERVICE OF THE
MUSKINGUM COMPREHENSIVE
MENTAL HEALTH CENTER**

SUICIDE AND CRISIS INTERVENTION SERVICE
GAINESVILLE, FLORIDA

Suicide & Crisis

Crisis Phone 376–4444

Hotline Phone 376–4447   Business 372–3659

II. STATISTICAL HISTORY OF SUICIDE:

- Once each minute, some American consciously tries to kill himself.

- Sixty to seventy suicide attempts result in death daily

- Each year over 26,000 people commit suicide

- Suicide is the third leading killer of college students

- Suicide is among the top ten causes of adult deaths in the U.S.

- Men kill themselves three times more frequently than women

- Women attempt to take their own lives three times more often than men

- 90% of all suicidal victims give some warning as to their intentions

- Fully 75% of all those who commit suicide have seen a physician within at least four months of the day on which they take their lives

III. WHAT CONSTITUTES A CRISIS?

A crisis is present when the pressures of life become so intense and intolerable, that the person views suicide as a solution.

Suicide can be grouped basically into four main types. First, when one is angry, frustrated, or disappointed, he might impulsively commit suicide. The person, in the heat of the moment, rashly tries to kill himself. This situation is the most severe because of the rapidity with which it happens.

143

SUICIDE PREVENTION CENTER
JACKSONVILLE, FLORIDA

SUICIDE PREVENTION CENTER

HELP IN TIME OF EMOTIONAL CRISIS

24 Hours a Day

CRISIS PHONE
384—6488

Please, answer the phone!

Suicide Prevention Center
Room 602   Herman Kiefer Hospital
1151 Taylor   Detroit, Michigan   48202

Crisis Intervention

Information   *Referral*

Help By Phone

For Emotional Problems

A 24 Hour Telephone Service
With Crisis Intervention Workers
Providing Information and Referral
To Community Resources of Prince George's County

Crisis Service

322 - 2606

A Cooperative Mental Health Program of Prince George's County Department of Health and the Prince George's General Hospital.

CRISIS HOTLINE
ZANESVILLE, OHIO

DO YOU NEED TO TALK

TO SOMEONE ABOUT A PROBLEM?

CALL THE CRISIS HOT LINE

THE SHORTEST DISTANCE TO A HELPING

HAND DURING EMOTIONAL CRISIS

CALL 452-8403

. CALL COLLECT IF OUTSIDE OF ZANESVILLE .

HELP WHEN YOU NEED IT!

CALLS ANSWERED 24 HOURS A DAY
7 DAYS PER WEEK

APPENDIX J

Volunteer Telephone Worker
Application Forms

SUICIDE PREVENTION OF DALLAS, INC.

CONFIDENTIAL INFORMATION
Volunteer Application Form

Date _____

Name _____ Sex _____ Age _____

Address _____ City _____ Zip _____

Home Phone _____ Business Phone _____

Employed? _____ Where? _____

Length of Time _____ In what capacity? _____

Spouse Employed? _____ Where? _____

Marital Status _____ Children: number _____ Ages _____

If married, how does your spouse feel about you doing volunteer work at Suicide Prevention?

_____

_____

Religious affiliation _____

Education _____

How did you hear about this program? _____

_____

_____

Past volunteer activities _____

_____

_____

Present volunteer activities _____

_____

_____

1.   What days and what hours will you be available to work at the Center? (the minimum requirement is 4 hours per week in direct service on the phone, plus 2 hours biweekly in training as long as you are on the phone.)

2.   Would you prefer a daytime or nighttime training group?

3.   Describe a time when you sought or received help from someone. Note your feelings about this.

4.   What do you feel are the strengths and weaknesses that you will bring to this program?

5. If you have ever been a participant in group or individual therapy or counseling, how do you feel this experience will help you to help others?

6. Note when you began and terminated therapy, giving the reasons for both events.

7. Write a brief statement on why you have chosen to work in the Suicide Prevention Center at this particular time in your life. (Use back of sheet if needed.)

8. Please list three personal references:

Name _____

Address _____ Zip _____

Phone _____ Relationship _____

Name _____

Address _____ Zip _____

Phone _____Relationship _____

Name _____

Address _____ Zip _____

Phone _____ Relationship _____

9. Please number in order of priority the areas where you would like to be involved in our agency.

_____ Telephone crisis-intervention counseling.
_____ Procedural assignments (telephoning, mailing, meeting arrangements, etc.)
_____ Typing
_____ Speakers Bureau
_____ Reviewing and writing summaries on research on suicide.
_____ Assisting in tabulating research data

10. Do you have any questions or concerns about this application form?

SUICIDE PREVENTION OF DALLAS, TEXAS

Dear Volunteer Applicant,

Your request to apply as a volunteer was received with enthusiasm and good cheer in our office. Your response to our need for volunteers is a boost to our faith that lay persons are willing to be a very important and valuable aid to the mental health field.

In checking through the volunteer responses, we have noted that you have not yet returned your application form. We are concerned and interested in why this has happened. If you are still interested in applying, we would like to help you in any way that we can. If you are no longer interested or have some concerns about our application process or program, we would like you to help us improve our procedure.

Please look over the enclosed check list and check what is appropriate for you. Please feel free to write on the back if necessary, write in your own category, whatever. Your candid and honest response will help us better serve your needs and the needs of future applicants.

May we say that your interest alone in such vital work as suicide prevention is encouraging to us because it lets us know that individuals in our community do care about the quality of life of other people.

Sincerely,

(Mrs.) Virginia Turner
Chairman, Personnel Committee
Board of Directors

aml

(Cont.)

SUICIDE PREVENTION OF DALLAS, INC.
P.O. Box 19651   Dallas 75219

Please read through the whole list checking the ones which are most appropriate for you. Feel free to write on the back if necessary, write in your own category, etc. Your honest response will be greatly appreciated.

_____ Never received the application.

_____ Received the application but can't find it.

_____ Sent in my application but have not heard from you yet.

_____ Made so many mistakes on the first copy that I need another.

_____ Your volunteer program requires more time than I have available for volunteer work.

_____ I do not have the time at present but will reapply at a future time.

_____ I do not plan to apply because of the other reasons checked or because:

_____ Indefinite family situation has involved my time.

_____ Indefinite work situation has involved my time.

_____ My family objects because:

_____ I have several questions about your program I would like answered before filling the application form. (Note: Please feel free to call our administrative office 521-9111 and talk with our staff or write your questions on the back of this form.)

_____ I hesitate because of the application form.
(Please help us by commenting on your concern.)

If you would like to continue application:
_____ I'll be sending the application shortly.

_____ Please send me another application form.

Name_____ Address _____

If you are indefinitely tied up at present and are still interested, please feel free to call us back whenever your time frees up again so that we can mail you another application.

Signature (Optional)

157

SUICIDE PREVENTION CENTER OF JACKSONVILLE

2627 Riverside Avenue   P.O. Box 6393

Jacksonville, Florida

S.P.C. WORKER PERSONAL DATA

Date _____

Name _____ Age _____ Female _____ Male _____

Address _____ Zip _____ Home Phone _____

Business Phone _____ Place of Birth _____

How long have you lived in this county? _____

Marital Status: Single _____ Married _____ Divorced _____ Separated _____

Widowed _____

Have you ever been divorced? _____ or your spouse divorced? _____

How many children do you have? _____ Boys _____ Girls _____ Ages _____

Any other dependents living in your home with you _____

Please give relationship and age _____

How many brothers and sisters do you have _____

EDUCATION AND OCCUPATION:

Circle the highest grade completed: 7 8 9 10 11 12

College: 1 2 3 4 5 6

If you finished college, what was your major _____

If you have professional training, in what field _____

List colleges or universities attended and degrees _____

_____

Have you been employed in the area of your training? Yes _____ No _____

If yes, where _____

If no, how long since you were last employed? _____

Have you held other types of positions now or in the past? Yes _____ No _____

If yes, please describe _____

Occupation of spouse _____ Religious Affiliation _____

Have you ever been in psychotherapy or psychoanalysis _____

When _____ How long _____ Have you ever made a suicide attempt

_____ If yes, when _____

Has anyone in your family or close friend been suicidal _____

If you could be any celebrity you wish, whom would you choose to be and why? _____

_____

_____

What would you do if you suddenly became so economically independent you could
change everything in your life that was possible? _____

_____

_____

_____

Please explain how you happened to become interested in the suicide prevention
program _____

_____

Community interest (List clubs, group work, etc.) _____

_____

_____

_____

DISCHARGE OF A STAFF AIDE

A person being considered for temporary leave or termination from the agency will be contacted by the director and be given a clear explanation of the director's concern. the director and the Staff Aide agree on some different approach, the Staff Aide would be given a period of time to work out whatever situation is stirring the question of discharge before a decision about discharge is finalized.

Rather than a set pattern, the director prefers to handle each situation quite individually, taking into account the needs and the concerns of the Staff Aide involved.

The agency director will take full responsibility for the decision of terminating a Staff Aide. The agency's director will cite his concern and clarify where he has received feedback regarding the Staff Aide. He will use the following feedback resources listed in order of priority:

1. The Staff Aide himself.
2. The group trainer.
3. The training group.
4. Their particular Staff Aide Consultant.
5. Case Review Committee.
6. Clients.

The director and the Staff Aide will mutually arrange any termination procedure.

Any termination from the agency will be followed by some formal expression of thanks from the Board of Directors.

It has been generally observed that Staff Aides terminate from our program when their energy level decreases significantly because of physical illness or change in environment.

The Staff Aides in our agency have been selected because of their internal stability and as a consequence this is seldom a factor in the termination of someone from the agency. If this is a factor, it will be clearly spelled out to the Staff Aide by the director.

The Staff Aides in our agency have been selected because of their internal stability and as a consequence this is seldom a factor in the termination of someone from the agency. If this is a factor, it will be clearly spelled out to the Staff Aide by the director.

Dallas, Texas, (Cont. p. 2.)

Interviews with the director or questions regarding his handling of cases by the review board are not indications of potential discharge from the agency. These are a natural part of our communications system that assures quality services to the client and maximizes goal setting in the training groups.

If at any time you have concern or question about the director's or the review committee's view of your work as a Staff Aide, please contact the director for clarification rather than allow this uncertainty to decrease your effectiveness in any way.

Dallas, Texas

SUICIDE PREVENTION SERVICE
INDIANAPOLIS, INDIANA

T O: Potential Applicants for
Clinical Associate Training

FROM: Rev. Kenneth E. Reed, Ph.D., Chairman
Suicide Prevention Service Committee

We are delighted you have contacted the Suicide Prevention Service of the Marion County Association for Mental Health requesting information and/or applications to become a volunteer "Clinical Associate", the title given to those who man the 24-Hour Telephone Answering Service.

It is our hope that this letter, the enclosed application form, and Statement of Policies for Clinical Associates, will answer many of the questions you might have.

The 24-Hour Telephone Answering Service operates in the following manner: A call for help is received initially by a telephone receptionist answering our well publicized number -- 632-7575. She takes the name (if able) and phone number of the caller, tells the caller that she will have a "Clinical Associate" ready to talk with him momentarily, has the caller wait while she calls the Clinical Associate on duty in his or her home or office to inform the Associate of the waiting call. The Associate confirms that he will return the call immediately; the receptionist then tells the caller to hang up in order to receive the Clinical Associate's return call.

From this description of how the Telephone Service works you can understand that the key persons in our Service are the volunteer Clinical Associates--who could be such a person as yourself. A Clinical Associate can be a professional, a student, or a lay person.

It is the job of the volunteer to present himself or herself as a sympathetic, concerned and interested person wanting to help the caller with his problem. Together, the volunteer and the caller discuss the problems causing distress, determine what can be done to relieve the tension and anguish, aid with the problems that might lead to any impulsive act, and assist the caller in securing the kinds of help needed to relieve the distress.

After reading the material, you may feel that volunteering for this kind of community service would not be "your cup of tea". However, we are equally sure there are those persons who, with training and constant back-up professional consultation available to you, could perform such an invaluable service.

Other criteria you will want to consider are:

1. Clinical Associates must have a private telephone at the location where they will perform their volunteer services.

2. The Clinical Associate's telephone must be one that can call any number within the Indianapolis exchange* toll free.

3. Clinical Associates serve a six-hour duty shift once a week and agree to stay with the Service at least 1 year (students 6 to 9 months).

4. Each applicant will have a personal interview prior to beginning a training program.

5. All persons must successfully complete the 20 to 25 hour initial training before being scheduled for phone duty.

6. Clinical Associates are required to attend monthly discussion meetings following initial training.

If, after reading this letter and the enclosed materials, you would like to submit your application for consideration to participate in the next series of training meetings, please return the application to the Mental Health Association.

Shortly before the next series of training meetings you will be contacted by Mrs. Patricia Jones, Co-ordinator of the Suicide Prevention Service, at which time an appointment for your personal interview will be scheduled.

If you have further questions, please contact Mrs. Jones at 636-2491 from 9:00 a.m. to 5:00 p.m., Monday through Friday.

We appreciate your consideration of volunteering for this most important service.

*Includes all telephones in grey area shown on page 2 of telephone director.

Indianapolis, Indiana
Marion County Association for Mental Health
Suicide Prevention Service

STATEMENT OF POLICIES FOR CLINICAL ASSOCIATES

1. Service, without charge, is offered to anyone who calls the Suicide Prevention Service of the Marion County Association for Mental Health, irrespective of the presenting problems or other qualifications.

2. Clinical Associates must keep the identity of and information from all callers in the strictest of confidence.

3. No Clinical Associate can be scheduled for telephone duty without fully completing the initial training sessions offered by the Suicide Prevention Service.

4. The Clinical Associate is required to attend the monthly discussion meetings. Repeated absences, without excuse may be considered sufficient cause for withdrawal from telephone duty.

5. No Clinical Associate may accept remuneration for any activity pertaining to the Suicide Prevention Service.

6. The Clinical Associate must exhibit responsible performance in relation to his duty hours. If the Clinical Associate cannot be available for a scheduled duty shift, it is the responsibility of the Clinical Associate to notify the co-ordinator well in advance.

7. If the Clinical Associate's duty shift is interrupted by an **emergency** the Clinical Associate **must** notify the co-ordinator of the Service.

8. If the caller is known to the Clinical Associate personally, the Clinical Associate should indicate this immediately, assuming recognition has not already taken place. Referral of the call to another trained Clinical Associate may be made in the manner prescribed by the Suicide Prevention Service.

9. The Clinical Associate will not give his home or office phone number to the caller.

10. The Suicide Prevention Service would prefer a Clinical Associate use his own name when on telephone duty. However, the use of your name, as a Clinical Associate, is optional and if a pseudonym is to be chosen by the Clinical Associate, such arrangements must be worked out with the co-ordinator.

11. The Clinical Associate will not personally meet any caller anywhere. If the caller states he cannot talk over the phone, he can be seen through the Referral Service of the Marion County Association for Mental Health between the hours of 9 a.m. and 5 p.m., Monday through Friday, or in the emergency room of a hospital.

12. Clinical Associates must submit all reports and records in the time and manner prescribed by the Suicide Prevention Service.

6/15/70

MARION COUNTY ASSOCIATION FOR MENTAL HEALTH
SUICIDE PREVENTION SERVICE
1433 North Meridian Street
Indianapolis, Indiana 46202
Phone 636-2491

APPLICATION FOR TRAINING AS A VOLUNTEER
CLINICAL ASSOCIATE

NOTE: The following questionnaire is designed to help us determine your suitability for working as a volunteer Clinical Associate for the Suicide Prevention Service of the Marion County Association for Mental Health. All applications will be considered confidential.

_____

Date _____ 19 _____

1.   NAME: _____
            (last)   (First)   (Middle)

2.   ADDRESS:_____
            (Street)   (City)   (State)   (Zip)

3.   TELEPHONES: _____ _____ Home
            (Home)   (Business)   _____ Business
                                             (Hours to call)

4.   BIRTH DATE: _____

5.   SINGLE _____ MARRIED _____ SEPARATED _____ DIVORCED _____
            (Years)   (Years)   (Years)   (Yrs.)
     WIDOWED _____
            (Years)

6.   NUMBER OF CHILDREN: _____ AGES: ___ ___ ___ ___ ___ ___ ___

7.   AMOUNT OF FORMAL EDUCATION: (Circle last completed year) 6, 7, 8, 9, 10, 11, 12, 13, 14, 15, 16, 17, 18

8.   ANY SPECIALIZED COURSES/TRAINING: _____

9.   EMPLOYMENT: (Circle) PRESENTLY EMPLOYED   UNEMPLOYED
     RETIRED   SELF-EMPLOYED

10. EMPLOYER: _____

     POSITION: _____

11. WORK EXPERIENCES: YEAR WORK
         FIRM   BEGAN   HOW LONG   POSITION

     _____ _____ _____ _____
     _____ _____ _____ _____
     _____ _____ _____ _____

165

12. HOW LONG HAVE YOU BEEN IN INDIANAPOLIS?

13. LIST ORGANIZATIONS FOR WHICH YOU HAVE WORKED IN A VOLUNTEER CAPACITY:

ORGANIZATION	YEAR WORK BEGAN	HOW LONG	DUTIES
_____	_____	_____	_____
_____	_____	_____	_____
_____	_____	_____	_____

14. LIST ANY SPECIAL SKILLS YOU HAVE WHICH YOU ARE WILLING TO USE IN VOLUNTEER WORK FOR US. (Interviewing, recording information, knowledge of community organizations, etc.) _____

15. HOW DID YOU LEARN ABOUT OUR ORGANIZATION? _____
_____

16. DOES YOUR HUSBAND/WIFE/FAMILY APPROVE OF YOUR DOING THIS WORK?   (Circle)   YES   NO

17. ARE YOU IN GOOD HEALTH?   (Circle)   YES   NO

18. DO YOU HAVE ANY PHYSICAL PROBLEMS WHICH MIGHT INTERFERE WITH YOUR WORK AS A CLINICAL ASSOCIATE? _____
_____

19. NO   YES
    ( ) ( )   Have you ever attempted suicide?
    ( ) ( )   Have you ever seriously considered suicide?
    ( ) ( )   Has anyone in your family committed suicide?
    ( ) ( )   Has anyone in your family attempted suicide in the last year?
    ( ) ( )   Have you ever been hospitalized for psychiatric reasons?
    ( ) ( )   Have you ever consulted a psychiatrist or other mental health professional about your own or your family's problems?

    If the answer to any question in 19 is yes, this does not eliminate you from consideration. However, we would like to discuss the situation with you in order to determine:

    1.   that working with us will not aggravate the problem, if any.
    2.   that the problem, if any, will not interfere with helping others.

    _____
    (Signature)

20. REFERENCES: (Please give names of people, such as ministers, teachers, supervisors, physicians, who know you personally, since they will be contacted by the Suicide Prevention Service.)

NAMES	ADDRESS	PHONES
_____	_____	_____
_____	_____	_____
_____	_____	_____

166

Indianapolis, Indiana

page 3

21. Although the Suicide Prevention Service provides a 24-hour, 7 days a week (holidays included) telephone service, most Clinical Associates volunteer for a regular weekly shift of six hours in their homes. After training is completed, Clinical Associates schedule, with the Co-ordinator, a mutually satisfactory time for a regular shift.

22. **Circle Shift Preferred:**

    12:01 a.m. to 6:00 a.m.   Mon. Tues. Wed. Thurs. Fri. Sat. Sun.

    6:00 a.m. to 12:00 noon   Mon. Tues. Wed. Thurs. Fri. Sat. Sun.

    12:00 noon to 6:00 p.m.   Mon. Tues. Wed. Thurs. Fri. Sat. Sun.

    6:00 p.m. to 12:00 midnight Mon. Tues. Wed. Thurs. Fri. Sat. Sun.

                                                          YES   MAYBE   NO

23. I can attend evening staff meetings at least once monthly. ____ ____ ____

24. I would always be available for my shift unless an ____ ____ ____
    emergency exists, in which case I would call in time to be
    replaced.

25. I am willing to come in for additional training sessions. ____ ____ ____

26. I intend to work for the Service at least one year ____ ____ ____
    (students 6 to 9 months) in the pattern that is most
    effective for me and for the Agency.

27. I have read and understand that I will not see or visit any person using the Suicide Prevention Service, nor to communicate with them in any way, except as authorized by the Marion County Association for Mental Health; that the records of an personal communications received by the Suicide Prevention Service staff and contained in the records or received by personal communication by staff or volunteers must not be divulged now or ever to any persons who have not themselves signed this statement of understanding.

SIGNED _____

4-13-70

SUICIDE PREVENTION & CRISIS HELP SERVICE
OF STARK COUNTY
CANTON, OHIO
Application Form For Volunteers

TO: Volunteers, Suicide-Prevention Service

The following is some basic information for volunteers to the Suicide Prevention and Crisis Help Service. Your interest in helping with this service is deeply appreciated.

1. The purpose of the service is to provide immediate, stop-gap help to persons facing crisis situations and to arrange referrals to the appropriate agencies or professional to assure continuing help toward a solution of their problems.

2. Anyone may volunteer - there are no restrictions as to age, occupation, education, etc.

3. All volunteers will have to take a screening-in test and an interview to determine their suitability for this kind of activity.

4. All volunteers will be required to attend training and orientation sessions before assuming duties. These may consist of six sessions of two hours each. Volunteers will be notified about exact dates.

5. Volunteers will be asked to serve one shift per week of at least four hours. Shifts can be arranged according to your schedule.

6. During normal working hours, the volunteer will be on duty in the office. On week-ends and at night, calls will be referred to the volunteer at any number the volunteer desires by an answering service or in the SPCH office.

7. Volunteers must furnish their own transportation when working at the clinic.

8. Because of the busy schedules of the professionals who are assisting in our recruitment and selection, it sometimes takes quite a while to get the reports and notify the volunteer whether he or she has been accepted or not. Do not be alarmed if you do not hear from us right away. You will be notified by mail as soon as possible concerning your application.

If you have questions please do not hesitate to contact us.

SUICIDE PREVENTION SERVICE
VOLUNTEER PERSONAL DATA SHEET

Name _____ Age _____ Female ( ) Male ( )

Address _____ City _____ Zip _____

Home Phone _____ Business Phone _____

Marital Status: Single ( ) Married ( ) Divorced ( ) Separated ( ) Widowed ( )

How many children do you have? _____ Boys _____ Girls _____ Ages _____

Any other dependents living in your home with you? _____ Please

Give their relationship and age _____

Circle the highest grade completed: 7 8 9 10 11 12

College 1 2 3 4 5 6 7

If you finished college, what was your major? _____

If you have professional training, in what field _____

Occupation _____

Occupation of spouse _____

Religious Affiliation _____

Do you speak any foreign language _____ Which _____

Community interests (List clubs, group work, etc.).

Briefly state why you are interested in this work

Date _____ Signed _____

Return this form to:
Suicide Prevention &
Crisis Help Service
c/o Stark County Mental
Health Association
106 High Avenue, N.W.
Canton, Ohio 44703

SUICIDE PREVENTION AND
CRISIS HELP SERVICE OF
STARK COUNTY, OHIO

BIOGRAPHICAL DATA OF VOLUNTEERS

(Confidential Information)

I. Identifying Information

    A. Name _____   E. Date _____

    B. Address _____   F. Sex _____

    C. Home Phone _____   G. Age _____

    D. Business Phone _____

II. Family Status

    A. Marital Status: (circle) single, Married, separated, divorced, widowed

    B. Number of years married: _____

    C. Number and ages of children:

	Child	Age
1.		
2.		
3.		
4.		
5.		
6.		

III. Occupational Status

    A. Employed, unemployed, student, housewife (circle)

    B. Name and address of employer:

        Name _____ Address _____

    C. Length of period of present employment _____

(Cont. p. 2)

D. History of previous employment:

	Place	From When to When
1.	_____	_____
2.	_____	_____
3.	_____	_____
4.	_____	_____
5.	_____	_____

E. Skill, Profession or area of training _____

F. Ever dismissed from a position, involuntarily? _____

IV. Educational Status

A. Are you a high school graduate? _____

B. Year of graduation from high school _____

C. Colleges or Special Training Programs attended:

1. _____
2. _____
3. _____

D. Subjects in high school and college, in which you were most successful?

1. _____
2. _____
3. _____

V. Medical and Health Status

A. Describe your present health status _____
_____

B. What chronic illnesses or disabilities do you have? _____
_____

C. Are you currently under physician's care? _____

(Cont. p. 3)

D. Do you experience any medical condition which may affect or be affected by your participation as a volunteer in this program? _____

If "yes," please explain _____

_____

_____

VI. Adjustment History

A. How would your friends describe you? _____

_____

_____

B. In the past have you required medical or counseling therapy for:

1. acute stress? _____   6. depression? _____

2. worry and anxiety? _____   7. neurosis? _____

3. nervousness? _____   8. sleepnessness? _____

4. migraine headache? _____   9. Any form of emotional

5. loss of appetite? _____   disturbance? _____

C. How would you describe your most common moods and feeling tones?

_____

_____

D. What circumstances are most likely to upset you? _____

_____

_____

VII. General Questions

A. How did you become aware of the program for which you are offering your service? _____

_____

B. Briefly describe the nature and development of your interest in being a volunteer in the program. _____

_____

172

(Cont. p. 4)

C. What days - and hours of the day could you be available for services?

Monday _____   Friday _____

Tuesday _____   Saturday _____

Wednesday _____   Sunday _____

Thursday _____

D. In what ways would you regard suicide as being of religious significance?

_____

_____

E. If today a neighbor called you, threatening to commit suicide, what approaches would you use?

_____

_____

_____

F. If, while you were serving as a telephone volunteer, a caller suggested a sexual proposition, how may the situation be handled? _____

_____

G. Do you feel quite confident in being able to convince each person, who threatens suicide, to preserve his own life? Explain: _____

_____

_____

_____

H. How will your husband (or wife) react to your volunteer efforts? _____

_____

_____

_____

I. Will your volunteer efforts place a strain upon other responsibilities you may have at home or at work? _____

VIII. What interests and hobbies do you find attractive to you? _____

_____

SUICIDE PREVENTION AND CRISIS HELP SERVICE
CANTON, OHIO
VOLUNTEER RECORD

NAME:

_____

	DATE	COMMENT
CONTACT		
APPLICATION		
TEST		
BIOGRAPHY		
INTERVIEW		
TRAINING		
SERVICE		

C.R.I. HOT LINE
APPLICATION

Return application to:
C.R.I.-Hot Line
232 East Front Street
Plainfield, New Jersey
(You will hear from us
promptly.)

(Please Print)

Name: _____ Age: _____

Mailing Address: _____ City _____ State _____

Home Phone: _____ Alternate Phone _____

Occupation: _____
        (If currently a student, specify year and/or major area of study, and name
        of school.)

Marital Status: _____

(Please use back of form for extended answers.)

1. Education and information to assist in evaluating your skills, talents, learnings in relationship to Hot Line needs -- special study, interests, therapy anything at all.

2. Please write something you find amusing or a joke.

3. What do you want from Hot Line involvement?

4. Anything you think might be particularly frightening for you in the program or training?

175

(cont. p. 2) C.R.I. Hotline

Do you agree to work regularly on the C.R.I. -Hot Line Program. ____Yes ____No

Shift Available

	Thurs.	Friday	Saturday	Sunday
2pm- 5pm	_____	_____	_____	_____
5pm- 8pm	_____	_____	_____	_____
8pm-11pm	_____	_____	_____	_____
11pm- 2am	_____	_____	_____	_____

(Please put your first and second choices.)

_____   _____
Date   Signature

                                             Thank you!

Plainfield, New Jersey

APPENDIX K

Recognition Award Certificates

Certificate of Appreciation

*The Muskingum Comprehensive Mental Health Center
hereby expresses appreciation for the work and efforts of*

_____

in the unselfish fulfillment of the responsibility of

_____

for the Crisis Hotline Service

*"Further progress in the difficult field of mental illness
and mental health will come only when millions of
Americans know enough, care enough, and are willing to
work together hard enough to make it ours."
William Menninger, M. D.
(1899 — 1966)*

Presented this _____ *day of* _____

_____

*Director, Muskingum Comprehensive
Mental Health Center*

Crisis Hotline - Zanesville, Ohio

APPENDIX L

Telephone Worker Evaluation
Forms of Training Program

C.R.I. - HOT LINE
PLAINFIELD, N.J.

EVALUATION FORM

NAME: ————————————————————————————

(1)   What are the satisfactions you are receiving from your work with Hot Line?

(2)   What are you finding to be your chief problems, complaints or areas of confusion in working for Hot Line?

(3)   What is your evaluation of the present recruiting program? Have you ideas to improve it?

(4)   What is your evaluation of the present training program?
      Please define your needs and proposals for improvement.

(5)   What do you think of our record-keeping system?

(6)   Will you be willing to call/visit several of our referral sources and make a brief report for all of us to use?

(7)   What suggestions have you for our further publicity and explaining our program to the public?

(8)   Do you plan on continuing as a volunteer on Hot Line?

(9)   What should we know/do that we have overlooked?

(10) Do you need/want closer supervision? How would you like this to be handled?

C.R.I. - HOT LINE - EVALUATION FORM - continued
PLAINFIELD, N.J.

(11) In recruiting we now (1) send out explanatory information to potential volunteers (2) If they return their application and seem interested and qualified we interview them on the phone or personally. What else should we be doing?

Potential volunteer's names are going to be accumulated until we have a training group of 10-15 people. Each group will have to participate in the following program:

a)   **Six hours** of orientation including guidebooks, possibly tapes, discussion, role-playing.

b)   Be assigned, briefly, to a shift as an observer with experienced Hot Liner.

c)   Be required to attend monthly training seminars with tapes, speakers, programs of special interest.

d)   Have, if desired, private conferences with Don.

Do you have any suggestions changes in this basic program?

(12) Would you like to become involved in other ways with Hot Line? Can you help with:

_____   Publicity, e.g., distributing flyers, cards or posters.
_____   Recruiting potential volunteers.
_____   Making contacts with community groups for possible speaking engagements for Hot Line.
_____   Serve on our Steering Committee.
_____   Fund-raising campaign.

Please return this form as soon as you can to Don at the "YW". Enclosed is an envelope you can use for this purpose.

Thanks,
(s) Don

SUICIDE PREVENTION CENTER
EVALUATION OF SUICIDE PREVENTION CENTER
TRAINING PROGRAM
JACKSONVILLE, FLORIDA

Please fill out the following questionnaire and return to:

Mrs. Roy Baker
2221 Segovia Street
Jacksonville, Florida 32217

1. How did you find out about Suicide Prevention Center workers? _____

    _____

2. How did you feel at the beginning of the initial training session (5 words or less?)

    _____

    _____

3. Did you feel four sessions were enough initial training? Yes _____ No _____

4. Would you prefer: (Check One)

    a. Four nightly sessions in one week

    b. Two nightly sessions one week, two sessions the following week

    c. Alternative arrangement of more hours, different schedule, etc., explain

5. Do you feel a ten minute break would be beneficial during session? Yes___ No___

6. Rate overall course content: Excellent _____ Good _____ Fair _____ Poor _____

7. Rate course instructors: Excellent _____ Good _____ Fair _____ Poor _____

8. Do you feel additional outside speakers should participate in initial sessions?

    Yes _____ No _____

    _____

9. Rate Handout information: Excellent _____ Good _____ Fair _____ Poor _____

Jacksonville, Florida (Cont.)

10. Check areas of information you feel strongest in:

    _____ Office Policies

    _____ History

    _____ Call Handling Procedures

    _____ General Knowledge of Suicide

    _____ Statistics Related to Suicide and Prevention

    _____ Community Resources

    _____ SPC Guidelines, Ethics

    _____ Others (Specify) _____

11. Are you satisfied with the standard SPC booklet? Yes ____ No ____

12. Would you prefer more detailed descriptions of:

    _____ Jacksonville SPC Programs

    _____ Workers Role

    _____ Local Statistics

    _____ Others (Specify) _____

13. Would you like to visit any of the Community Resource Agencies? Yes __ No __

Specify _____

14. Rate value of role playing to you in training session: Excellent ____ Good ____

Fair ____ Poor ____

15. Would you enjoy?

    _____ More Movies

    _____ More Staged Situations

    _____ Others (Specify) _____

16. For the coming monthly inservice education meetings, suggest topics and speakers that would complement your present knowledge: _____

_____

17. Are you thoroughly familiar with:

    Office procedures Yes _____ No _____

    Home duty procedures Yes _____ No _____

18. What further experience after your final session, if any, do you prefer before handling a Hotline Call? _____

_____

19. How do you feel at the end of this final training session? (5 words or less)

_____

20. Comments, Suggestions _____

_____

_____

_____

_____

_____

_____

APPENDIX M
Training Manual of
Abilene Suicide Prevention Service
Abilene, Texas

SUICIDE
PREVENTION
SERVICE

Abilene, Texas

The Abilene Suicide Prevention Service is a voluntary citizens' organization functioning under the administrative sponsorship of the Abilene Association for Mental Health.

ABILENE SUICIDE PREVENTION SERVICE
OPERATION MANUAL

prepared by

SPS STAFF

October 1970

Abilene Suicide Prevention Service
P.O. Box 2707
Abilene, Texas 79604

Telephone (915) 673-3132

1970 EDITION

SOMEONE CARES . . .
24 HOURS A DAY!

Three years of operation by the Abilene Suicide Prevention
Service have passed during which we have learned a great deal, weath-
ered some crises, and hopefully have done a better job to help people
in need.

There is no magic in all this. The dramatic emergency is
rarely part of the scene. In fact, we can make no claim to having
saved any one from suicide. All we can say is that each year the
crisis calls have increased and because someone was there who really
cared, people found hope and the help to choose life instead of death.
Perhaps that is enough.

SPS Volunteers come from many walks of life and differ greatly
in age, religion, and background. The quality of being a "caring person" is perhaps the one thing they have in common. Trained, mature, and
capable, they are the key to an effective suicide prevention service.

Therefore, it is fitting and proper that this Second Edition be
dedicated to the Volunteers of the Abilene Suicide Prevention Service.

SPS STAFF

The Reverend William W. Eastburn, Chairman
Mrs. Bob Todd, Director of Volunteers
Ben Zickefoose, Director of Training
B.D. Beall, M.D. Medical Consultant
William N. Fryer, Ed.D., Psychological
    Consultant

October 1970
Abilene, Texas

Cartoons - Art by Leo

Abilene, Texas

CONTENTS

Don't Betray Confidence!

ETHICAL STANDARDS OF VOLUNTEER SERVICE

The volunteer believes in the dignity and worth of the individual human being. He is committed to an increasing understanding of himself and others. While pursuing this endeavor, he protects the welfare and confidence of any person who may seek his help. He does not use his volunteer service position or relationships, nor does he knowingly permit his own service to be used by others, for purposes inconsistent with these values.

Principle 1. Responsibility. The volunteer, committed to an increasing understanding of man, places high value on integrity and maintains high standards.

Principle 2. Competence. The maintenance of high standards of competence is a responsibility shared by all volunteers, in the interest of public service and of volunteerism as a whole.

Principle 3. Moral and Legal Standards. The volunteer shows sensible regard for the social codes and moral expectations of the community, recognizing that violations of accepted moral and legal standards on his part may involve others in damaging personal conflicts, and impugn his own name and the reputation of volunteerism.

Principle 4. Misrepresentation. The volunteer avoids misrepresentation of his own qualifications, affiliations, and purposes, and those of the institutions and organizations with which he is associated.

Principle 5. Confidentiality. Safeguarding information about an individual which has been obtained by the volunteer in the course of his service, is a primary obligation of the volunteer.

FABLE: People who talk about suicide don't commit suicide.
 FACT: Of any ten persons who kill themselves, eight have
       given definite warnings of their suicidal intentions.

FABLE: Suicide happens without warning.
 FACT: Studies reveal that the suicidal person gives many clues
       and warnings regarding his suicidal intentions.

FABLE: Suicidal people are fully intent on dying.
 FACT: Most suicidal people are undecided about living or
       dying, and they "gamble with death," leaving it to
       others to save them. Almost no one commits suicide
       without letting others know how he is feeling.

FABLE: Once a person is suicidal, he is suicidal forever.
 FACT: Individuals who wish to kill themselves are "suicidal"
       only for a limited period of time.

FABLE: Improvement following a suicidal crisis means that the
       suicidal risk is over.
 FACT: Most suicides occur within about three months follow-
       ing the beginning of "improvement," when the individ-
       ual has the energy to put his morbid thoughts and feel-
       ings into effect.

FABLE: Suicide strikes much more often among the rich - or,
       conversely, it occurs almost exclusively among the poor.
 FACT: Suicide is neither the rich man's disease nor the poor
       man's curse. Suicide is very "democratic" and is repre-
       sented proportionately among all levels of society.

FABLE: Suicide is inherited or "runs in the family."
 FACT: Suicide does not run in families. It is an individual pat-
       tern.

FABLE: All suicidal individuals are mentally ill, and suicide al-
       ways is the act of a psychotic person.
 FACT: Studies of hundreds of genuine suicide notes indicate
       that although the suicidal person is extremely unhappy
       he is not necessarily mentally ill.

From SOME FACTS ABOUT SUICIDE by E.S. Shneidman and N.L. Farberow,
Washington, D.C., PHS Publication No. 852, U.S. Printing Office.

6

ABILENE SUICIDE PREVENTION SERVICE
OPERATION MANUAL

This manual has been prepared to acquaint you with the problems and procedures in working with suicidal people, especially by means of the telephone. It is intended as a guide only and aims to give information which will aid you to function effectively and comfortably, and cannot possibly cover all situations.

I. THE SUICIDAL SITUATION

Involvement in the suicidal situation is a frightening experience. Concern about life and death becomes so sharply focused that it may produce anxiety feelings in the telephone worker and may inhibit his ability to help. Experience has shown that the problems inherent in the suicidal crisis are really no greater than or much different from other crises of life, but are only more sharply focused.

<u>The Suicidal Person</u>

Suicide is complex. There is no single cause and no single "cure". There are common methods of approach, however, which can be modified to fit individual cases. In general, the suicidal person is in a disorganized, chaotic state. He feels helpless, hopeless, and is looking desperately for assistance. He is usually anxious, confused, and frequently hostile. He feels rejected, isolated and lonely, and thinks that no one loves him. His suicidal behavior can best be understood as an expression

7

Don't "play God." Assumption that you can solve all problems is presumptuous.

of his severe emotional stress. His calling for the Suicide Prevention Service (SPS) should be seen as a "cry for help." In reality, it is an extension of his attempts to communicate how deeply distressed he is.

The Telephone Volunteer

The Volunteer comes to the situation with motivations and feelings which also need to be understood. The suicidal situation may arouse strong reactions in him. These feelings usually fall into three main areas: (1) feelings of anxiety, (2) feelings of omnipotence, and (3) feelings about death.

1. Feelings of anxiety. One area relates to the Volunteer's feelings of anxiety, and his questions of adequacy and competence to work with the suicidal situation. A moderate level of anxiety is, of course, appropriate. Too much anxiety will interfere, and will also be transmitted to the caller who may begin to doubt whether he can be helped by anyone. Most of the feelings of anxiety and concern about competence will be relieved by training and experience.

2. Feelings of omnipotence. The contrasting area lies in his feelings of omnipotence. The "playing God" role must be avoided. Assumption that all problems can be solved by you is presumptuous. While a death is actually rare, it is always a possibility. Its occurence should not be taken as an indication of the Volunteer's personal failure.

3. Feelings about death. Feelings about death are very important. The Volunteer should have thought through and should be honestly aware of his own feelings about death, i.e., his views of it and his attitudes toward it. Death is a reality of life. The note of finality cannot be avoided. Obtaining death by means of self-destruction is a useless waste of human life. Death by choice is far too often selected as the final answer to a temporary problem. We need to give thought to our personal feelings about the popular prejudices regarding suicide as our conscious thoughts may affect our appraisal of the suicidal crisis situation.

II. THE TELEPHONE CALL SITUATION

In taking calls for the Suicide Prevention Service, you will be talking with people who are seeking help in a suicidal crisis. One of the most important features of the situation is that an individual has called, offering you the opportunity to help. The call also shows that he has mixed feelings about dying; although threatening to destroy himself, he wants to be stopped. All calls, however, should be interpreted as evidence of conscious suicidal intent. Particular attention should be given to third person calls, in which the caller may actually be the suicidal individual.

10

III. THE VOLUNTEER'S TASK IN HANDLING CALLS

The task, in taking a call, can be divided into four major aspects once rapport has been established with the caller:

1. <u>Listen</u> - To obtain information.

2. <u>Record</u> - To make notes on information you have obtained.

3. <u>Evaluate</u> - To evaluate the suicidal potential.

4. <u>Refer</u> - To decide upon and recommend a course of help.

1. Listen - to obtain information.

The best way to get specific information is to ask specific questions. Your own openness and willingness to confront the caller directly with the problem of suicide can be very helpful in reducing the caller's anxiety. Inquire about the suicidal aspect of the behavior in a routine or matter-of-fact manner. Ask about:

1. Prior attempts.
2. When attempts occurred.
3. Whether he is presently planning an attempt.
4. If so, specifically, what his plans are.
5. Whether he has the means available to carry out his plans.

11

Abilene, Texas

In general, your conversation should denote patience, interest, self-assurance, hope, and helpfulness. You want to communicate by your attitude that the person has done the right thing by calling, and that you are willing and able to help. To repeat, remember that you <u>must</u> have information in order to evaluate the suicidal potential. Therefore, do not hesitate to ask questions which will enable you to make an evaluation. (See Appendix B - The SPS Contact Form, p. 37).

2. Record - To make notes on information you have obtained.

Always begin a call by identifying yourself, giving your code name and asking how you may be of help. Allow the caller, then, to tell his story in his own way, listening to obtain the name, address, and telephone number of the caller, as well as the names and phone numbers of other interested persons. Asking for identifying information may occur at any time in the conversation. Do not be obvious in your note taking as this action may create distrust on the part of the caller, and he may doubt the confidentiality of his call.

3. Evaluate - To evaluate the suicidal potential.

Having gathered the information by listening and taking notes, your next task is to evaluate the suicidal potential. The criteria listed in the next section have been developed from research and experience at the Los Angeles Suicide Prevention Center. You should be thoroughly familiar with these criteria before beginning to answer calls as a telephone volunteer for the Abilene Suicide Prevention Service.

12

██

CRITERIA FOR ASSESSMENT OF SUICIDAL POTENTIALITY

With the possible exception of the one item, i.e., having a very lethal and specific plan for suicide, no single criterion should be alarming. Rather, the evaluation of the suicidal potential should be based on the general pattern within the framework of the ten criteria which follow: (See Appendix B - Sample Case, p. 36).

1. Age and sex. Suicidal communications from males are usually more dangerous than from females. The older the person, the higher the probability of suicidal intention. Both age and sex should be considered. A communication from an older woman is more dangerous than one from a younger boy. Note, however, that younger people do make attempts, even if the aim is to manipulate and control people.

2. Mood. If the caller sounds tired, depressed, "washed out", then the suicidal risk is higher than if he seems to be in control of himself. Exuberance, flight of ideas, screaming and yelling are to be considered ominous signs, also. Strong denial of suicidal intention should be considered a definite danger signal. If the caller's mood undergoes marked change for the better during the conversation, this is an important positive sign of suicidal potentiality.

3. Prior attempts or threats. Recent studies show that in about 75 per cent of actual suicides, there have been previous attempts.

4. Acute or chronic situation. An acute situation is a sign of greater immediate danger than would be chronic recurring situations. An acute event, although a sign of immediate danger, has a better prognosis for improvement (once the crisis has been dealt with) than is true of chronic, recurring situations.

██

14

5. <u>Means of possible self-destruction</u>. The most deadly means are shooting, hanging and jumping. If the caller has used or is threatening to use any of these methods, and the means are available, you <u>must</u> consider the threat to be serious and that the suicidal danger is high. Other methods can be lethal and should not be discounted because they appear to be slower and less dangerous, such as barbiturate ingestion, carbon-monoxide poisoning, and wrist cutting.

6. <u>Specific details of the method</u>. If the caller not only has specifically named the method he intends to use, but also goes on to give details about time and place, he should be considered to be in danger.

7. <u>Recent loss or separation from a loved one</u>. If death of a loved one and/or divorce and separation come into the picture, the danger goes up. The separation need not have already taken place, but he may feel that it is impending and he is therefore depressed. If there is any actual or pending loss of a loved one, suicidal danger rises.

8. <u>Medical symptoms</u>. If such facts as unsuccessful surgery, chronic debilitation, cancer or fear of cancer, asthma, fatigue, impotence, loss of sexual desire or any medical symptom come into the picture, the suicidal danger goes up. This is especially true in older persons who may be fearful they will never be well again. They may be lonely and feel that nobody cares for them, which will help to exaggerate the importance of their physical ailments.

9. <u>Diagnostic impressions</u>. Making a psychiatric diagnosis is a professional task; however, record any symptoms given you so that a professional evaluation may be made later. Obvious signs such as hallucinations, delusions, loss of "contact with reality", will reveal a disoriented state. If such states as depression, anxiety, alcoholism, homosexuality enter into the picture then the suicidal danger rises.

10. <u>Resources</u>. If the caller is under financial stress, if he has no friends, or if he is all alone and has few or no social contacts, then the suicidal danger is high.

15

4. Refer - To decide upon and recommend a course of help.

    The fourth task is to decide an appropriate recommendation for help. Generally, the course of action will fall into three categories, (1) emergency, (2) non-referral and (3) referral.

    Emergency. In the highly unusual event that you have a call about a suicide that is occurring, or has just occurred, you should obtain as much information as is necessary to identify the victim or the caller. The informant should then be instructed to follow any of the following procedures: take the patient to an emergency hospital; call his personal physician; call an ambulance; or call the police. Give the police both the name, number and location of the informant as well as the name, number and location of the possible suicide. (The purpose of providing police with the name of the informant is to reduce possible prank situations).

    Since there is no police jurisdiction over suicide, the Volunteer should stand by after notifying the police, to make any appropriate follow-up calls which the emergency may require. It is most important that the police be given any known information concerning dangerous weapons (guns, knives) and other lethal means (drugs, gas) which the suicidal individual may have at his disposal. The aim at that time must be to provide the person in danger with immediate attention.

    Non-referral. Sometimes a person will call and will talk about a problem which is not suicidal or has no suicidal implications.

17

Abilene, Texas

Many calls will be received from persons who simply want to talk and unburden themselves. It is often sufficient and important to LISTEN SYMPATHETICALLY.

Referral. Some cases require minimal action, such as suggestions or guidance. As a general recommendation, it is usually helpful to suggest that the caller communicate his crisis to someone in his personal environment, such as a family member, a friend, family physician, minister, or others. It is useful to encourage the caller to make these contacts or, if necessary, to make contacts for him with his approval. The Directory of Health, Welfare and Social Services in Taylor County gives useful referral information.

People

Helping

People

18

IV. RESOURCES

You may need all the help you can get.

The Suicide Prevention Service staff or professional consultant will be available for you to call if the need arises. Initially, you may feel the need to call often. It is anticipated, however, that this need will soon be reduced. When in doubt, call the SPS staff or consultant.

These are some of the resources which can be used to handle the situation.

1. Family. The family may be one of the most valuable re-
    sources at the time of crisis. The caller could be en-
    couraged to discuss his situation with his family. If he
    is reluctant, but you feel it is important to have some-
    one with him, you should call upon family members and in-
    form them of the situation. The caller should be told first

19

that you are going to call his family because you judge
it best. Generally the family should be involved in accepting responsibilities for emergencies and seeing to it that
the caller gets help.

2. Friends. Close friends may often be used the way families
   are used, as described above. In addition, the caller may
   be encouraged to have a friend stay with him during a particularly bad night. Also, he might ask a friend to talk
   things over with him.

3. Family Physician. People often turn to a physician for
   help, usually their family physician. The caller should
   be encouraged to discuss his problems with the physician.

4. Clergy. If the caller seems religious, he may be encouraged to discuss his situation with a minister.

5. Employer. If the patient's occupation is involved, the
   caller may be encouraged to talk about his problems with
   his employer or with a co-worker.

6. Police. Police should be notified only in cases of clear
   and immediate emergency: (1) if the caller reveals the
   fact that he is actually in the act of attempting suicide,
   (2) if the caller hangs up abruptly, without logical reason,
   and upon calling back there is no answer, and (3) if a third
   person report of a suicide in progress is received. (See
   Emergency, p. 17).

7. Abilene Association for Mental Health. In those cases where
   it is felt there is a high suicide potential and where there
   is need for more intensive, careful referral and further
   interview, the caller can be asked to make an appointment
   with the AAMH during the next regular office hours. Asking
   the person to make an appointment gives him a task to perform, helping him to a goal and purpose in his immediate
   future.

   In cases where you find the suicide danger is not high, or
   perhaps not even the primary problem, but in which there is
   an underlying problem such as marital discord, family conflict, or chronic personal and social maladjustment, a referral may also be made to the Association.

8. Abilene Council on Alcoholism. The alcoholic is often
   troubled with suicidal intentions. It is anticipated that
   you will be talking with numerous persons who have a

20

drinking problem. The Abilene Council on Alcoholism
maintains a 24 hour emergency service and may be called
at any time to assist the alcoholic, suicidal individual.

9. <u>Family Service Counsel</u>. This program offers educational,
informational, and supportive services in the areas of
marital problems, emotional disturbances, mental illness,
child guidance, retardation, and family stress.

At the present writing, this program is staffed part time
by a psychiatric nurse. Expansion of the service into a
full-time counseling agency is anticipated in the future.
The Family Service Counsel shares offices with the Mental
Health Association.

10. <u>Resources Available to Military and Their Dependents</u>.
A Volunteer who receives a call from an active member of
any military service, or his dependents, should be aware
of facilities of Dyess Air Force Base. An emergency phone
is manned 24 hours a day at the base hospital in case of
any medical emergency. A staff duty officer is on call
after duty hours to assist with other type problems. He
can refer you to a chaplain who is always on call, or to
other staff people if the need exists.

                Dyess Information - - - - - - - -   696-3113
                Dyess Hospital Emergency - - - -   696-2333
                Officer of the Day - - - - - - -   696-2123
                Chaplain on call - - - - - - - -   696-2123

21

Abilene, Texas

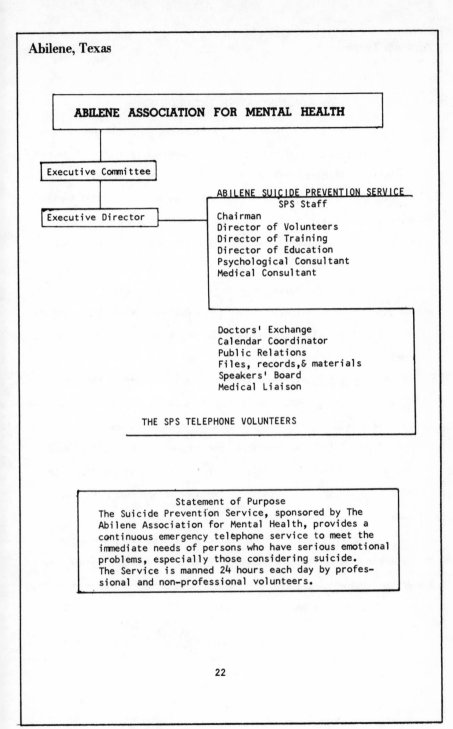

ABILENE ASSOCIATION FOR MENTAL HEALTH

Executive Committee

Executive Director

ABILENE SUICIDE PREVENTION SERVICE
SPS Staff
Chairman
Director of Volunteers
Director of Training
Director of Education
Psychological Consultant
Medical Consultant

Doctors' Exchange
Calendar Coordinator
Public Relations
Files, records,& materials
Speakers' Board
Medical Liaison

THE SPS TELEPHONE VOLUNTEERS

Statement of Purpose
The Suicide Prevention Service, sponsored by The
Abilene Association for Mental Health, provides a
continuous emergency telephone service to meet the
immediate needs of persons who have serious emotional
problems, especially those considering suicide.
The Service is manned 24 hours each day by professional and non-professional volunteers.

22

207

V. ADMINISTRATIVE PROCEDURES

1. Checking In. It will be your responsibility to report on time to the Doctors' Exchange that you are on duty. Phone 672-2811.

2. The SPS Contact Form. You will have a supply of SPS Contact Forms, which will also serve as guides for your telephone interview. These may be filled out while you are taking the call. Any rough notes you make during the call may also be helpful in compiling data. SPS Contact Forms and rough notes for each call should be mailed as soon as possible to the AAMH office, P.O. Box 2707, Abilene, Texas 79604. Remeember that all information is confidential. Your case reporting will be reviewed by the SPS staff.

3. Shift Changes. Feel free to call any member of the SPS staff for consultation and guidance regarding referrals and any partic-ular problems relating to your duty as a telephone Volunteer.

If you must change your time, please make every effort to make arrangements with another SPS Volunteer to cover your shift. Notify the Calendar Coordinator and the Doctors' Exchange of any change in your schedule.

4. Checking Out. When your tour of duty is over, alert the Doctors' Exchange if you have a case pending. Provide the Exchange with any information which might be needed by the Volunteer on the next shift, such as a high risk or emergency situation.

23

BASIC LIBRARY ON SUICIDOLOGY

Volunteers are encouraged to read the studies in the field of Suicidology. All books and materials listed below are available at the Mental Health Association. In addition, several unpublished materials, including graduate research papers, training tapes, and various manuscripts developed by the Abilene SPS staff and volunteers, are available for your use at the Association.

BOOKS

SUICIDE: A SOCIOLOGICAL AND STATISTICAL STUDY - Louis I. Dublin
THE CRY FOR HELP - Norman L. Farberow and Edwin S. Shneidman, Eds.
THE MEANING OF DEATH - Herman Feifel, Ed.
DYING - John Hinton
MAN AGAINST HIMSELF - Karl A. Menninger
SUICIDAL BEHAVIORS: DIAGNOSIS AND MANAGEMENT - H.L.P. Resnik, Ed.
ESSAYS IN SELF DESTRUCTION - Edwin S. Sheidman, Ed.
CLUES TO SUICIDE - Edwin S. Shneidman and Norman L. Farberow, Eds.
SUICIDE AND ATTEMPTED SUICIDE - Erwin Stengel
PREVENTION OF SUICIDE - World Health Organization
THEORY OF SUICIDE - Maurice L. Farber
AS CLOSE AS THE TELEPHONE - Alan Walker
THE PSYCHIATRIC EMERGENCY - The Joint Information Service

PAMPHLETS AND PERIODICALS

HOW TO PREVENT SUICIDE - Edwin S. Shneidman and Philip Mandelkorn
SUICIDE IN THE UNITED STATES, 1950-1964 - Public Health Service
SOCIAL AND PSYCHOLOGICAL ASPECTS OF SUICIDE - Jack D. Douglas,
    Edwin S. Shneidman and Norman L. Farberow
TECHNIQUES IN CRISIS INTERVENTION: A TRAINING MANUAL - Norman L.
    Farberow, Samuel M. Heilig, and Robert E. Litman
INVESTIGATIONS OF EQUIVOCAL SUICIDES - Robert E. Litman, Theodore
    Curphey, Shneidman, Farberow, and Norman Tabachnick
THE TRAGEDY OF SUICIDE IN THE U.S. - Stanley F. Yolles
SOME FACTS ABOUT SUICIDE - National Institute of Mental Health
BULLETIN OF SUICIDOLOGY - National Clearinghouse for Mental Health
    Information
SYMPOSIUM ON SUICIDE - Abilene Suicide Prevention Service
SUICIDE PREVENTION SERVICE: A TRAINING MANUAL - Abilene SPS
SUICIDE PREVENTION: THE BURDEN OF RESPONSIBILITY - Roche Laboratories

24

APPENDIX A

1. SPS VOLUNTEER APPLICATION PROCEDURE

2. SPS TRAINEE CALENDAR AND REQUIREMENTS

3. STATEMENT OF AGREEMENT
   SPS TRAINEE AND SPS VOLUNTEER

4. SUMMARY OF CALLS TO SPS FROM 1967

25

SPS VOLUNTEER APPLICATION PROCEDURE

1. Application sent to interested individual from the office of the Abilene Association for Mental Health.

2. Application returned to AAMH office for processing by the executive director.

3. Executive director presents application to SPS psychological consultant for initial screening. If desired, the SPS staff meets with consultant.

4. After the applicant's references have been received, the psychological consultant makes an appointment with the applicant through the AAMH office. The consultant may request other SPS staff to be present.

5. At this initial meeting, the following will be included:

   a. Personal interview
   b. Orientation of SPS
      1) Function and policy
      2) Training Calendar and Requirements

6. The SPS chairman notifies the applicant if he is accepted as an SPS trainee. If rejected, individual is notified by the AAMH executive director after consultation with SPS staff.

7. SPS trainee is informed of assignments and requirements which must be completed in a satisfactory manner before individual may be considered an SPS volunteer.

26

SPS TRAINING CALENDAR AND REQUIREMENTS

You have been accepted as an SPS trainee. Your initial training will take approximately six months. When training has been satisfactorily completed, you will be assigned regular telephone duty. During your time as a trainee and as a volunteer, you should feel free to call any member of the SPS staff for guidance and support.

The assignments include required reading, listening, testing, and in-service training.

1. Reading assignments (completed within 30 days)

   THE CRY FOR HELP - Farberow and Shneidman
   ABILENE SUICIDE PREVENTION SERVICE TRAINING MANUAL
   HOW TO PREVENT SUICIDE - Shneidman and Mandelkorn
   SYMPOSIUM ON SUICIDE - Abilene SPS
   DIRECTORY OF HEALTH, WELFARE, AND SOCIAL SERVICES IN
       TAYLOR COUNTY - Abilene Association for Mental Health

2. Trainee meets with SPS staff to evaluate first phase of training. Examination will include oral discussion of the reading material with an emphasis on the Do's and Don'ts and Questions for Thought.

3. Listening assignments (tapes and recorder at AAMH office)

   CALL TO LEADERSHIP (3)
   VOLUNTEER TRAINING TAPE (4 & 5)
   TRAINING RECORD IN SUICIDOLOGY

4. Attend In-service Training. (Volunteers are expected to attend at least two of four In-service sessions each year. Absences must be cleared with the Director of Volunteers; otherwise, you will be placed on inactive status).

5. Director of Volunteers assigns your telephone duty. You will serve one month on regular shift with SPS volunteer available as back-up. Director of Volunteers determines when you are ready for SOLO DUTY.

6. Trainee meets with SPS staff for final evaluation. If accepted as SPS volunteer, you are encouraged to take a regular shift with a minimum of 24 hours per month.

27

Don't diagnose. Your job is to Listen - record - evaluate - refer.

STATEMENT OF AGREEMENT
SPS TRAINEE AND SPS VOLUNTEER

1. I agree that I will not make face-to-face appointments with any suicidal SPS caller, except as authorized by a member of the SPS staff or its consultants, in which case I assume legal and personal responsibility for my actions.

2. I hereby free the Abilene Association for Mental Health and the Abilene Suicide Prevention Service which it sponsors, of any and all responsibility for loss or injury during the course of my work or duty tour as an SPS trainee and as an SPS volunteer.

3. I understand that the records and communications received by the Suicide Prevention Service in the course of its work are strictly confidential, and that such information must not be divulged at any time to any unauthorized person. I understand that safeguarding information about an individual, which has been obtained during my course of service, is a primary obligation which I assume as a volunteer.

4. I have read with understanding and agree to abide by the ETHICAL STANDARDS OF VOLUNTEER SERVICE as defined in the SPS Manual.

_____	_____
date	SPS Trainee - Volunteer

Approved as Trainee: _____

	date	Psychological consultant

Approved as Volunteer: _____

date	Director of Training

_____	_____
date	Director of Volunteers

29

APPENDIX B

1. DO'S AND DON'TS

2. QUESTIONS FOR THOUGHT

3. HOW TO REACH A PERSON WITH AN
   UNLISTED NUMBER

4. CASE STUDY

5. SPS CONTACT FORM

6. TWENTY USEFUL HINTS FOR TELEPHONE
   VOLUNTEERS

31

DO'S AND DON'TS

This list of Do's and Don'ts was prompted because of a need for a summary of the SPS Manual. These ideas were compiled during many hours discussion, debate, and friendly persuasion by the SPS staff over a three year period.

DO'S

1. LISTEN - RECORD - EVALUATE - REFER!
2. BE OPEN-MINDED.
3. THINK - STAY ALERT.
4. MAKE NOTES.
5. DEVELOP CONFIDENCE.
6. BE DISCREET WITH OPPOSITE SEX.
7. ASK SPECIFIC QUESTIONS WHEN DESIRING SPECIFIC INFORMATION.
8. BE HELPFUL.
9. BE PATIENT.
10. USE CONSTRUCTIVE QUESTIONS.
11. MOBILIZE PEOPLE IN CALLER'S ENVIRONMENT IN EMERGENCY.
12. GIVE RESPONSIBILITY TO CALLER REGARDING HIS CASE.
13. BE POSITIVE AND POINTED ABOUT THE ACTION(WHEN NECESSARY) WHICH YOU TAKE. KNOW WHY AND WHAT TO DO.
14. KEEP INFORMATION CONFIDENTIAL.
15. MAKE REFERRALS QUICKLY.
16. CHECK IN AND OUT WITH THE DOCTORS' EXCHANGE.
17. MAKE ARRANGEMENTS FOR YOUR SHIFT IF YOU HAVE A CONFLICT.
18. KNOW THE SPS STAFF AND ITS RESPONSIBILITY.
19. COMPLETE SPS CONTACT FORM AND MAIL WITH ROUGH NOTES TO AAMH.
20. ASK HOW YOU CAN HELP OR WHAT YOU CAN DO.
21. ERR ON THE CONSERVATIVE SIDE. CALL FOR HELP WHEN NEEDED.
22. KNOW WHEN TO CALL THE POLICE.
23. ABIDE BY THE ETHICAL STANDARDS OF VOLUNTEER SERVICE.
24. STAY INFORMED ABOUT SUICIDOLOGY.
25. ATTEND IN-SERVICE TRAINING.

32

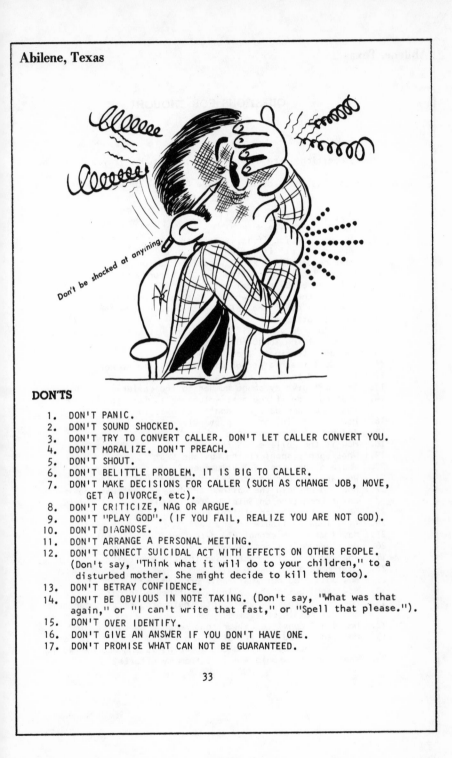

Don't be shocked at anything.

DON'TS

1. DON'T PANIC.
2. DON'T SOUND SHOCKED.
3. DON'T TRY TO CONVERT CALLER. DON'T LET CALLER CONVERT YOU.
4. DON'T MORALIZE. DON'T PREACH.
5. DON'T SHOUT.
6. DON'T BELITTLE PROBLEM. IT IS BIG TO CALLER.
7. DON'T MAKE DECISIONS FOR CALLER (SUCH AS CHANGE JOB, MOVE, GET A DIVORCE, etc).
8. DON'T CRITICIZE, NAG OR ARGUE.
9. DON'T "PLAY GOD". (IF YOU FAIL, REALIZE YOU ARE NOT GOD).
10. DON'T DIAGNOSE.
11. DON'T ARRANGE A PERSONAL MEETING.
12. DON'T CONNECT SUICIDAL ACT WITH EFFECTS ON OTHER PEOPLE. (Don't say, "Think what it will do to your children," to a disturbed mother. She might decide to kill them too).
13. DON'T BETRAY CONFIDENCE.
14. DON'T BE OBVIOUS IN NOTE TAKING. (Don't say, "What was that again," or "I can't write that fast," or "Spell that please.").
15. DON'T OVER IDENTIFY.
16. DON'T GIVE AN ANSWER IF YOU DON'T HAVE ONE.
17. DON'T PROMISE WHAT CAN NOT BE GUARANTEED.

33

QUESTIONS FOR THOUGHT

These questions were designed for your study. If you don't know the answers, discuss the problem with the Director of Volunteers.

1. What is the first thing I say?
2. How do I say it?
3. How do I decide if it is an emergency?
4. Whom do I call if I need assistance?
5. What records do I keep? What information?
6. How do I get information for the records if it's not volunteered by the caller?
7. Who get the records when I am through with them?
8. What do I do if the caller has already made the suicide attempt?
9. What do I do or say if the caller just wants to talk and keeps talking 30-40-60 minutes?
10. How do I terminate a call?
11. How do I reach a person with an unlisted number?
12. Do I need to use a code name?
13. Should I give my phone number to the caller?
14. What do I do if the next volunteer is late for shift?
15. What are some do's and don'ts to observe.
16. How do I decide on the best referrals?
17. To whom am I responsible?
18. How is the Abilene SPS financed?
19. What agency sponsors the Abilene SPS?
20. Who are the other SPS Volunteers?
21. Who are members of the SPS staff and what is its job?
22. How and why did the Abilene SPS begin? What was the Joint Committee on Suicide Prevention?
23. What is considered ethical conduct?
24. Am I legally liable in any way?
25. May I make a personal (face-to-face) appointment?
26. Do I accept collect calls?
27. What do I do if I must leave the phone area?
28. Do I make a follow-up call?
29. How do I find out what their problem is?
30. How can I build the caller's confidence in me?
31. How can I project myself into their problem so I can help and yet remain objective?
32. How can I convince caller that someone cares for him?
33. How can I find out if caller has worked out details for his suicide? How can I find out where he is and who he is?
34. What success should I expect from my efforts?

34

Abilene, Texas

HOW TO REACH A PERSON WITH AN UNLISTED NUMBER

The procedures described below were developed by an SPS

Volunteer as the result of an emergency situation which involved reach-

ing a person with an unlisted number.

FOR EMERGENCY USE ONLY

Recently, a volunteer was hampered in giving quick assistance
because the subject's phone was not obtained, and the subject hung up.
He did get the name and address in record time. After attempting to
secure help from a phone operator, with no success, he ended up calling
for police assistance. The phone number was unlisted.

If you haven't run into this problem yet, you probably will
soon. As of today, almost one third of the phone numbers in Abilene are
unlisted. These numbers are under lock and key. Only the Dial Administrator or the Chief Operator have keys.

The phone official I contacted suggested this procedure:
Between 8 and 5 Monday through Friday, call the Dial Administrator at
677-3300. After hours and on week-ends, call Chief Operator, 677-7258.

Your procedure in presenting your problem might be as follows:

> "This is an emergency. I am a Suicide Prevention
> Service Volunteer. I have a potential suicide call
> that hung up before I could get the phone number.
> The name is _____. Would you please get
> the number and connect me with this party?"

This procedure can also be used in the event the phone is not listed
in the book. It would save a call to information in the case of an
emergency.

The telephone operator cannot by law give you the unlisted
number of any individual. But they can connect you to the number. This
will take between five and eight minutes. The telephone company personnel
is well versed in emergencies. But remember the procedure. This will
speed up their service to you.

35

Abilene, Texas

CASE STUDY

Prepared for
SPS In-Service Training

This case is a compilation of actual situations.

LINDA, a female, age 18, in contact with the SPS volunteer began by expressing that she did not want to live, but she realized that she needed help. Her attitude in the telephone conversation was sad and often tearful. Linda expressed that she was considering taking some of her mother's sleeping pills and just "going to sleep to get out of it all."

About 2½ years ago when she had been involved with a boy whom she had planned to marry, Linda became pregnant. Her baby was placed for adoption. When she had found out about the pregnancy, she had slashed her wrists in an unsuccessful attempt at suicide. About six months earlier, she had taken an overdose of sleeping pills. Her mother discovered her in time to save her life.

She seemed insecure of herself and of her relation to other people. Apparently, she had no trouble with boy friends, for she had just recently broken up with 7 or 8 boy friends. Each time she would begin to become attached to a boy she would break up in a fit of anger at the slightest provocation from the boy.

Linda had trouble making her grades; math was particularly a problem. She attended a local high school and was in grade 11. She had no goal for what she wanted to do when she finished high school. She expressed fear that no matter what she tried to do, she would fail at it. She thought she was not bright enough to succeed.

Her father was an outside salesman and was away from home much of the time. Her mother was a beautician. Her only brother was 20 years old and now at the University of Texas. Her parents did not get along well. Her relationship to her mother was poor. Linda found herself frequently becoming angry with her mother and almost raging. Her father was apathetic to her situation, but she did not have these anger fits toward him. Her mother constantly criticized her: "Don't act so stupid." "Your dress is not right." "That long stringy hair looks icky." Her mother was the dominant personality in the family.

Her older brother and she had quarreled frequently when he was home. He never wanted her to go along whenever he went anywhere.

PROBLEM: WHAT RECOMMENDED ACTION AND REFERRAL IS INDICATED?

36

Abilene, Texas

ABILENE SUICIDE PREVENTION SERVICE CONTACT FORM   CASE #_____

Volunteer _____

Code Name _____   time   day   date

I. SOURCE OF CALL

A. _____   E. _____
     Third party caller   Re: Individual in crisis   Name

B. _____   F. _____
     Address   Phone   Address   Phone

C. _____   G. _____
     Relationship to individual   age   sex   race   occupation

D. _____   H. Marital status: I. Children:
     Nature of request   married single

     _____   divorced widowed   No.   ages

     _____   separated other

     _____   J. Nature of Call: (circle)

     _____   suicide threat   actual suicide

     _____   suicide emergency attempted

     _____   emotional crisis information

II. EVALUATION OF INDIVIDUAL IN CRISIS

A. Mood? crying calm drunk in-
     coherent hostile withdrawn
     Other _____

B. Prior attempts? ___ ___ ___
                yes no unk.
     When? 3mo 6mo 1yr 2yr 5yr 10yr
     Date most recent attempt _____
     Methods? _____

C. Suicide means at hand now?
     Yes _____ No _____ Unk _____
     What? (circle) jumping hanging
     gun poison cutting drowning
     pills car accident carbon
     monoxide other

D. Details worked out? Yes _____
     No _____ Explain _____

E. Recent loss or separation from
     loved one? Yes _____ No _____
     Explain _____

F. Evaluation: _____
            high risk low risk

G. Emergency action taken _____

     Other action taken _____
     NOTE: Use additional pages
     for a brief narrative of call.
     Mail report and rough notes to
     P.O. Box 2707
     Abilene, Texas   79604

III. PROBLEM AREA (circle primary)

1. Marital _____
2. Physical _____
          illness   can't work
3. Addiction _____
          drugs   alcohol
4. Emotional_____
          lonely fear depression
5. Family _____
         relatives money parent/
                       child
6. Work _____
         job school unemployed
7. Sexual conflicts _____
8. Other _____

IV. RESOURCES   Prior help ___ ___
                       no   yes

Nature of prior help _____

A. _____
     minister   physician

B. _____
     important others: family friend
     counselor agencies

V. REFERRAL MADE TO _____

Circle resource: minister   AA
physician   clinic   AAMH
Coun on Alco   hospital   FSC
Hotline   welfare   Other
friends   Voc Rehab
police   Counselor

37

TWENTY USEFUL HINTS FOR TELEPHONE VOLUNTEERS

1. Consider the following qualities in yourself:

empathy	persuasive power
warmth	judgment
imagination	knowledge of drugs
referral facility	motivation
self-disclosure	insight
emergency equilibrium	self-appraisal
public relations	responsibility
voice quality	maturity
initiative	experience

2. Never say "I'm just a volunteer."

3. Be patient. Being available 24 hours a day, 7 days a week is an essential part of SPS responsibility. As one caller put it, "It''s good to know you are there if I need you."

4. First establish trust; then mobilize resources.

5. Never be satisfied with a caller's own evaluation of his trouble. Explore, in order to make the most appropriate referral.

6. When a caller can not, through distress or otherwise, artic-ulate his problem, reassure him. Let him set the pace. Intro-duce discussion of various subjects to him:

doctor/clergy	health
parents	money
children	suicide attempts
religion	travel-vacations
pets	other people in home
friends	sex life
neighbors	sleep
work	meals
his house	hobbies
age	time of decision to call
prior help	handicaps

7. Silence is useful. Do not talk more than the caller.

8. Be alert for any opportunity to stress caller's positive qualities, accomplishments, and hidden strengths.

38

9. Make frequent use of the words HOPE, HOPEFUL, but at the same time make sure not to use them in such a way as to suggest the opposite.

10. Be realistic in your appraisal. Do not give unrealistic reassurances; "He'll come back.", etc.

11. Do not change a caller's therapist or make derogatory statements about his choice of minister, doctor, counselor.

12. Keep the spotlight on the caller.

13. Four useful questions:
    "What are your ideas concerning the causes of your difficulty?"
    "What have you done so far to improve the situation?"
    "What stands in the way of working things out?"
    "Do you have someone to whom you can take your problems?"

14. Careful paper work is extremely important. Another volunteer may depend upon what you write about a caller in a later emergency.

15. Watch details. A reversed digit in an emergency could lose a life.

16. After a client's trust has been won, ask: "What is your name?' You will usually get it.

17. All information relating to another volunteer is strictly confidential; protect your colleagues.

18. Caller's often tell a great deal about themselves. Be sure to put down the important facts contained in his narrative: his weight, age, etc. In your write-up, the following scaled descriptions are useful: Was the client: indifferent, excited, emotional, eager, warm, friendly, matter-of-fact, moody, silent, anxious, complaining, irritable, cold, hostile, frightened, lamenting, angry, raging, hyper-sensitive, intelligent, academic, average, slow, dull, retarded, hearty, forthright, steady, tired, sleepy.

19. Tell the truth by answering the real questions. Are you hearing what is being said?

20. Do not promise what can not be guaranteed.

This list was adapted from materials developed by the San Francisco SPS.

39

APPENDIX N
Brief Suggested List of
Materials for Training

Blum, D., Lester, D. "The Chronic Caller to a Suicide Prevention Center: Report of a Case." **Crisis Intervention. 2** (1) 1970.

Brockopp, G.W. "The Masturbator." **Crisis Intervention** 1969, **1**, (1).

Brockopp, G.W. "The Silent Caller." **Crisis Intervention** 1970, **2**, (3).

Brockopp, G.W. "The Telephone Call-Conversation or Therapy." **Crisis Intervention,** 1970, **2**, (3).

Brockopp, G.W. "Training the Volunteer Telephone Therapist." **Crisis Intervention,** 1970, Vol. 2, (3).

Brockopp, G.W. "I'll Be Here Tuesday, If you Need Me." **Crisis Intervention,"** 1971, **3**, (1).

Farberow, N.L. Crisis, Disaster and Suicide: Theory and Therapy in **Essays in Self Destruction** (Ed.) E. Shneidman. Science House, New York, 1967.

Grollman, E. **Suicide: Prevention, Intervention, Postvention.** Boston: Beacon Press, 1971.

Lester, D. "Chronic Callers To A Suicide Prevention Center." **Community Mental Health Journal,** 1970, **6**, (3).

Lester, G. & Lester, D. **Suicide and the Gamble with Death.** Englewood Cliffs, New Jersey: Prentice-Hall, 1971.

Litman, R.E., Shneidman, E.S., Farberow, N.L. "First Aid in Suicidal Crisis." Zeroxed paper from the Los Angeles Suicide Prevention Center.

Litman, R.E. "Emergency Response to Potential Suicide." **The Journal of the Michigan State Medical Society. 62,** 1963, pp. 68-72.

Litman, R.E., Farberow, N.L., Shneidman, E.S., Heilig, S.M., Kramer, J. "Suicide Prevention Telephone Service." **The Journal of the American Medical Association,** 1965, **192,** pp. 21-25.

Litman, R.E. "The Prevention of Suicide." **Current Psychiatric Therapies,** 1966, **VI.**

Shneidman, E.S., Farberow, N.L. & Litman, R.E. **The Psychology of Suicide.** Science House, New York, 1970.

APPENDIX O

Examples of Training Program Format

LOS ANGELES SUICIDE PREVENTION CENTER

However, certain fundamentals are included in all the programs. The four fundamental components of all training in suicide prevention are (1) basic concepts of suicide prevention, (2) recognition of suicidal persons and evaluation of lethality, (3) use of the telephone and techniques and (4) mobilization of resources to implement an appropriate helping response.

The basic concepts of suicide prevention include (1) ambivalence, (2) communication, (3) lethality, (4) stress, (5) helplessness and hopelessness, (6) the significant other, and (7) action response.

Verbal clues, behavioral clues, and symptomatic clues are elaborated to teach how to recognize persons in suicidal crises. The most important single component for training in suicide prevention is to teach how to make a careful evaluation of the danger, once a suicidal situation has been identified.

The criteria used for evaluation of suicide potential are (1) character, (2) current psychological status or symptoms, (3) suicide method or plan, (4) precipitating stress, and (5) available resources.

In teaching the principles of telephone interviewing, we cover such items as (1) maintaining contact and establishing a relationship, (2) obtaining necessary information, (3) evaluation of suicide potential, (4) clarification of stress and focal problem, (5) assessment of strengths and resources, (6) recommendation and initiation of an action plan, and (7) closure. The use of the telephone in getting collateral persons to both provide information and help in the crisis is also discussed.

Mobilization of resources is on three levels: (1) personal resources, such as family, friends and co-workers, (2) professional resources available to a particular patient such as doctors, clergy, therapists and lawyers, and (3) the broad range of community resources, such as clinics, hospitals and social agencies are also covered.

DIAL HELP TRAINING PROGRAM - BANGOR, MAINE

Note: Throughout training there is an emphasis on discussing the trainees' performance in role-played calls. Constructive criticism is constant. Trainees understand that they may drop out if at any time they become aware that they are uncomfortable with, or unsuited for, this type of work. They also understand that they are not accepted as volunteers until completion of the training and successfully passing the taped final exam. Throughout training trainees practice role-playing and writing up calls.

Session 1:

A get-acquainted, ice-breaking session which also introduces trainees to the basic skills we will be learning namely: reflecting accurate empathy, genuineness, non-possessive warmth, facilitating communication, establishing relationships, making fast and accurate assessments, formulating plans with callers. We talk about ways of being our most effective selves, about the feelings of people calling and what sorts of responses they might be looking for or find helpful. We practise accurate listening by pairing off trainees and having them tell each other about their day, or about someone, and then see if the listener heard how the talker **felt** about the day, or the someone. Finally, a tape of a previous role-play session is played and we discuss what was happening, how both parties felt, how they were communicating, etc.

Session II:

We discuss our feelings prior to, during and after the first session; the importance of being aware of one's feelings; trust, lack of trust, and it's importance in intercommunication. Then background is given on The Counseling Center and its services, the origins and varieties of help lines; the mental health professions, and the difference between a volunteer telephone worker's job and that of a psychotherapist. We then practise listening and responding, using taped examples of types of (role-played) callers. Trainees are asked to identify feelings expressed and then to respond in such a way as to indicate that they've heard the caller's feelings.

Session III:

Trainees practise establishing communication, using telephone role-plays of withdrawn, depressed, and otherwise difficult-to-draw-out callers. Tapes of previous role-plays may also be played for illustrative purposes.

Session IV:

Trainees practise non-possessive warmth, role-playing with callers whose situations call for non-critical acceptance and a minimum of active prejudices. We then review and discuss a list of questions which are almost always essential in assessing caller's situation (such as the personal and public resources available to him), and practise role-playing calls with a view to assessing caller's situations.

Session V:

We discuss the possible outcomes of calls and the planning stage, covering personal and community resources and the importance of follow-up. We then practise this stage of the call, describing a call up to this stage and role-playing the final stages.

Session VI:

Crisis intervention theory is reviewed, stressing crisis as a time of opportunity. We then role-play a crisis. The "caller" is stopped at various points and different trainees try their own approaches on him and they play out the results of the different approaches.

Session VII:

Different types of calls are described and briefly role-played with trainees, drawing on Richard Hall's categorization of callers to a suicide prevention center.

Session VIII:

Three short papers are discussed: "Chicken Soup is Poison" by Robert Resnick, "The Knight-Errant, The Dragon and the Maiden" by G. Wilson, and "Telephone Therapy" by Charles Lamb. Around the first we discuss what is meant by "help" and the balance between helping too much and not enough; around the second, the caller who doesn't **want** to be helped, forms this may take, and how to deal with this; around the third, the games that callers and answerers, engage in, role-playing alternative counter-moves.

Session IX:

We discuss suicide: assessing lethality, the suicide-in-progress, the attempter, local statistics, etc. The film "Cry for Help" is shown and discussed.

Session X:

Hospitalization in the local area is reviewed, with visits to Bangor State and The Counseling Center's psychiatric ward at Eastern Maine Medical Center. Trainees talk with representatives of the facilities regarding appropriate patients, emergency admission procedures, types of therapy offered, commitment, etc.

Session XI:

Trainees rap with young people representing various segments of "the youth culture" and with a few adults who work with young people (probation officers, guidance counselor, etc.) about the problem of youth today and the communication gap between generations.

Session XII:

Staff members with experience in dealing with drug problems talk about drugs, the local scene, and local resources. A staff member role-plays "talking down" a caller on a bad trip.

Session XIII:

The director of The Counseling Center's Alcoholic Rehabilitation Program talks to trainees about the stages of alcoholism, and the calls that might be expected from alcoholics and their family members. Role-playing.

Session XIV:

Discussion of what has been learned and of practical procedures, forms, etc. A summing-up.

Trainees then schedule appointments to take a tape-recorded exam. This exam tests knowledge and skills by presenting "callers" to whom they "respond" on another tape. "Callers" make requests necessitating knowledge of resources and skill in the areas trainees have practised. Upon passing the exam, trainees are assigned to training shifts with experienced workers, where they first listen in on and discuss calls, then take calls under supervision of the trained worker.

Suicide Prevention and Crisis Service

of Erie County, Buffalo, N.Y.

In-Service Training

Though there are on-going opportunities for the volunteer to upgrade and continually develop his telephone counseling skills (see Part 3) if a volunteer remains at SPCS beyond 6 months he/she is required to attend a series of at least three (3) refresher training conferences which are offered by the Center staff periodically throughout the year. This requirement can be waived for a volunteer who has regularly attended case conferences and other refresher sessions. The refresher sessions may be chosen according to need as perceived by the volunteer himself or as recommended by his supervisor.

Section II (1 session)

> The nature of communication
> Listening and responding
> The response of the counselor
> Telephone communication
> Practice in Communication
> Telephone Counseling Method

Section III (1 session)

> Emergencies, Crisis, and Stress
> The nature of crisis
> Crisis intervention, what, when, and how
> Practice in Crisis Intervention

Section IV (2 sessions)

> Suicide, Homicide and Death
> Assessment of Lethality
> Suicide Prevention
> Film - "The Cry for Help."

Section V (3 sessions)

> Special Problems in Telephone Counselling
> Counselling the Adolescent
> Emergencies, Crises, and Problems related to drugs

Section VI (2 sessions)

> Community Resources & the Referral Process
> SPCS policies for counselors
> The record system: its maintenance and use, including taping
> Supervision and Consultation

TRAINING PROGRAM FOR VOLUNTEERS
OF THE
SUICIDE PREVENTION AND CRISIS CENTER OF
PORTSMOUTH, VIRGINIA

The following is a tentative outline for our training program. It is urged that each volunteer plan to attend at least six (6) of the following sessions. Although we plan to cover all of the topics outlined, the order of the topics may be changed to handle questions as they come up, and we may wish to spend more time on any one area when appropriate. Also, our discussions may be interrupted to listen to phone calls as they come into the center when it is in operation.

Session I SATURDAY JANUARY 10, 1970 1:00 P.M. Dr. Dozoretz

Introduction and Orientation: Introduction of ourselves and what we bring to the SPCC, understanding of this center and it's operations in relation to the volunteer program.

1. Introduction--interests, previous experiences, motivation for becoming a volunteer.
2. Impressions and expectations--what is our understanding of the work of this center, out impressions from observing phone work, what do we expect of a volunteer.
3. Overview of the SPCC--its history--relationship to community, research, personnel, etc.
4. Preliminary discussion of crisis and the problems of suicide.

Session II WEDNESDAY JANUARY 14, 1970 7:30 P.M. Dr. Barnard

The role of the volunteer-what is a "helping person," and how are services given via telephone.

1. Role of the helper--what do you bring as a non-professional person, what are your qualifications and what level of competency is expected, the limitations of any helping person.
2. Phone as modality--how do we provide services via telephone, difference from person-to-person contact, helper as listener, resolution of crisis via phone.
3. Communication--how do we understand and respond to what someone else is telling us in a way which is most beneficial to them.

Special emphasis on;

a. Interactional process--flow between two people.
b. Response on more than one level--content, affective, dynamic, etc.
c. Assessment--going on bits of information we have, how do we begin to understand what is going on with a caller.

Session III WEDNESDAY JANUARY 21, 1970 7:30 P.M. Dr. Mingione

Interviewing--techniques of gathering information in a way which is therapeutic to the caller.

1. Purpose of interviewing.
2. Non-directive and directive approach.
3. Beginning, continuing, closing.
4. The problem-solving approach.
5. Role playing-simple crisis discussed.

Session IV WEDNESDAY JANUARY 28, 1970 7:30 P.M. Dr. Rosin

Crisis and Suicide: what is the nature of a crisis, and in particular, a crisis involving suicide, and how do we deal with it.

1. Crisis--what does a crisis mean in terms of one's psychological makeup, implications of crisis for the helping person.
2. Suicidal audio material where available.
3. Suicide--general facts about suicide and suicidal populations, the meaning of suicide to the suicidal caller, ambivalence, comments, our own personal feelings about suicide.

Session V WEDNESDAY FEBRUARY 4, 1970 7:30 P.M. Dr. Mingione

Practicing and Using of the skills and handling the crisis situation.

1. Group role playing--acting out phone situations in the group with comment and discussion.
2. Diads--role play in twos. Attention to specific procedures, roladex, contact sheets, case records, referral book, etc.
3. Beginning to deal with resources available in immediate family and in community.

Session VI WEDNESDAY FEBRUARY 11, 1970 7:30 P.M. Dr. Barnard and/or Mr. Vance Foster

Resources--when and how do we refer caller to an agency, what resources may be helpful in the resolution of a crisis.

1. When is a referral made--type of problem, motivation of caller.
2. Mobilization of caller's own resources-relatives, friends, clergymen, doctors, etc.
3. Emergency procedures--police, operators, hospitalization, centers of activity.
4. Referral to agencies--agencies which may give treatment, advice in specific area, material help, etc.
5. Use of referral book enabling caller to use referral.

Session VII WEDNESDAY FEBRUARY 18, 1970 7:30 P.M. Dr. Kornblut

Police role in an acute crisis--use of a consultant as a resource for the volunteer person.

1. Repeaters, depressed callers, hostile callers, "crank" calls, etc.
2. Adolescent calls--what is "normal" for adolescents, what are problems most common with adolescents.

Session VIII WEDNESDAY FEBRUARY 25, 1970 7:30 P.M. Dr. Dozoret

Summing up.

1. A pulling together of what we have learned and evaluation of the training program.
2. Feelings about our own competency.
3. Strengths, weaknesses, and suggestions for future training programs.
4. Statement that this is considered a broad outline for the training program which we feel is essential to each volunteer.

It is the feeling of the Board that no volunteer should be considered acceptable until completion of the training program at which time the Board members will meet and make a firm decision as to the acceptability of all volunteers. Each volunteer will then be notified by letter from the Suicide Prevention and Crisis Board.

If you have any questions, please feel free to call upon me.

Sincerely,

Ronald I. Docoretz, M.D.

RID;bk

ALL TRAINING SESSIONS WILL BE HELD AT MARYVIEW HOSPITAL SCHOOL OF NURSING

CRISIS CLINIC ORIENTATION PROGRAM FOR VOLUNTEERS SEATTLE, WASHINGTON

I. **FIRST ORIENTATION SESSION: INTRODUCTION TO CRISIS CLINIC HISTORY AND SERVICE**

    A.   Introduction
        1.   Introductions.
        2.   Tour and orientation to Crisis Clinic.
        3.   History and description of Crisis Clinic: the roles of the volunteers and professionals.
        4.   Philosophy of Crisis Clinic.

Coffee Break

    B.   The Creative Use of Self.
        1.   Over-view and philosophy of training.
            a.   Training is for the purpose of opening doors to personal growth.
            b.   Continuous personal growth of volunteers is essential.
        2.   Preparation for role playing: technique and expectations.
        3.   Training tape: "The Telephone"
        4.   Role playing - how to conduct a call.
            a.   How to introduce yourself on the phone.
            b.   Dealing with simple information calls.
            c.   How to close the call.
        5.   Role playing of simple information calls.
        6.   Recording the call.
            a.   The importance of paper work.
            b.   The steps for recording calls.
        7.   Playback of role playing tapes: discussion and suggestions for voice and language development.

    C.   Summary.
        1.   Limitations and advantages of the Crisis Clinic Service.
            a.   Responsibility to clients.
            b.   The use of community resources.
        2.   Evaluation and discussion of first training session.
        3.   Preparation for first training shift: play training tape number two: "The Technique of Listening."
        4.   Schedule first training shift before second orientation session.

TRAINING SESSIONS WITH VOLUNTEER TRAINER

(The first four-hour **observation and training shift** should be complete before the second **orientation** session).

II. **FIRST TRAINING SHIFT.**

    A.   The Equipment.
        1.   How to use phones and buttons on phones.

Crisis Clinic (Cont. p. 2)

    2.   How to use the answering service.
    3.   How to use the Intercom system.
    4.   How to use the buzzer.
    5.   The purpose of the clipboard.
    6.   The purpose of the bulletin board.
    7.   Using the large note pad.
    8.   Shift schedules.

B.   The Calls.
    1.   Listen to at least three calls.
    2.   While listening take notes and write summary of each call (this is not the regular written format, but an exercise in listening).
    3.   Discuss summary with trainer.
        a.   Did you get correct name, address and telephone number?
        b.   What was the spoken problem? What kind of service was asked for?
        c.   What was the real problem?
        d.   What would you have considered with the caller?

C.   The cases.
    1.   Information and referral call (case name to be given).
    2.   Request for help - crisis call (case name to be given).
    3.   Potential suicide (case name to be given).

D.   Acquaint yourself thoroughly with Rolodex File A through F.

E.   Read: "Crisis Intervention," article by Dr. Louis Paul.

III. **SECOND ORIENTATION SESSION: DEVELOPING AN EFFECTIVE RELATIONSHIP ON THE PHONE.**

A.   Review of first orientation session and first training shift.

B.   Introduction of and playing of training tape: "The Opening Minutes."

C.   Review and discuss "Frame of Reference" paper.

D.   Role playing: Identifying the real rather than the spoken problem.
    1.   Staff will role play both parts.
    2.   Half the training group will role play both parts, followed by discussion.

Coffee Break

E.   Crisis Theory and Crisis Intervention: Dr. Carrold Iverson.

F.   Role playing of specific crisis situations by second half of trainees.

G.   Summary and discussion.

IV. **SECOND TRAINING SHIFT** (4 hours)

A.   How to prepare a case folder and write up case contacts.
    1.   Face sheet and follow-up sheets, IBM, etc.
    2.   Files for callers, IBM sheets, Volunteer file, Volunteer Case File, Incoming Call Sheet.

B. Case reading: trainer will have ready a suggested list of callers that will give trainee an idea of overall kinds of calls that Crisis Clinic receives.

C. Listen to at least three Crisis calls, taking notes and organizing the written summary as follows:
    1. What is the spoken problem?
    2. How did caller feel about asking for help?
    3. What seemed to be the real problem?
    4. What would have been your plan if you were actually receiving the call?

D. Discuss summary with your trainer and place in your file to discuss with Social Worker.

E. Review Persistent Caller List and "Points to Remember." Role play with trainer two typical persistent caller approaches and response.

F. Review Rolodex File G to L.

G. Read: "How to Prevent Suicide."

V. THIRD ORIENTATION SESSION: WHAT TO DO WHEN THE PROBLEM HAS BEEN IDENTIFIED.

A. Resources and referrals.
    1. The danger of referral based upon the spoken problem.
    2. Establishing priority in multi-problem calls: what happens when too many referrals are given.
    3. Public and private resources: legal, financial, social, religious, physical, emotional, etc.

B. Emergency Calls.
    1. What to do and say during an emergency.
    2. How, when, and where do refer for emergency help.
    3. Considerations in dealing with a dying person.
    4. Emergency second party calls.
    5. Role playing to obtain pertinent information.

C. Other emergency requests: financial, medical, food, shelter, transportation, and others.

Coffee Break

D. Other things to consider.
    1. Persistent callers and points to remember.
    2. The inarticulate caller under great emotional stress.
    3. Pertinent information regarding individuals with drug, alcohol, marital, and sexual problems.

E. Suicide prevention and assessing the lethality risk.
    1. The question of ambivalence.
    2. Communication of intent.
    3. Search for the significant other.
    4. Universal reactions to death and dying.

5. Religious, social, economic, and psychological implications of suicide.
6. Role playing to assess lethality risk and summary of available resources.

F. Discussion and summary for evaluation of trainees in training program.

VI. THIRD TRAINING SHIFT (four hours)

A. Review training notes on emergency services. Role play at least two such experiences with trainer.

B. Outline all steps in proper case recording.
1. Listen to at least three calls that would be a case.
2. Make a mock record following all steps, using a different name so that mock record will not be confused with real record, and discuss the mock record with the trainer and file for later discussion with Social Worker.

C. Review Rolodex File M through S.

D. Review points to consider in evaluating suicide risk. Particularly note what volunteer can do! Role play at least one such situation. Discuss with trainer.

VII. FOURTH TRAINING SHIFT

A. Review Rolodex File T through Z. Review Private Practice file and Clergy and Hospital Emergency Room file. Note and discuss use of professional back-up staff. Discuss when night consultants are used.

B. Begin taking calls and prepare case records.

C. Discuss when to use and how to use professional staff.
1. Discuss written notes in records.
2. Discuss cases and resources about which you have question.

D. Schedule appointment with Social Worker to evaluate training and work as volunteer.

E. Trainer will write a brief summary, which trainee will have seen, and submit to Social Worker before scheduled appointment with trainee.

VIII. TRAINING SHIFTS FIVE AND SIX

A. Take calls and prepare case records appropriately.

B. Discuss problems and feelings with trainer.

C. Attend staff meetings and in-service training sessions.

D. Schedule interview with trainer and Social Worker to evaluate trainee's progress and "graduation" to volunteer status.

VOLUNTEER COURSE FOR SUPPORT - AKRON, OHIO

1969

Time: Thursday nights, 7:30-9:30
Duration: Six Weeks
Place: Fallsview Mental Health Center

Class I   October 9, 1969

    A.   Introduction to SUPPORT (A. Koplin)
        1.   Introduction of teaching team
        2.   Rules for training sessions
        3.   Outline of course

    B.   Need for SUPPORT (A. Koplin)
        1.   Description of suicide crisis in Summit County
        2.   History and organization of SUPPORT

    C.   Questions and Answers (Professional Staff)

    D.   Policy of confidentiality (N. Ross)

    E.   The Role of the Volunteer (H. Bair)
        1.   Unique qualifications of volunteers
        2.   How different and complimentary to physicians, psychologists, social workers.
        3.   Why need volunteers to provide service
        4.   Place of SUPPORT in matrix of provision of service to citizens and social agencies (see enclosed chart)

    F.   Use of Community Resources (H. Bair, and Panel)
        1.   Hypothetical Case example, Part 1

Class II   October 16, 1969

    A.   Causes of bizarre and destructive behavior (W. Holloway)

    B.   Movie "Cry for Help"
        1.   Police procedures (Lt. Cunningham)
        2.   Management of bizarre and destructive behavior (W. Holloway)

Class III   October 23, 1969

    A.   Community Resources: Hypothetical case example, Part II, (H. Bair and Panel)

    B.   Techniques in Listening (P. Jackson)
        1.   How to make an assessment of lethality
        2.   How to win caller's trust, (sympathetic listening, confidence, reassurance, looking for areas of agreement, etc.) illustrative role play by staff and/or volunteers.
        3.   Emergency plans for lethal caller.

Support (Cont. p. 2)

Class IV   October 30, 1969

    A.   Phone techniques continued. Review measuring lethality (P. Jackson)

    B.   Further techniques in listening (P. Jackson) (encourage to state problem, not pushing to far; classifying problem-problem not unique; outline needs, non-judgemental attitude.

    C.   Appropriate plans for semi and non-lethal calls (T. Flower; H. Bair)

    D.   Using call report sheet (P. Jackson)

    E.   Third party and/or complaint call (A. Koplin)

    F.   Professional consultation back-up. (A. Koplin) In order to ensure adequate practice in handling phone calls, there will be one small group meeting in addition to the regular Thursday night meetings. This small group practice will allow everyone some individual practice. The times will be announced a few weeks in advance.

Class V   November 6, 1969

    A.   Special problems of younger people (L. Kacalief)

    B.   Special problems of senile adult (To be announced)

    C.   The hostile caller (To be announced)

    D.   Special problems of drugs and alcoholism (P. Jackson)

    E.   Office procedures (A. Koplin)

    F.   Coverage of important items missed (Staff)

    G.   Questions and answers

Class VI   November 13, 1969

    Practice calls

    November 17, 1969

    SUPPORT begins operations

APPENDIX P

Examples of Log Sheets

MONTH: _____ YEAR _____ PROBLEM:

PROBLEM:
1. Family
2. Drinking
3. Disturbed
4. Lonely
5. Depressed
6. Suicidal Tho'ts
7. Suicide attempt
8. Other

DATE	DAY	HOUR AM/PM	CITY OR AREA	INIT. OR ANONY.	MAR. STAT.	M / F	AGE teen 30-40 40-60	WHO CALLED	EMP OR UNEMP	PROB-LEM	CONV. ENOUGH YES NO	REFERRAL	COMMENTS

LOG OF PHONE CALLS-SP&CH SERVICE

DAY _____ DATE _____

TIME	VOLUNTEER	CALLER	M/F	I/R	R/U	TYPE OF CALL

TALLY SHEET FOR CALLS WITH LITTLE OR NO SIGNIFICANCE- S.P. & C.H.S.

DATE	WRONG NUMBERS	HANG UPS	INFORMATION	BUSINESS	TOTAL

LOG RECORD — Form 3

DATE _____ Day _____ Date _____

Listener's _____ Caller's Case _____

Walk In	Phone	Time		Name	Name	#	Subject of Call	Code #	Referral
		Start	Close						

Code Numbers: 1. Boy-girl 2. Parents, family 3. Social relationships (loneliness, popularity, etc.) 4. Sexual 5. Pregnancy 6. Venereal Disease 7. Medical 8. Drugs 9. School 10. Information 11. Click 12. Other

Bridgeport Suicide Prevention Telephone Service - 5/71
Bridgeport, Conn.

Date _____ A.M. _____ A.M. _____ VOLUNTEER _____
                  P.M.   P.M.

TIME OF CALL ST./FIN.	NAME & AGE	ADDRESS & PHONE NO.	CALLER'S RELATION TO PATIENT	NATURE OF CRISIS AND DISPOSITION	CHECK ONE out-going	in-coming

OPERATION: HOTLINE
MANHASSET, N.Y.
Statistical
Analysis

CALL FREQUENCY RECORD

PERIOD OF TIME	YEAR

HOUR	SUNDAY # ___	MONDAY # ___	TUESDAY # ___	WEDNESDAY # ___	THURS. # ___	FRI. # ___	SAT. # ___
7-7:59 pm							
8-8:59 pm							
9-9:59 pm							
10-10:59 pm							
11-11:59 pm							
12-12:59 pm							
1-1:59 am							
2-2:59 am							
AVERAGE CALLS A NIGHT							

Miscellaneous Comments _____

HOTLINE CALL RECORDS MANHASSET, N.Y. Statistical Analysis				SU MO TUE WE TH FR SA			DATE OF MONTH			YEAR

HOUR REC'D	BOY	GIRL	CALL LENGTH	CALLER'S LOCATION	NICK-NAME	AGE	How Heard	Staff Listr.	PROBLEM CLASSIFI-CATION
1									
2									
3									
4									
5									
6									
7									
8									
9									
10									
11									
12									
13									
14									
15									
16									
17									
18									
19									
20									
21									
22									
23									
24									
25									
26									
27									
28									
29									
30									
31									
32									
DAILY TOTALS		____ Av ____ ____%		WEATHER:		____ ____ ____			TEAM SUPPORTER: _____

RUNNING BOYS ___ TOTAL CALLS ___ TOTAL CALLS AVG. PER DAY ___
TOTALS   GIRLS ___ SUBSTANTIVE ___ SUBSTANTIVE AVG. PER DAY ___
DAYS   % Substantv.   ___%

9/10/71

248

APPENDIX Q

Examples of Caller Report Forms

DALLAS, TEXAS
OUTLINE FOR NARRATIVE RECORDING
Recording for Initial Contact

All recording should be categorized under these six captions:

I. **Present problem and Present Treatment**

— Reason for calling the center
— Describe problem most important to client
— Note recent efforts to get professional help

II. **Present Living Situation**

Note any pertinent information about this person's environment (both strengths and weaknesses) which have influences on the problem:

— Employment, training, and schooling
— Financial situation
— Residence with significant others
— Level and quality of social intercourse
— Significant changes in life style (moves, losses, promotions, etc.)

III. **Personality of the Client**

— Describe the way the client relates to you on the phone
— How did client make you feel
— Voice quality (low, brisk, monotonous, emotional, etc.)
— Describe the client's pattern of coping with his problems (note past suicidal feelings or actual attempts and past efforts for improvement)

IV. **Recommendations**

List the things you recommended to the client with the reasons for these recommendations.

V. **Follow Up**

— Note any contact you have with community resources or family
— Also note follow up contacts with client

Recording for Call Backs

All recording should be categorized under these two captions:

I. **Reason for Call**

II. **Summary of Contact**

Note any change or lack of change in the client's situation considering the material of the initial interview.

SUICIDE PREVENTION CENTER – DALLAS, TEXAS

CLIENT SHEET

CASE NO. _____

How did you hear of us? _____   Date _____   Staff Member _____

Prior contact with SPC? _____   Time: in _____ out _____   Problem Category _____
                                                  (initial call)

Name _____ _____ _____   Age _____ Sex _____
      Last   First

Address _____
How long at this address? _____   in city _____ Phone _____ in state _____

Occupation _____   Business address _____   Business Phone _____

Occupation of Spouse _____   Business address _____   Business Phone _____

How long at this job? _____   If unemployed, how long? _____   Financial Status _____

Marital History _____

Children: Number _____ Sex and ages _____
Immediate family in home _____
Other family in home _____   immediate area _____

Education _____

Religious Affiliation _____   Minister _____

Health _____

Physician or Clinic _____   Address _____   Phone _____

Present Medication _____

Previously used resources _____

Potential resources _____

Referral _____

Instructions _____

_____

Caller other than client:

Name _____

Address _____

Phone _____

Relationship _____

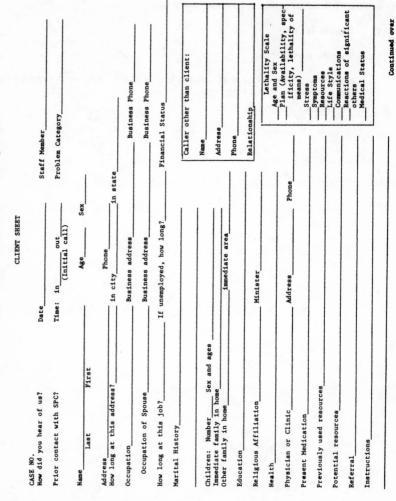

Lethality Scale
  Age and Sex _____
  Plan (Availability, specificity, lethality of means) _____
  Stress _____
  Symptoms _____
  Resources _____
  Life Style _____
  Communications _____
  Reactions of significant others _____
  Medical Status _____

Continued over

Client's Name _____ Supervisory Staff Aide _____

(Code Name)

Case Number _____

CASE SUMMARY SHEET for CHRONIC CALLERS

I. Definition of Supervisory Staff Aide: The person who supervises all work done with this client. This Staff Aide is not on call to the client even in emergencies, unless specified on this sheet. This Staff Aide is available for consultation to other Staff Aides who have received calls from this client. The supervisory Staff Aide fills out these instructions and decisions are to be followed by other Staff Aides working on this case.

II. Instructions:

A. Please date each entry and cross out **obsolete** instructions.

B. Explain why your recommendation will be effective with the Client.

(a) The approach we should have in relating to the client:

(b) Route we should take to involve client with the community resources:

Note: Use back of sheet if necessary.

CAN HELP — TOPEKA, KANSAS

CASE HISTORY "CAN HELP" 24-HOUR TELEPHONE ANSWERING SERVICE

CASE NO. _____

DATE: _____   NAME: _____

DAY OF WEEK: MON. _____   ADDRESS _____ PHONE _____
TUES _____ WED _____ THURS _____   TYPE OF CALL: __ EMPLOYMENT
FRI _____ SAT _____ SUN _____   __ HEALTH __ LEGAL
                                        __ MARITAL __ FINANCIAL __ EMO-
TIME OF DAY, LENGTH OF CALL   TIONAL __ ALCOHOLISM __ DRUGS
                                        __ HOMOSEXUAL
8 AM — 12 Noon _____   __ PARENT-CHILD RELATIONS:
12 Noon — 4 PM _____   __ HOMICIDAL __ SUICIDAL
4 PM — 8 PM _____   __ CONCERNING SOMEONE ELSE
8 PM — 12 MIDNIGHT _____   __ OTHER _____
12 MIDNIGHT — 4 AM _____   REFERRED TO: _____
4 AM — 8 AM _____   APPOINTMENT KEPT _____

Sex: ____ Male ____ Female
AGE ____ MARITAL STATUS _____   VOLUNTEER'S PSEUDONYM _____

OCCUPATION _____   MEDICAL DOCTOR _____
EMPLOYED ___ YES ___ NO ___

SEX AND AGES OF CHILDREN _____
RELIGION _____ MINISTER _____
NEAREST RELATIVE AND/OR FRIEND (Name, Address and Phone Number)
_____
WHAT MADE THIS PERSON CALL AT THIS TIME _____
_____

LIST ANY PREVIOUS HELP CALLER HAS RECEIVED (Problem, Source of help,
Feeling about help received or lack of it)
_____

REFERRALS SUGGESTED (List all and indicate if accepted: P-positively;
T-tentatively; R-refused)
_____
IF THIRD PARTY: NAME _____ PHONE _____
          ADDRESS _____
          REASON FOR CALL _____
HOW DID CALLER LEARN OF CAN HELP __ TV __ RADIO __ NEWSPAPER
__ OTHER

NARRATIVE (Please include following areas, if pertinent: confusion, withdrawal,
physical symptoms, homicidal target, financial problems, alcoholism, hostility,
delusional thinking, paranoid thoughts, suicidal plan, steps taken to help self, your
reaction to the call) _____
SUGGESTIONS TO OTHER VOLUNTEERS REGARDING THIS CALLER: _____
_____

254

SUICIDE REFERRAL SERVICE of El Paso County, Inc.

Date of Call:									
Name of Volunteer:									
Name of Caller:	Phone No. of Caller:						Phone:		

Time Start: a.m. p.m. | Time Stop: a.m. p.m. | Total Time:

If other caller, Name:

Relationship to Person called about:

Information below applies to subject of call.

		Under 25	26-30	31-35	36-40	41-45	46-55	56-65	66 up	Unknown
Sex:	Age:									
Subject's Location:	Zip:	NE NW	SE SW	Down-town	Black Forest	Security	Ft. Carson	Fountain		Unknown
				Military:			Active Duty			
Occupation:	Race:						Dependt	Active Duty	Retired	Unknown
Marital			Single	Married	Common-Law		Sept'd	Widowed	Divorced	Unknown
Problem		Info Only	Unwed Preg	Drugs	Marital Probs	Term. Illness	Alcohlsm	Depresn	Suicide	Unknown
Plan or Method		None	Jumping	Cutting	Hanging	Car Wreck	Home Gas	Drugs/Pills	Gun	Unknown
Prior Attempt		None	Over 20 yr ago	Over 15 yr ago	Over 10 yr ago	Over 5 yr ago	1 to 5 yr ago	Recent	At Present	Unknown
Family History		None		Close Friend	Family Member	Family Member	Brother Sister	Spouse	Parent	Unknown
Caller is			Non-suicidel		Chronic			Acute		Unknown
Lethality is		←— LOW —→		←— MEDIUM —→			←— HIGH —→			Unknown

Prior Hospitalization:	When?		Where?		Results?	
Now under care of MD or therapist?	Who?		Called by Subject?		Results?	
Prior SRS Contact?	When?		Results?		Repeat Caller?	
Referred to?	Priest Minister	Family Member	Piks Pk MH Ctr	Family Csling	M.D.	Therapst	Police	C.O.D.E.	Sunshine Terros

RESUME:

OPERATION HOTLINE — MANHASSET, N.Y.

CALL RECORD
(CONFIDENTIAL)

Check box with initial:
Action; Followup;
Emergency; Suicide.

7/71

Operation-Hotline, Town of North Hempstead, 220 Plandome Road, Manhasset, N.Y. 11030

TIME START :	TIME STOP :	TOTAL Minutes	Nickname or Code	AGE	DAY: SU MO TU WE TH FR SA (Circle)

___MAN ___BOY
___WOMAN ___GIRL
___New Caller
___Repeater

Call Location (optional)

How Heard of HL?

DATE _____ Year____
LAST NAME OF STAFF _____
PHONE # ___ -5005 -5006
Received
(Circle) -5007 -5008

DESCRIBE THE CALL IN DETAIL (PRINT)	YOUR ACTION OR ATTITUDES

USE BACKSIDE TO CONTINUE NOTES

REFERRAL MADE (IF ANY)
To_____
At_____

Phone(s)_____
Code(s)_____

STRATEGY
___Referral
___Handled on phone
___Will call again
___No Help
___ _____

LISTENER'S REACTIONS:

Check here if you wish staff review of this call.

MAIN PROBLEM DESCRIPTION:

ADDITIONAL DESCRIPTIONS:

Indianapolis, Ind.

MARION COUNTY ASSOCIATION FOR MENTAL HEALTH
SUICIDE PREVENTION SERVICE
CLINICAL ASSOCIATE CASE REPORT
(PLEASE PRINT)

CASE NUMBER_____

$\overline{1}$ $\overline{2}$ $\overline{3}$ $\overline{4}$ $\overline{5}$

1. Clinical Associate's Name_____

$\overline{6}$ $\overline{7}$ $\overline{8}$

2.   CLIENT/PATIENT   CALLER

NAME		
ADDRESS		
CITY		
PHONE		

3. Sex:_____ 4. Stated Age:_____ 5. Estimated Age:_____

$\overline{9}$ $\overline{10}$ $\overline{11}$ $\overline{12}$

6. Time Call Started:_____AM-PM, Ended_____AM-PM
          Day of

$\overline{13}$ $\overline{14}$ $\overline{15}$ $\overline{16}$

7. Date: Mo._____Day_____Year_____Week_____

$\overline{17}$ $\overline{18}$ $\overline{19}$ $\overline{20}$ $\overline{21}$ $\overline{22}$

8. Present Suicide Risk? High Medium Low None Undetermined
                    (Circle One)

$\overline{23}$

9. Referred to:_____Agency or Person. Give Name_____

$\overline{24}$

   Suggested:_____Agency or Person. Give Name_____

   Refused:_____Explain_____

   None:_____Why?_____

$\overline{25}$ $\overline{26}$

10. Caller-Client Relationship:_____

$\overline{27}$ $\overline{28}$

11. Referred By:_____ 12. Called S.P.S. Before?_____

$\overline{29}$ $\overline{30}$ $\overline{31}$

13. Was Suicide Attempt Being Made During Call?_____

$\overline{32}$

14. How Many Previous Suicide Attempts?_____

$\overline{33}$ $\overline{34}$

15. Approximate Date of Last Suicide Attempt? (Mo. & Yr.)_____

$\overline{35}$ $\overline{36}$ $\overline{37}$

16. Marital Status:_____17. Living Arrangement:_____

$\overline{38}$ $\overline{39}$

18. Estimated Income/Year:_____

$\overline{40}$

19. Number Supported by Income (Including Client):_____

$\overline{41}$ $\overline{42}$

20. Source(s) of Income:_____

$\overline{43}$ $\overline{44}$

21. Present Employment:_____

$\overline{45}$ $\overline{46}$ $\overline{47}$

22. Number of Jobs Currently Held:_____

$\overline{48}$

23. Usual Occupations: (Principal)_____

$\overline{49}$ $\overline{50}$

                     (Other)_____

$\overline{51}$ $\overline{52}$

24. Education:_____ 25. Religion:_____

$\overline{53}$ $\overline{54}$

MARION COUNTY ASSOCIATION FOR MENTAL HEALTH
SUICIDE PREVENTION SERVICE
CLINICAL ASSOCIATE CASE REPORT
INCOMPLETE CALL

Clinical Associate's Name _____

CLIENT/PATIENT	CALLER

NAME

ADDRESS

CITY

PHONE

Sex: _____ Stated Age: _____ Estimated Age _____

Time Call Started: _____ AM-PM, Ended _____ AM-PM

Date: Mo. _____ Day _____ Year _____ Day of Week _____

RESUME OF ACTION TAKEN: _____

_____

_____

_____

_____

_____

_____

_____

(Continue on Back)

Indianapolis, Ind.

SUICIDE PREVENTION CENTER
LOS ANGELES, CALIFORNIA

SPC CONTACT WORK SHEET

Serial No. _____

Day _____ Date ____ ____ ____ Time _____ PM AM Duration _____
                          Day Mo. Year   Hrs.   Min.

Patient _____ Tel. No. _____
        Last   First   Initial

Address _____ City _____
        No.   Street   Apt. No.

Sex M F   Age _____   Race C N O R M   Education _____ 1 2 3 4 G
                                                                       Yrs H.S.   College

Marital Status U M D S MM W CL   Religion None P C J M O

Current problem (reason for call, current stress) **USE REVERSE FOR ADDITIONAL DATA**

Recent Symptoms (mood, phys. & psych. symptoms, unusual behavior, attitudes)

Suicide plan (method, timing, location, details)

Previous suicidal behavior (threats, attempts, seriousness & when)

Current / previous psychiatric or medical treatment

LETHALITY RATING (1 – 9) _____

Disposition (includes calls to relatives, friends, police, physician,
                 hospital, recommendations to patient or caller.) **USE REVERSE FOR ADDITIONAL DATA**

WORKER _____   SPC CONSULTANT _____
S2 – 1270

SUICIDE PREVENTION CENTER
LOS ANGELES, CALIFORNIA

SPC CONTACT WORK SHEET

Caller if other than patient:

Name _____   Tel. No. _____
       Last   First   Initial

Address _____   City _____
       No.   Street   Apt. No.

Relationship: Spouse ☐   Friend ☐   Family ☐

                Professional ☐   Cleric ☐   Neighbor ☐

Current Problem (cont.)

Resources (other than above)

Name _____   Relationship _____   Tel. No. _____

Name _____   Relationship _____   Tel. No. _____

Name _____   Relationship _____   Tel. No. _____

Disposition (Cont.)

Additional data (Include recommended action for SPC)

SUICIDE PREVENTION REPORT
ST. JOSEPH STATE HOSPITAL

Follow-Up _____

No Follow-Up _____

_____
Your Name

SELF CALLERS (B)

1.   Date _____ Time - Began _____ Ended _____
2.   Phone _____ Name _____
Address _____ City _____
Sex ____ Age ____ Given ____ Race ____ Marital Status
                                         S M W D Se
          Guess ____ Guess ____ (Circle One)

Living Arrangements: Alone _____
                      With Spouse _____
                      With Relative (s) _____
                      With Non-relative (s) _____
                      Don't know _____
                      Housewife _____
                      Employed _____
                      Unemployed _____
                      Retired _____
                      Don't know _____

Attempt just made? _____

3.   Main Problem (Use extra sheet if necessary) _____
4.   How did they learn about S.P.S.

     Friend ____ Newspaper Ad ____ Radio ____ Professional Person ____

5.   Others Talked to or Contacted:

     Back Up Name: _____ Time _____
     Family Name _____ Phone _____ Relationship _____
     Physician Name _____ Phone _____
     Psychiatrist Name _____ Phone _____
     Other Name _____ Phone _____ Relationship _____
                    (circle one)

6.   Referral   a) Own Md or Therapist Name _____
                b) SPS listed psychiatrist Name _____
                c) Psychiatric Clinic Name _____
                d) Other   Name _____
                e) None _____ Why _____
                f) Refused by caller _____

7.   Suicide Risk Estimate: High ____ Medium ____ Low ____ None ____
     Underdetermined ____
8.   Comments of Associate (About call of caller)
9.   Was an assessment sheet filled out? Yes ____ No ____ Why not ____

DIALOGUE PHONE CALL SUMMARY

_____   _____   From _____ PM to _____
(Volunteer-Real Name)   (Date)   (Time of Call)

_____   S M T W Th F S   Age (Check One)
(Alias, if used)   (Circle One)   _____

                                                      _____ 10 or below
_____   Sex: _____ 11 thru 13
(Caller's Name)   _____ 14 thru 18
                          Male   Female   _____ Over 18
                             (Circle One)

BASIC PROBLEM (Check those appropriate)

____ Boy/girl relations   ____ Drug information   ____ Pregnancy information
____ Parent/child conflict   ____ General information   ____ General depression
____ School concerns   ____ Sexual concerns   ____ Loneliness ("just to rap"
____ Drug crisis.   ____ Draft, armed
____ Other   services, war
     (Please describe) _____

_____

SUMMARY OF CALL

Caller's Presentation of Concerns (Describe as briefly as possible the problem(s) as presented by caller: _____
_____
_____

Volunteer's Approach (What direction did you take in trying to help him/her deal with
the situation?)
_____
_____
_____

Describe what referral was made, if any: _____
_____

VOLUNTEER'S REACTION TO CALL   **CALLER'S REACTION**
I feel that the call (check one)   I feel that he/she (check one)
____ (a) Was generally successful   ____ (a) Was satisfied
____ (b) Was directionless   ____ (b) Was neutral-unaffected
____ (c) Went poorly   ____ (c) Was frustrated and dissatisfied
____ (d) Other _____

                                          ____ Check here if you wish this call
                                               reviewed by team.

IF TEAM MEMBERS WISH TO COMMENT, PLEASE DO SO ON REVERSE AND
SIGN YOUR NAME.

Fairfield, Cal.

SUICIDE CRISIS INTERVENTION SERVICE-HOTLINE

Palm Springs Mental Health Clinic,   161 Civic Drive, Suite 8

Palm Springs, Calif.

Date: _____ Day: _____ Time: _____   AM Answering   Length

PM Staff Person _____ of Call _____

Name of Caller: _____ Location of Caller _____

Tel. # calling from: _____ Home Phone: _____

Resident or Visitor: R V

Home address: _____

Prior knowledge of SCIS-Hotline _____ Age _____ Sex: F M

Marital Status: S M W D Sep. Race: _____ Occupation: _____

Education: Years Completed _____ Religion _____ Income _____

Sex, number, ages of children _____

Closest relative or friend _____ Telephone _____

Statement of Problem: (Current situation - feelings - suicide, etc.) _____

_____

_____

_____

Suicide Potential: High _____ Moderate _____ Low _____

Any previous suicidal behavior: _____

Current medical and/or psychiatric help: _____

Previous medical and/or psychiatric help: _____

_____

Disposition: (Include recommendations to caller, calls to relatives, friends, referrals to police, medical, legal, treatment resources, back-up consultation, etc.

_____

_____

Follow-up Information (App't kept?, etc.) _____

_____

Additional Comments: _____

_____

_____

PSMHC 9

(USE OTHER SIDE IF NEEDED)

Suicide Prevention Center-Jacksonville, Florida

(Do not use pencil)

SUICIDE PREVENTION CENTER OF JAX.

CLIENT _____

ADDRESS _____

TEL. # _____

What/Who referred caller to SPC?

_____

AGE _____ SEX _____ RACE _____
SEP. ____ SING. ____ MAR. ____ WID. ____
DIV. ____

OCCUPATION: _____

Working now? Yes _____ No _____

Prev. counseling or therapy? _____

When? _____ Therapist _____

Medical Doctor _____

Religion _____ Minister _____

Other pertinent names & Phone numbers:

_____

CHART NUMBER

Who Called? _____

Relationship _____

Tel. # _____ Address _____

Prev. Attempts? Yes _____ No _____
        # X's _____
Means available? Yes _____ No _____
METHOD PLANNED _____
Lethality: High ____ Med ____ Low ____

" "

SPC WORKER _____

DATE _____ TIME _____ AM OR PM
" "

SPC REFERRAL _____

Follow-up Needed? Yes ____ No ____
Suggested Follow-up: _____

_____

##

PROBLEM: (briefly stated) _____

DETAILS OF CALL: _____

_____

_____

_____

CJ 01 71 r-7/16

264

SUICIDE PREVENTION AND CRISIS HELP SERVICE
CANTON, OHIO

Caller _____ Case Number _____

Address _____ Volunteer _____

Telephone _____ Day _____ Date _____

Age _____ Sex _____ Call Began _____ ( )am ( )pm

Marital Status _____ Call Ended _____ ( )am ( )pm

Calling for - Self - Other - If other, Who? _____

* *

PROBLEM AREAS - CIRCLE THOSE PRESENT   COMMENTS

Abortion   ....

Aggression   ....

Alcoholism

Anorexia   ....

Anxiety   ....

Apathy   ....

Delinquency   ....

Delusions

Depression   ....

Desertion   ....

Discord   ....

Divorce   ....

Employment   ....

Family

Financial   ....

Guilt   ....

Helplessness   ....

Heroin   ....

Homicidal   ....

Homesexual

Hopelessness   ....

Insomnia   ....

Loneliness

Loss   ....

Marihuana   ....

Nervousness   ....

Physical Illness

Pills   ....

Prev. Psychiatry ....

Rape   ....

Separation

Sex   ....

Suicide Attempt   ....

Suicide Plan
                  ....

....

Volunteer's Evaluation _____

Action Taken _____

Follow Up _____

265

SP & CH CASE SUMMARY

Caller	Case No.
Address	1st Vol.
Community	Date
Telephone	Day
Sex & Age	Hour
Marital	

Data
Family
Children
Housing
Occupation
Education
Problems

Present
Crisis
and Cause

Previous
and
Present
Professional
Therapy

Evaluation
and
Action Taken

Repeat calls, contacts, follow-ups, referrals, etc.
Dates and Vols.

_____   _____

_____   _____

_____   _____

_____   _____

SUICIDE PREVENTION & CRISIS HELP SERVICE - CANTON, OHIO

SUICIDE PREVENTION & CRISIS HELP SERVICE
CANTON, OHIO
FOLLOW-UP CALL TO BE MADE

NAME _____   CASE NO. _____

ADDRESS _____   VOLUNTEER _____
INITIAL CONTACT
PHONE _____   DATE _____

WHO TO CALL _____   WHEN TO CALL: DAY _____

DATE _____

TIME _____

PURPOSE OF CALL:

ABSTRACT OF FOLLOW-UP CONVERSATION

By Volunteer _____ Date _____

CRISIS CALL REPORT RECORD
NASHVILLE, TENN.

Call In   Call Completed

Case No. _____
CA Name & No. _____
New _____ Former _____

Name _____ Age _____ Sex _____ Student _____

Address _____ Phone _____ - _____
                                                          (home)   (other)

Person calling if not patient:
    Name _____ Address _____
    Teleph. _____ Relationship to patient _____

Marital Status: Sing. Mar. Sept. Div. Wd. Remar. Children: _____

Education _____ Occupation/Profession _____

Other relevant patient information:

Medications available: _____

Suicide data:

    Suicide case: Yes _____ No _____ Uncertain _____
    Current Lethality Assessment: High Moderate Low
    Present Attempt: Yes No
    Suicide Attempt History:

	Date:	Method	Outcome
1.			
2.			
3.			

Nature of Present Crisis:

Initial Action Plan:

Transfer:
Case Closed: _____   _____
                    Date   Closed By
PLEASE COMPLETE CASE DATA SHEET
CRISIS CALL-NASHVILLE, TENN.

268

CRISIS CALL-NASHVILLE, TENN.

Basic problem: _____
Referral: _____

	Date		Day of week	Hour
month	day	year	S M T W T F S	_____ am pm _____

CALLER name   '   **VOLUNTEER**
       address   '
       teleph.   '
       relationship   '

CLIENT name   age   race   sex
       address
       teleph.
       directions to reach home

---

marital status (circle)   marital relationship   Education
m s wid. sep. div. other   good fair poor NK   grade   HS   Coll.
                                             coll. grad.   NK

Next of Kin   religion   church
name
(address if diff.)

Occupation: employed now: '   DOCTOR'S name
                              '   address
               Yes ___ No ___   '   teleph.
                              '

Reason for calling:
(use quote)

	Yes	No	
Specific stress			prior **medical** care
loss of loved person	___	___	(state illness) _____
loss of job or status	___	___	hospitalized? _____
illness	___	___	
change in environment	___	___	prior **psychiatric** care ___
other _____			hospitalized? _____

---

prior suicidal record: prior suicidal action:
considered   yes ___ No ___
attempted   ___   ___   serious ___ light ___ NK _
means   ___   ___
hospitalized?   ___   ___

Suicidal **now**
plans (means)
attempted
hospitalized

Action taken by volunteer: follow-up if referral was made
                                         yes ___   no ___
                            agency contacted
                                  will help   ___   ___
                              cannot help   ___   ___

ADDITIONAL INFORMATION CAN BE CONTINUED ON REVERSE SIDE OF
THIS SHEET

SUICIDE PREVENTION REPORT SHEET
BRIDGEPORT, CONN.

Date: _____   Time of Call ____ AM/PM to ____ AM/PM

Suicide Potential: 1-2 Low   3-4-5-6 Medium 7-8-9 High

CLIENT: _____   CALLER: _____
          Name   Name

Address _____   Relation to Patient _____

_____ Phone No.   Address _____

Age Sex Religion Education   Phone No.

                                         NAMES, ADDRESSES AND PHONE
MARITAL STATUS S M W D Sep.   NUMBERS OF SIGNIFICANT OTHERS:
                    (Circle One)   _____
NO. OF CHILDREN
(INCLUDE AGES) _____ _____   _____
                Male   Female
OCCUPATION _____ INCOME _____   _____

PERTINENT MEDICAL HISTORY   _____
(List Illnesses, Dates and Duration)

_____   _____

_____   FAMILY PHYSICIAN: _____

_____   PSYCHIATRIST: (or Other
                                         Therapist:
PSYCHIATRIC HISTORY (Indicate Dates
and Duration of Therapy and/or Hospitali- _____
zation; Note any Prior Suicidal Attempts   HOUSEHOLD COMPOSITION
and Dates)   (Mark all which apply)
_____   Lives alone _____ With
                                         With Spouse _____ siblings _____
_____   With Children _____ With Other
                                         In Institution   Relatives _____
_____   With Others _____
                                         With Parents _____
_____   DATES OF ADDITIONAL CALLS TO
                                         SPS (Attach Explanation)
_____   _____

_____   _____

NATURE OF CRISIS AND DISPOSITION:

Bridgeport 9/70   (Continue on reverse side)

Bridgeport Suicide Prevention Center-Bridgeport, Conn.

SUICIDE PREVENTION DATA SERVICE

NAME _____ DATE: _____ DAY <u>M. T. W. TH. F. S. SUN.</u>

TIME _____ AM: _____ PM: _____

ADDRESS _____ SEX _____ AGE _____

TELEPHONE _____ WORKER _____

CONTACTS: RELATIVES OR NEIGHBORS: _____
NAME _____ ADDRESS _____ PHONE _____
NAME _____ ADDRESS _____ PHONE _____
PHYSICIAN: _____ MINISTER _____

IF NO ANSWER OR PRANK DESCRIBE CIRCUMSTANCES _____
_____

REASON GIVEN FOR CONTEMPLATING SUICIDE: _____
_____

DESCRIPTION OF PROBLEM: (SYMPTOMS, STRESSES, CONFLICTS, CHRONOCITY, MEDICAL STATUS, OTHERS INVOLVED) _____
_____

METHOD: _____

AVAILABILITY OF METHOD PROPOSED: READILY AVAILABLE _____
AVAILABLE WITH DIFFICULTY: _____ NOT READILY AVAILABLE _____

CURRENT STATUS: VAGUE THOUGHTS _____ LOOSE PLANS ____
CLEAR PLANS _____
PRIOR ATTEMPTS: YES ____ NO ____ RATING OF LETHALITY: LOW ____
MIDDLE _____ HIGH _____

ACTION TAKEN: _____
_____

_____

FOLLOW UP _____
_____

_____

271

SUICIDE PREVENTION OF SACRAMENTO COUNTY

FIRST CALL

Date: _____   Caller: _____
      Month   Day   Year   First Name   Last Name

Volunteer Name _____   Anonymous: MALE   FEMALE

Time: _____ AM   PM   Telephone: _____

Length: _____ hrs _____ min.   Address: _____

Lethality: LOW   MODERATE   HIGH   _____

Contacted:

POLICE AMBULANCE EMERGENCY CAB TRACE CONSULTANT FIRE DEPT.

Referred to: _____ Notified: YES   NO
            _____ Notified: YES   NO
            _____ Notified: YES   NO

Other calls made by us: _____

Background: Professional Care: PRESENT

Age: _____   PAST THERAPY MEDICATION
Religion: _____ Active: YES NO
                                           M.D. CLERGY
SING. MARR. SEPAR. DIV. WID.
                                           Details: _____
Children _____
                                           Present Problem: MARITAL ALCOHOL
Spouse's name: _____   FINANCIAL MEDICAL LEGAL
Age: _____   PARENTS DRUGS SEX ALONE
Alone or living with: _____   Other: _____
UNEMPLOYED or Occupation: _____
_____   Suicide Attempts? When: _____

How long: _____   _____

                YES   **FOLLOW-UP**
May we call back? NO   When: _____ Which referral taken:
Call back made? Dates: _____
Reports back from referrals. Seen: _____ No Show _____ Explain: _____

Suicide Prevention Service of Sacramento County, Inc.

10/68- #1 #113

272

REFERENCES

Albee, G.W. "Emerging Concepts of Mental Illness and Models of Treatment: The Psychological Point of View." **American Journal of Psychiatry,** January, 1969, 125, (7).

Albee, G.W. "The Sickness Model of Mental Disorder Means a Double Standard of Care." **Research Bulletin,** Michigan Mental Health, Winter, 1970, IV, (1).

Anderson, D.B., McClean, L.J. **Identifying Suicide Potential.** New York: Behavioral Publications, Inc., 1969.

Ansel, E.L., McGee, R.K. "Attitudes Toward Suicide Attempters." **Bulletin of Suicidology,** Fall, 1971, (8).

Asbell, B. "I Don't Know Why I'm Calling . . .Nobody Can Help Me." **Redbook,** June, 1970.

Baatz, R.J., Haddad, S.C., Hartman, M., Richardson, F.R., Roller, A.B., Stuart, C.L. "The Seattle Crisis Clinic Volunteer Training Program-A Descriptive Study." A Research project submitted in partial fulfillment of the requirements for the degree of Master of Social Work, University of Washington, 1968. Unpublished.

Bagley, C. "The Evaluation of a Suicide Prevention Scheme by an Ecological Method." **Social Science & Medicine,** 1968, 2.

Bell, D. The Crisis Clinic of Seattle, zeroxed paper, 1969.

Blum, D.L. "The Chronic Caller to a Suicide Prevention Center: Report of a Case." **Crisis Intervention,** 1970, 2, (1).

Bourne, N. Unpublished material from the Erie County Suicide Prevention and Crisis Service, Buffalo, New York, 1969.

Brockopp, G.W. "The Masturbator." **Crisis Intervention,** 1969, 1, (1).

Brockopp, G.W. "Seven Predictions for Suicide Prevention in the Seventies." **Crisis Intervention,** 1970, 2, (1).

Brockopp, G.W. "The Silent Caller." **Crisis Intervention,** 1970, 2, (3).

Brockopp, G.W. "The Telephone Call-Conversation or Therapy." **Crisis Intervention,** 1970, 2, (3).

Brockopp, G.W. "Training the Volunteer Telephone Therapist." **Crisis Intervention,** 1970, 2, (3).

Brockopp, G.W. "I'll Be Here Tuesday, If You Need Me." **Crisis Intervention,** 1971, 3, (1).

Caplan, G. **Principles of Preventative Psychiatry.** New York: Basic Books, 1964.

Cavan, R.S. **Suicide.** New York: Russell & Russell, 1965.

Cockrell, M.S. et al. "A Study of Seattle's Crisis Clinic." A Research project submitted in partial fulfillment of the requirements for the degree of Master of Social Work, University of Washington, 1970. Unpublished.

Dublin, L.I. Suicide: A Sociological and Statistical Study. New York: Ronald Press, 1963.

Dublin, L.I. "Suicide Prevention" in On The Nature of Suicide. (Ed. by E.S. Shneidman). San Francisco: Jossey Bass, 1969.

Farberow, N.L. and Shneidman, E.S. The Cry for Help. New York: McGraw-Hill, 1961.

Farberow, N.L. Problems in the Creation and Organization of a Suicide Prevention Center, Presented at the International Association for Suicide Prevention, Copenhagen, Denmark, 1963.

Farberow, N.L. Concepts and Conceptions of Suicide Prevention Services, zeroxed paper, June 12, 1968.

Farberow, N.L., Heilig, Samuel, M., Litman, R.E. "Techniques in Crisis Intervention: A Training Manual." Suicide Prevention Center, Inc. Los Angeles, Calif., December, 1968.

Farberow, N.L. Bibliography on Suicide, and Suicide Prevention. Chevy Chase, Maryland: National Institute of Mental Health, 1969.

Farberow, N.L. "Ten Years of Suicide Prevention--Past and Future." Bulletin of Suicidology, Spring, 1970.

Fisher, S.A. The Establishment of the Suicide Prevention and Crisis Help Service of Stark County, Masters Thesis, 1970, unpublished.

Fowler, D.E., McGee, R.K. "Assessing the Performance of Telephone Crisis Workers: The Development of a Technical Effectiveness Scale." Bulletin of Suicidology, Fall, 1971, (8).

Fox, R. The Samaritan Contribution to Suicide Prevention, Paper delivered to Sixth International Congress on Suicide Prevention: Mexico, December 5-8th, 1971.

Frederick, C.J. "Current Directions for Suicide Prevention and Crisis Intervention." Crisis Intervention, 1970, 2, (1).

Garrard, Mrs. R.L. "Community Suicide-Prevention Activities, Greensboro, North Carolina." (Ed. by H.L.P. Resnik). Suicidal Behaviors.

Greer, S. Bagley, C. "Effect of Psychiatric Intervention in Attempted Suicide: A Controlled Study." British Medical Journal, Feb. 6, 1971.

Grollman, E.A. Suicide: Prevention, Intervention, Post-vention. Boston: Beacon Press, 1971.

Hall, R. Unpublished report, 1969.

Haughton, A. "Suicide Prevention Programs in the United States--An Overview." **Bulletin of Suicidology,** July, 1968.

Heilig, S.M., Farberow, N.L., Litman, R.E., Shneidman, E.S. "The Role of Non-professional Volunteers in a Suicide Prevention Center." **Community Mental Health Journal,** 1968, **4,** (4).

Heilig, S.M. "Training in Suicide Prevention." **Bulletin of Suicidology,** Spring, 1970.

Jaffee, D.T., Beyer, M., Clark, T., Cytrynbaum, S., Quinlan, D. & Reed, H. "Responses to Youth Problems at a Crisis Center." Unpublished, No. 9., New Haven, Conn., 1971.

Kiev, A. (Ed. by Anderson & McLean). "Suicide Prevention in Identifying Suicide Potential." **Behavioral Publications, Inc.,** 1969.

Klugman, D.J., Litman, R.E., Wold, C.I. "Suicides: Answering the Cry for Help." **Social Work,** October, 1965.

Knickerbocker, D.A. & McGee, R.K. Clinical Effectiveness of Non-professional and Professional Workers in a Crisis Intervention Center, Unpublished paper, 1971.

Knickerbocker, D.A. & Fowler, D.E., A System for Evaluating the Performance of Crisis Workers. Unpublished paper 1971.

Kolker, H.B. & Katz, S. "If YOu've Missed the Age You've Missed a Lot." **Crisis Intervention,** 1971, **3,** (2).

Lester, D. "Characteristics of Those Who Call the Suicide Prevention and Crisis Service of Buffalo." **Crisis Intervention,** 1969, **1,** (1).

Lester, D. "Suicidal Behavior in Men and Women." **Mental Hygiene,** 1969, **53,** (3).

Lester, D. "Chronic Callers to a Suicide Prevention Center." **Community Mental Health Journal,** 1970, **6,** (3).

Lester, D. "The Obscene Caller." **Crisis Intervention,** 1970.

Lester, D., Brockopp, G.W. "Chronic Callers to a Suicide Prevention Center." **Community Mental Health Journal,** 1970, **6,** (3).

Lester, D. "Biographical Location of Callers to a Suicide Prevention Center: Note on the Evaluation of Suicide Prevention Programs." **Psychological Reports,** 1971, **28.**

Lester, D. "Suicide: Aggression or Hostility?" **Crisis Intervention,** 1971, **3,** (1).

Lester, D. "The Chronic Caller To a Crisis Hotline: An Example of An Institution "Creating" the Problem Stockton State College, Pomona, N.J." **Crisis Intervention,** 1971.

Lester, D. "The Suicide Prevention Contribution to Mental Health." **Psychological Reports,** 1971, **28.**

Lester, D. "Suicide Prevention and Crisis Service." Crisis Intervention, Buffalo, 1971.

Lester, G. & Lester, D. Suicide and the Gamble with Death. Englewood Cliffs, New Jersey: Prentice-Hall, 1971.

Litman, R.E., Shneidman, E.S., Farberow, N.L. "Suicide Prevention Center." Current Psychiatric Therapies, 1961.

Litman, R.E. "Emergency Response to Potential Suicide." Journal of the Michigan State Medical Society, 1963, 62.

Litman, R.E. Shneidman, E.S., Farberow, N.L., Heilig, S.M., Kramer, J.A. "Suicide Prevention Telephone Service." Journal of American Medical Association, 1965, 192.

Litman, R.E. "Acutely Suicidal Patients." California Medicine, March, 1966.

Litman, R.E. "Police Aspects of Suicide." Police, January-February, 1966.

Litman, R.E. "The Prevention of Suicide." Current Psychiatric Therapies, 1966, VI.

Litman, R.E. Workshop in Suicidology, San Francisco, 1970.

Litman, R.E. "A Decade of Suicide Prevention, Secretary General." International Association of Suicide Prevention, Vita, December, 1971.

Mann, P.A. "Establishing a Mental Health Consultation Program with a Police Department." Community Mental Health Journal, 1971, June, 7, (2).

Maris, R.W. "The Sociology of Suicide Prevention: Policy Implications of Differences Between Suicidal Patients and Completed Suicides." Social Problems, 1969, 17, (1).

McGee, R.K. "The Suicide Prevention Center as a Model for Community Mental Health Programs." Community Mental Health Journal, 1965, 1, (2).

McGee, R.K. Development and Organization of Suicide Prevention Centers, Paper presented at the First Annual Symposium Community Mental Health Services, Atlanta, Georgia, 1966.

McGee, L.L. & Hiltner, S. "The Role of the Clergy." Suicidal Behaviors. (Ed. by H.L.P. Resnik), Boston: Little Brown, 1968.

McGee, R.K. "Community Mental Health Concepts as Demonstrated by Suicide Prevention Programs in Florida." Community Mental Health Journal, 1968, 4.

McGee, R.K. "Some Basic Considerations in Crisis Intervention." Community Mental Health Journal, 1968, 4.

McGee, R.K. Some Reflections on the Character of Suicide Prevention Centers in 1968. Progress report of Grant No. MH 14948, National Institute of Mental Health.

McGee, R.K., McGee, J.P. "A Total Community Response to the Cry for Help: We Care, Inc. of Orlando, Florida." **Suicidal Behaviors.** (Ed. by H.L.P. Resnik), Boston: Little Brown, 1968.

McGee, R.K. "Toward a New Image for Suicide and Crisis Services." **Crisis Intervention,** 1970, **2,** (3).

McGee, R.K. Professional Consultants, From Case History: Development of We Care, Inc., Suicide Prevention Center of Orlando, Fla., 1971.

McGee, R.K. Report of Study Presented at Institute on Suicidology, Washington, D.C., 1971.

McGee, R.K. "Suicide Prevention Programs and Mental Health Associations." **Mental Hygiene.** 1971, **55.**

Meerloo, J.A. "Hidden Suicide." **Suicidal Behaviors.** (Ed. by H.L.P. Resnik), Boston: Little Brown & Co., 1968.

Motto, J.A. "Newspaper Influence on Suicide-A Controlled Study." Proceedings from Fifth International Association for Suicide Prevention, London, 1968.

Motto, J.A. "Development of Standards for Suicide Prevention Centers." **Bulletin of Suicidology,** 1969, March.

Motto, J.A. "Newspaper Influence on Suicide." **Archives of General Psychiatry,** August, 1970, **23.**

Motto, J.A. "Evaluation of a Suicide Prevention Center by Sampling the Population at Risk." **Life-Threatening Behavior,** Spring, 1971, **1,** (1).

Moyer, E.A. A Descriptive Analysis of the Use of a Personal Emergency Telephone Service in Crisis Intervention for Youth in Richmond, Virginia. A Masters Thesis, Unpublished, 1971.

Murphy, G.E., Robins, E. "The Communication of Suicidal Ideas." **Suicidal Behaviors.** (Ed. H.L.P. Resnik), Boston: Little Brown & Co., 1968.

Murphy, G.E. "Who Calls the Suicide Prevention Center: A Study of 55 Persons Calling on Their Own Behalf." **American Journal Psychiatry,** 1969, **126,** (3).

Murphy, G.E., Walbran, B., Clendenin, W., Robins, E. The Role of the Police in Suicide Prevention: Analysis of 380 Consecutive Cases Involving Police (from Session 105) Proceedings from Fifth International Association for Suicide Prevention, London, 1969.

Neleigh, R., Newman, F.L., Madore, C.E., Sears, W.F. "Training Non-professional Community Leaders." **Community Mental Health Journal Monograph,** 1971, Series #6.

Noyes, R., Jr. "Shall We Prevent Suicide?" **Comprehensive Psychiatry,** 1970, **11,** (4).

Peck, M.L. Police Training in Handling Emotionally Disturbed and Suicidal Persons, **Suicide Prevention Center, Los Angeles, Calif.,** June 3, 1969.

Reiff, R., Riessman, F. "The Indigenous Non-professional." **Community Mental Health Journal Monograph,** 1965, #1.

Resnik, H.L.P. "A Community Anti-Suicidal Organization." **Suicidal Behavior,** (Ed. H.L.P. Resnik) Boston: Little Brown & Co., 1968.

Resnik, H.L.P. "Center Comments." **Bulletin of Suicidology,** Fall, 1971, National Institute of Mental Health, Washington, D.C.

Richard, W.C., McGee, R.K. "An Answer to Need for Suicide Prevention Center Outreach Program." **American Association of Suicidology,** Washington, D.C., 1971.

Rioch, M.J. "National Institute of Mental Health Pilot Study in Training Mental Health Counselors." **American Journal of Orthopsychiatry,** 1963, 33.

Robins, E., Schmidt, E.H., O'Neal, P. "Some Interrelations of Social Factors and Clinical Diagnosis in Attempted Suicide: A Study of 109 Patients." **American Journal of Psychiatry,** 1957.

Robins, E. "The Communication of Suicidal Intent: A Study of 134 Consecutive Cases of Successful (Completed) Suicide." **American Journal of Psychiatry,** February, 1959, **115.**

Selkin, J., Morris, J. "Some Behavioral Factors Which Influence the Recovery Rate of Suicide Attempts." **Bulletin of Suicidology,** 1971, (8).

Shneidman, E.S., Farberow, N.L. **Clues to Suicide.** New York: McGraw-Hill, 1957.

Shneidman, E.S., Farberow, N.L., Litman, R.E. "The Suicide Prevention Center." **The Cry For Help,** (Ed. N.L. Farberow, E. Shneidman) New York: McGraw-Hill, 1961.

Shneidman, E.S., Mandelkorn, P. "How to Prevent Suicide." **Public Affairs Pamphlet,** 1967, No. 406.

Shneidman, E.S. **On the Nature of Suicide.** San Francisco: Jossey Bass, 1969.

Shneidman, E.S. "Los Angeles Suicide Prevention Center, Ten Years in Retrospect." **Bulletin of Suicidology,** Spring, 1970, (6).

Shneidman, E.S., Litman, R.E. **The Psychology of Suicide.** New York: Science House, 1970.

Snyder, J.A. "Use of Gatekeepers in Crisis Management." Presented at American Association of Suicidology, 1970.

Sudak, H.S., Hall, S., Sawyer, J.B. "The Suicide Prevention Center as a Coordinating Facility." **Bulletin of Suicidology,** Fall, 1970.

Suicide in the United States, 1950-1964," Department of Health, Education and Welfare, National Center for Health Statistics, August, 1967, Series 20, (5).